CHANGING PARADIGMS IN HISTORICAL AND SYSTEMATIC THEOLOGY

General Editors
Sarah Coakley   Richard Cross

This series sets out to reconsider the modern distinction between 'historical' and 'systematic' theology. The scholarship represented in the series is marked by attention to the way in which historiographic and theological presumptions ('paradigms') necessarily inform the work of historians of Christian thought, and thus affect their application to contemporary concerns. At certain key junctures such paradigms are recast, causing a reconsideration of the methods, hermeneutics, geographical boundaries, or chronological caesuras which have previously guided the theological narrative. The beginning of the twenty-first century marks a period of such notable reassessment of the Christian doctrinal heritage, and involves a questioning of the paradigms that have sustained the classic 'history-of-ideas' textbook accounts of the modern era. Each of the volumes in this series brings such contemporary methodological and historiographical concerns to conscious consideration. Each tackles a period or key figure whose significance is ripe for reconsideration, and each analyses the implicit historiography that has sustained existing scholarship on the topic. A variety of fresh methodological concerns are considered, without reducing the theological to other categories. The emphasis is on an awareness of the history of 'reception': the possibilities for contemporary theology are bound up with a careful rewriting of the historical narrative. In this sense, 'historical' and 'systematic' theology are necessarily conjoined, yet also closely connected to a discerning interdisciplinary engagement.

This monograph series accompanies the project of *The Oxford Handbook of the Reception of Christian Theology* (Oxford University Press, in progress), also edited by Sarah Coakley and Richard Cross.

CHANGING PARADIGMS IN HISTORICAL AND SYSTEMATIC THEOLOGY

General Editors: Sarah Coakley (Norris-Hulse Professor of Divinity, University of Cambridge) and Richard Cross (John A. O'Brien Professor of Philosophy, University of Notre Dame)

RECENT SERIES TITLES

Calvin, Participation, and the Gift
The Activity of Believers in Union with Christ
J. Todd Billings

Newman and the Alexandrian Fathers
Shaping Doctrine in Nineteenth-Century England
Benjamin J. King

Orthodox Readings of Aquinas
Marcus Plested

Kant and the Creation of Freedom
A Theological Problem
Christopher J. Insole

Blaise Pascal on Duplicity, Sin, and the Fall
The Secret Instinct
William Wood

Theology as Science in Nineteenth-Century Germany
From F. C. Baur to Ernst Troeltsch
Johannes Zachhuber

Georges Florovsky and the Russian Religious Renaissance
Paul L. Gavrilyuk

Balthasar on the Spiritual Senses

Perceiving Splendour

MARK McINROY

OXFORD
UNIVERSITY PRESS

OXFORD
UNIVERSITY PRESS

Great Clarendon Street, Oxford, OX2 6DP,
United Kingdom

Oxford University Press is a department of the University of Oxford.
It furthers the University's objective of excellence in research, scholarship,
and education by publishing worldwide. Oxford is a registered trade mark of
Oxford University Press in the UK and in certain other countries

© Mark McInroy 2014

The moral rights of the author have been asserted

First Edition published in 2014

Impression: 1

All rights reserved. No part of this publication may be reproduced, stored in
a retrieval system, or transmitted, in any form or by any means, without the
prior permission in writing of Oxford University Press, or as expressly permitted
by law, by licence or under terms agreed with the appropriate reprographics
rights organization. Enquiries concerning reproduction outside the scope of the
above should be sent to the Rights Department, Oxford University Press, at the
address above

You must not circulate this work in any other form
and you must impose this same condition on any acquirer

Published in the United States of America by Oxford University Press
198 Madison Avenue, New York, NY 10016, United States of America

British Library Cataloguing in Publication Data
Data available

Library of Congress Control Number: 2014936657

ISBN 978-0-19-968900-2

As printed and bound by
CPI Group (UK) Ltd, Croydon, CR0 4YY

Links to third party websites are provided by Oxford in good faith and
for information only. Oxford disclaims any responsibility for the materials
contained in any third party website referenced in this work.

To my mother and father

Acknowledgements

This study would not have been possible without scholarly guidance from a number of different quarters. In its initial form as a doctoral dissertation at Harvard Divinity School, it was shaped by an exceptionally generous and insightful committee of examiners. The late Ronald Thiemann was a terrifically stimulating conversation partner as my work developed; Kevin Madigan could not have been more supportive of my scholarly endeavours throughout my doctoral study; Francis Schüssler Fiorenza provided an invaluable sense of the thought-world out of which Balthasar's theology arises. Most of all, Sarah Coakley gave her unflagging support throughout the writing of the doctoral thesis and its revision thereafter. I have benefitted enormously from her incisive commentary, her close attention to texts, and her keen eye for the relevance of this topic for the contemporary theological climate. I owe a great deal to other Harvard faculty members, especially François Bovon, Francis X. Clooney, Karen King, David Lamberth, and Stephanie Paulsell.

My friends and colleagues at Harvard helpfully responded to numerous chapter drafts throughout the years. Special thanks go to Mary Anderson, Faye Bodley-Dangelo, Tim Dalrymple, Sutopa Dasgupta, Philip Francis, George Gonzalez, Brett Grainger, Paul Dafydd Jones, Tamsin Jones, Piotr Malysz, Cameron Partridge, Mark Scott, John Senior, Katherine Shaner, Rachel Smith, Charles Stang, Robert St Hilaire, Bryan Wagoner, and Mara Willard.

A Frederick Sheldon Traveling Fellowship from Harvard University funded a year of research at Albert-Ludwigs-Universität Freiburg, where Hansjürgen Verweyen generously gave my project his time and penetrating insight. Helmut Hoping not only kindly agreed to serve as my *Doktorvater* for the 2007–2008 academic year, he also invited me into his circle of doctoral students and allowed me to present a chapter of my study in his doctoral colloquium. I also benefitted from a number of stimulating conversations about Balthasar's thought within German-speaking academic circles. My gratitude extends to Martin Bieler, Antonio Cimino, Benjamin Dahlke, Markus Enders, Gisbert Greshake, Julia Knop, Aaron Looney, Thomas Möllenbeck,

Robin Stockitt, Klaus von Stosch, Magnus Striet, Jan-Heiner Tück, and Andrej Wierzinski.

Cornelia Capol at the Balthasar Archiv and Hans-Anton Drewes at the Barth Archiv, both in Basel, Switzerland, made archive work immensely enjoyable. Special thanks also to Lois Rankin for her translation of Agnell Rickenmann's article from the original Italian.

More recently, I had the good fortune of discussing this project at the University of Cambridge while on a postdoctoral fellowship there. Especially helpful were discussions with David Ford, Raphael Cadenhead, Ashley Cocksworth, Samuel Kimbriel, Robbie Leigh, Jon Mackenzie, Richard McLauchlan, Elizabeth Powell, Darren Sarisky, Simon Ravenscroft, Giles Waller, Nicki Wilkes, and Simeon Zahl.

My colleagues at the University of St Thomas have been my latest set of valued conversation partners, and I have particularly benefitted from discussions with Cara Anthony, John Boyle, Thomas Bushlack, Mark DelCogliano, Massimo Faggioli, Paul Gavrilyuk, Michael Hollerich, Sherry Jordon, Billy Junker, Anne King, Robert Koerpel, Amy Levad, John Martens, Steve McMichael, Terence Nichols, Philip Rolnick, Barbara Sain, Kimberly Vrudny, and Paul Wojda.

Richard Cross, one of the series editors, offered his exceptionally insightful commentary and generous support of this project. At Oxford University Press, Tom Perridge, Alex Johnson, Karen Raith, Lizzy Robottom, and others have shown the very height of professionalism.

Last, I would like to take this opportunity to thank my family. To my mother, Jan, my debts and gratitude are immeasurable. In particular regard to this project, she has not only generously offered her professional editorial expertise in reviewing multiple chapter drafts, she has also inspired in me a delight in the English language that, I hope, manifests itself on the pages of this study. My father, John, stands behind this work in countless ways. My brother, Adam, has simply been an inspiration to me throughout my life. And to Suzanne I am so very grateful for her unfailing love and support. She, more than anyone else, has been with me through every step of this project. Without her it never would have been completed.

Contents

Abbreviations	xi
Introduction	**1**
On the 'Doctrine of the Spiritual Senses'	3
Why the Neglect of the Spiritual Senses in Balthasar's Thought?	4
Balthasar's Interest in the Spiritual Senses	7
Progression of Argument and Chapter Outline	10
Implications	13
1. 'In the Spirit of Origen': Balthasar's Exploration of Patristic Versions of the Spiritual Senses	**16**
The Patristic Ideal: Origen of Alexandria	18
Two Cautionary Tales: Evagrius of Pontus and Diadochus of Photice	37
Pseudo-Macarius, the Spiritual Senses, and Death and Resurrection	39
Augustine of Hippo and the Perception of Beauty	43
Maximus the Confessor and the Liturgical Setting for the Spiritual Senses	47
Curious Neglect: Gregory of Nyssa and Pseudo-Dionysius	49
Conclusion	53
2. Balthasar's Reading of Medieval and Early Modern Versions of the Spiritual Senses	**55**
The Heights of the Tradition: Bonaventure	56
Ignatius of Loyola	84
Conclusion	91
3. The Spiritual Senses in a Modern Idiom: Balthasar's Contemporary Interlocutors	**94**
Karl Barth	95
Romano Guardini	105
Gustav Siewerth	111
Paul Claudel	116
Conclusion	120

4. Balthasar's Distinctive Rearticulation of the Doctrine of the Spiritual Senses	122
The 'Personalist' Dimension to Balthasar's Doctrine of the Spiritual Senses	123
The Unity of Spiritual and Corporeal Perception in Balthasar's Thought	125
Balthasar on the Place of the Spiritual Senses in the Life of Faith	129
The Aesthetic Dimension to Spiritual Perception	132
Conclusion	133
5. Perceiving Splendour: The Role of the Spiritual Senses in Balthasar's Theological Aesthetics	134
At the Roots of Reality: Beauty as a Transcendental Property of Being	135
Being Appears: Balthasar on Form (*Gestalt*)	143
Beauty is 'Seen': On the Importance of Perception (*Wahr-nehmung*)	154
Perceiving Splendour: The Role of the Spiritual Senses	156
Conclusion	159
6. Seeing (Spiritually) Is Believing: The Spiritual Senses and Faith	161
Seeing God in All Things: The Spiritual Senses and Natural Theology	162
The Spiritual Senses and Fundamental Theology	167
Given, Yet One's Own: The Spiritual Senses, Nature, and Grace	178
Conclusion	184
Conclusion	**186**
Bibliography	193
Index	215

Abbreviations

THE WORKS OF HANS URS VON BALTHASAR

CL	Cosmic Liturgy: The Universe According to Maximus the Confessor
Ep.	Epilogue
ET I-IV	Explorations in Theology, vols I–IV
GL I-VII	The Glory of the Lord: A Theological Aesthetics, vols I–VII
KB	The Theology of Karl Barth
LA	Love Alone is Credible
OSF	Origen: Spirit and Fire
TD I-V	Theo-Drama: Theological Dramatic Theory, vols I–V
TL I-III	Theo-Logic: Theological Logical Theory, vols I–III

OTHER WORKS

ANF	Ante-Nicene Fathers
Brev.	Bonaventure, Breviloquium
CCSL	D. Eligius Dekkers, OSB, and Johannes Fraipont, eds. *Corpus Christianorum Series Latina*
CD	Karl Barth, Church Dogmatics
Conf.	Augustine, Confessions
De Civ. Dei	Augustine, City of God
De Gen.	Augustine, De Genesi ad Litteram
De Prin.	Origen, De Principiis
De Ver.	Thomas Aquinas, De Veritate
DS	Denzinger-Schönmetzer, eds., Enchiridion Symbolorum
Enarr. in Ps.	Augustine, Expositions of the Psalms

GCS	W. A. Baehrens, ed., *Origenes Werke. Die Griechischen Christlichen Schriftsteller*
GNO	H. Langerbeck, ed., *Gregorii Nysseni Opera*
Hom.	Pseudo-Macarius, *The Fifty Spiritual Homilies*
In Cant.	Origen, *In Canticum Canticorum*
Itin.	Bonaventure, *Itinerarium Mentis in Deum*
PG	Jacques-P. Migne, ed., *Patrologiae Cursus Completus, Series Graeca*
PL	Jacques-P. Migne, ed., *Patrologiae Cursus Completus, Series Latina*
SCG	Thomas Aquinas, *Summa Contra Gentiles*
SD	Paul Claudel, 'La Sensation du Divin'
Sent.	Bonaventure, *Sentences Commentary*
SRE	Romano Guardini, *Die Sinne und die religiöse Erkenntnis*
ST	Thomas Aquinas, *Summa Theologiae*
SW	Gustav Siewerth, *Die Sinne und das Wort*
WB	Gustav Siewerth, *Wort und Bild*

Introduction

The theology of Hans Urs von Balthasar (1905–88) has significantly shaped Catholic and Protestant thought for some time. He is most widely known for the particular manner in which his thought confronts the anthropocentrism of many modern theological schemes: namely, through the use of aesthetic categories in mediating divine revelation to humanity. At the heart of this 'theological aesthetics' stands the task of perceiving the absolute beauty of the divine form (*Gestalt*) through which God is revealed to human beings.

Although extensive scholarly attention has focused on Balthasar's understanding of revelation, beauty, and form, what remains curiously overlooked is his heavy reliance on the classic Christian doctrine of the 'spiritual senses' in his theological aesthetics.[1] Balthasar expresses the significance of the doctrine in a crucial section of *The Glory of the Lord*, in which he claims that his theological anthropology actually 'culminates' with his treatment of the spiritual senses.[2] And yet Balthasar's secondary commentators have for the most part missed this vital point, in part because the doctrine has a 'capillary' quality: it is present throughout Balthasar's corpus, but it manifests subtly, and attention is seldom drawn to it (excepting the one portion of his aesthetics noted above).[3] Indeed, the spiritual senses theme has been hidden from view because, although the language of sensation certainly permeates Balthasar's aesthetics, he does not consistently make clear to his reader that it is 'spiritual' sensation of which

---

[1] The doctrine of the spiritual senses has been interpreted in the Christian tradition in a variety of ways. In its epistemological sense, it claims that human beings can be made capable of a mode of perception that exceeds the physical plane and takes place in an extra-corporeal, 'spiritual' register.

[2] Balthasar devotes the third and final section of his examination of Christian experience (titled 'The Spiritual Senses') to the doctrine. See *The Glory of the Lord*, vol. 1: *Seeing the Form*, 365–425.

[3] I borrow this term from Boyd Taylor Coolman, who so characterizes the easily overlooked character of the spiritual senses in William of Auxerre. See *Knowing God by Experience: The Spiritual Senses in the Theology of William of Auxerre* (Washington, DC: Catholic University of America Press, 2004), 3.

he speaks. For instance, he discusses 'seeing the form' of divine revelation throughout *The Glory of the Lord*, but one must be attuned to the spiritual senses motif in order to discern that it is actually *spiritual sight* that performs this task.

Highly significant in this connection are the numerous interpretive difficulties that the doctrine of the spiritual senses presents to contemporary scholarship; the spiritual sense of scripture as a hermeneutical strategy is much more widely known, and the idea of the spiritual senses as perceptual faculties remains relatively unfamiliar.[4] As a result, many scholars misread discussions of the spiritual senses as pertaining to biblical interpretation. Furthermore, because Balthasar is often read in opposition to Karl Rahner as adopting the revelation-centred theological method of Karl Barth, Balthasar's theological anthropology (of which the spiritual senses are a crucial component) has been largely occluded from scholarly view.

I argue in this study that Balthasar's account of the reception of revelation can only be effectively explained by reference to his reliance on the doctrine of the spiritual senses. At the very core of Balthasar's aesthetics lies the idea that our perceptual faculties must become 'spiritualized' if we are to perceive the splendour (*Glanz*) of the form through which God is revealed. The spiritual senses tradition therefore emerges as an essential resource for Balthasar's articulation of this spiritual aesthesis; it serves as the anthropological correlate to the splendour of revelation. These findings significantly revise regnant understandings of Balthasar's aesthetics, anthropology, and epistemology, and they also demonstrate the surprising contemporary relevance of this long-obscured aspect of the Christian tradition.

It should additionally be said that, in deploying the spiritual senses in his theological aesthetics, Balthasar is not content simply to repristinate the doctrine out of its patristic and medieval versions. Instead, Balthasar places traditional understandings of the spiritual senses in conversation with the thought of his contemporaries, most particularly Karl Barth (1886–1968), Romano Guardini (1885–1968), Gustav Siewerth (1903–63), and Paul Claudel (1868–1955). What emerges from this dialogue is a re-forged model of the doctrine that displays noteworthy discontinuities from its previous instantiations. Balthasar

---

[4] For a recent attempt to remedy this situation, see Paul Gavrilyuk and Sarah Coakley, eds., *The Spiritual Senses: Perceiving God in Western Christianity* (Cambridge: Cambridge University Press, 2012).

Introduction 3

thus uses his contemporary interlocutors to advance a highly creative and *modern* rearticulation of the doctrine that diverges significantly from its historical precedents. It is only when the spiritual senses have been recast in a modern form that they will serve Balthasar's project in the manner described above.

ON THE 'DOCTRINE OF THE SPIRITUAL SENSES'

A preliminary question must be faced at the outset of this study: what exactly is the 'doctrine of the spiritual senses'? Although the term is not used univocally throughout its long history, the phrase frequently denotes a set of five 'spiritual' perceptual faculties that function in a manner analogous to their corporeal counterparts. In other words, just as there are corporeal senses of sight, hearing, taste, touch, and smell that apprehend physical objects, there are also spiritual senses of sight, hearing, taste, touch, and smell that perceive 'spiritual' entities (God, Christ, angels) in an extra-corporeal register. Augustin Poulain and Karl Rahner, in separate, highly influential studies, developed a 'definition' of the spiritual senses as fivefold, 'analogical' uses of the language of sensation.[5] In other words, they argued that there are indeed

---

[5] Augustin Poulain, SJ, *Des grâces d'oraison* (Paris: V. Retaux, 1901). Published in English as *The Graces of Interior Prayer*, trans. Leonora L. Yorke Smith from the 6th edition, and corrected to accord with the 10th French edition (London: Kegan Paul, Trench, Trübner & Co., 1950). Karl Rahner, SJ, 'Le début d'une doctrine des cinq sens spirituals chez Origène', *Revue d'ascetique et de mystique* 13 (1932), 112–45. The article was translated into German and printed in abridged form in Karl Rahner, *Schriften zur Theologie,* Band XII: *Theologie aus Erfahrung des Geistes,* ed. Karl Neufeld, SJ (Zürich: Benziger Verlag, 1975), 111–36, then later published in English as 'The "Spiritual Senses" According to Origen', in Karl Rahner, *Theological Investigations*, vol. 16: *Experience of the Spirit: Source of Theology*, trans. David Morland, OSB (New York: Crossroad, 1979), 81–103. Karl Rahner, 'La doctrine des "sens spirituels" au moyen-âge, en particulier chez S. Bonaventure', *Revue d'ascetique et de mystique* 14 (1933), 263–99. Rahner wrote another essay on Bonaventure published in 1934: 'Der Begriff der Ecstasis bei Bonaventura', *Zeitschrift für Aszese und Mystik* 9 (1934), 1–19. These two articles were combined by Karl Neufeld and published as 'Die Lehre von den "geistlichen Sinnen" im Mittelalter', in *Schriften zur Theologie,* Band XII: *Theologie aus Erfahrung des Geistes,* ed. Karl Neufeld, SJ (Zürich: Benziger Verlag, 1975), 137–72. The English translation is from this 1975 German version, 'The Doctrine of the "Spiritual Senses" in the Middle Ages', in *Theological Investigations*, vol. 16: *Experience of the Spirit: Source of Theology*, trans. David Morland, OSB (New York: Crossroad, 1979), 104–34.

five discrete spiritual senses, and they further insisted that exponents of the doctrine used the language of sensation in a manner that was not 'merely metaphorical'.[6] Instead, they claimed that we observe in these descriptions of mystical encounter a 'stronger', 'analogical' use of sensory terms.[7] It was this version of the spiritual senses tradition that Balthasar inherited and utilized, though not—as we shall shortly show—without added novelties of his own.

WHY THE NEGLECT OF THE SPIRITUAL SENSES IN BALTHASAR'S THOUGHT?

In spite of the repeated (albeit often scattered) references to this theme throughout his corpus, Balthasar's appropriation of the doctrine remains largely unexamined at present. Only a handful of scholars have observed that the spiritual senses are a noteworthy feature of Balthasar's aesthetics,[8] and even among those who are aware of the

---

[6] Poulain emphatically holds, 'With the mystics, the words to *see* God, to *hear*, and to *touch* Him are not mere metaphors. They express something more: some close analogy' (*The Graces of Interior Prayer*, 90). Spiritual seeing, for example, is in an important way quite similar to physical seeing. A 'merely metaphorical' use of such terms, by contrast, bears only a 'distant or restricted resemblance', on Poulain's analysis. Rahner adopts Poulain's criteria and employs them in examining a vast range of patristic and medieval texts. For the methodological prologue to Rahner's analysis, see 'The "Spiritual Senses" According to Origen', 81–2. Of course, some will find this particular understanding of metaphor reductive. A 'metaphorical' use of sensory language, on these accounts, simply indicates a use of sensory language that does not actually retain any sensory or perceptual dimension. For example, in the colloquial expression, 'I see what you mean', the term, 'seeing' is used in a sense that Poulain and Rahner would regard as metaphorical. For purposes of this examination, I use the term in the manner in which it has been used in scholarship on the spiritual senses, the various shortcomings of such a limited concept of metaphor notwithstanding.

[7] Of what, one might ask, does this 'close analogy' consist? Poulain draws on the notion of 'presence' in order to outline the necessary conditions for a 'strong resemblance' between the spiritual and corporeal senses. He explains, 'Does the soul possess intellectual spiritual senses, having some resemblance to the bodily senses, so that, in an analogous manner and in diverse ways, she is able to perceive the *presence* of pure spirits (*la présence des purs esprits*), and the presence of God in particular' (*The Graces of Interior Prayer*, 88)? For Poulain, it is precisely when one speaks of detecting an immaterial *presence* that he or she is using sensory language in an 'analogous', 'non-metaphorical' manner.

[8] Balthasar's use of the spiritual senses receives brief mention in the following works: Hansjürgen Verweyen, *Ontologische Voraussetzungen des Glaubensaktes* (Düsseldorf: Patmos Verlag, 1969), 172. Manfred Lochbrunner, *Analogia Caritatis*:

doctrine's significance, only Stephen Fields and Agnell Rickenmann have undertaken article-length investigations of the topic.[9] Rickenmann provides an excellent summary of Origen's position on the spiritual senses (from which Balthasar draws) and a helpful exposition of Balthasar's overall goals in his theological aesthetics. Fields offers an instructive account of key points of contrast between the readings of Bonaventure advanced by Balthasar and Rahner. However, due in large part to of the brevity of any article-length treatment of the issues, neither Fields nor Rickenmann gestures toward the wide array of influences on Balthasar's creative rearticulation of the doctrine, nor do they investigate the systematic significance of the spiritual senses in relation to Balthasar's theory of aesthetic form. As the essays by Rickenmann and Fields are the only articles on the topic, and there is at present no full-length study of Balthasar's use of the spiritual senses tradition, the secondary literature on this aspect of Balthasar's thought remains unexpectedly incomplete.

At the risk of oversimplifying the reasons for this lacuna, much can be explained by reference to Balthasar's well-known emphasis on resuscitating an *objective* revelatory claim for modern theology. That is, Balthasar's resistance to theologies that follow Immanuel Kant's 'turn to the subject' has influenced many commentators on his texts to focus on the *object* of theology in his thought, and as a result examinations of his model of the human *subject* have been comparatively minimal. Indeed, the most notable point of contrast between Balthasar and Rahner is often said to be that, whereas Rahner (and,

---

Darstellung und Deutung der Theologie Hans Urs von Balthasars (Freiburg: Herder, 1981), 175. Peter Casarella, 'Experience as a Theological Category: Hans Urs von Balthasar on the Christian Encounter with God's Image', *Communio* 20 (Spring 1993), 118–28, at 122. Roland Chia, *Revelation and Theology: The Knowledge of God in Balthasar and Barth* (Bern and New York: Peter Lang, 1999), 82–6. Victoria Harrison, '*Homo Orans*: von Balthasar's Christocentric Philosophical Anthropology', *Heythrop Journal* 40 (1999), 280–300, at 299. D. C. Schindler, *Hans Urs von Balthasar and the Dramatic Structure of Truth* (New York: Fordham Press, 2004), 279–85. Anthony Cirelli, 'Form and Freedom: Patristic Revival in Hans Urs von Balthasar' (doctoral dissertation: Catholic University of America, 2007), 225–9. Although Louis Dupré does not address Balthasar's use of the spiritual senses tradition specifically, he does take up similar themes in his 'The Glory of the Lord: Hans Urs von Balthasar's Theological Aesthetic', in David L. Schindler, *Hans Urs von Balthasar: His Life and Work* (San Francisco, CA: Ignatius Press, 1991), 183–206.

[9] Stephen Fields, 'Balthasar and Rahner on the Spiritual Senses', *Theological Studies* 57 (1996), 224–41. Agnell Rickenmann, 'La dottrina di Origene sui sensi spirituali e la sua ricezione in Hans Urs von Balthasar', *Rivista Teologica di Lugano* 6 (2001), 155–68.

more broadly, all of so-called 'transcendental Thomism') is concerned with the transcendental structure of the human subject, Balthasar is deeply critical of this approach, and he instead focuses his theological attention on that which lies *beyond* the human being.[10] The spiritual senses, then, may have gone largely unnoticed because of the fact that they, as epistemological features of the human being, do not occur to many Balthasar scholars as especially pertinent to the broader themes of his theology.

It should additionally be noted that interpreting Balthasar on any topic is a notoriously difficult task, and elucidating his many comments on the spiritual senses proves to be no exception to this general rule. In characteristic Balthasarian fashion, a frequently opaque account of the spiritual senses is put forward in *The Glory of the Lord*, and as a result it is not immediately obvious to Balthasar's readers how carefully his reading of the spiritual senses tradition is considered, nor how well it serves many of Balthasar's overarching aims. Although we will find in some instances that Balthasar simply does not provide his reader with sufficient clarity, I also suggest that a number of claims in Balthasar's texts that may at first glance appear to be overly epigrammatic can in fact be shown through careful analysis to have highly developed theoretical backing.

Also significant on this question of scholarly neglect, as mentioned briefly above, are the numerous hermeneutical difficulties the doctrine of the spiritual senses presents to its interpreters. The very term, 'spiritual senses', tends to disorient more than illuminate, and it often initially brings to mind the spiritual sense of scripture as a hermeneutical approach to the Bible. The notion of the spiritual senses as a set of perceptual faculties analogous to the physical senses remains

---

[10] Balthasar contrasts his approach with that of Rahner in an interview late in life, commenting as follows: 'Rahner has chosen Kant, or, if you prefer, Fichte: the transcendental starting point. And I—as a Germanist—have chosen Goethe, [who stressed] the form (*Gestalt*), the indissolubly unique, organic, developing form (*Gestalt*)—I am thinking of Goethe's poem *Die Metamorphose der Pflanzen*—this form (*Gestalt*) [is] something that Kant, even in his aesthetics, never really dealt with.' Hans Urs von Balthasar, 'Geist und Feuer', *Herder Korrespondenz* 30 (1976), 72–82, at 75. English translation in Edward T. Oakes, SJ, *Pattern of Redemption* (New York: Continuum, 1994), 72–3. Balthasar's theological method, then, emphasizes the object of theology over against any 'Kantianism', and he is quite clear in claiming that this object itself sets the terms for encounter and delimits its possibilities. To ascribe the synthetic power of which Balthasar speaks to the subject alone undermines the self-organizing nature of the object of theology on Balthasar's model.

Introduction

relatively unknown, and even to those familiar with the idea, a number of interpretive issues complexify contemporary understandings of the doctrine.

Most pressing among these difficulties is the fact that, throughout the long history of the doctrine, an exceptionally broad constellation of phrases is used to describe spiritual perception. The term 'spiritual senses' certainly receives the most attention in modern scholarship, but more prevalent in patristic and medieval texts themselves are phrases such as 'inner senses', 'interior eyes', 'eyes of the soul', 'eyes of faith', 'eyes of the mind', 'eyes of the heart', 'eyes of the spirit', 'ears of the heart', 'touch of the spirit', 'divine sense' and many others. This variety of terms—which itself often changes from one historical period to the next—makes it extremely difficult to identify when an author is speaking of spiritual perception, properly understood.

Additionally, various figures in the spiritual senses tradition respond differently to even the most basic questions about how spiritual perception functions. For example, what, exactly, do the spiritual senses perceive? One finds that they have different objects, depending on whom one consults. Do they operate purely *independently* of the corporeal senses, or are they joined with them? Does one receive them through grace alone, or does practice play a role in developing one's spiritual senses? Who receives spiritual senses: only 'mystics', or all Christians? What are they good for, theologically speaking? The fact that there are wide-ranging answers to each of these questions means that any academic treatment of the spiritual senses will need to investigate an unusually large number of variables to determine how the doctrine is understood.

BALTHASAR'S INTEREST IN THE SPIRITUAL SENSES

Despite the challenges associated with our enquiry, one thing is clear: Balthasar himself regarded the spiritual senses as highly significant for his theology. His interest in the doctrine can even be observed as early as 1934: in October of that year he wrote a letter to the German philosopher Josef Pieper, to whom he commented on Rahner's recently published studies on Origen and

Bonaventure.[11] Just a few years later, in his 1939 Origen anthology, Balthasar grouped together over 150 passages from Origen's works that describe, in Balthasar's terms, 'spiritual "super-sensibility"' (*geistliche Übersinnlichkeit*).[12] In that same year Balthasar published an article titled 'Seeing, Hearing, and Reading within the Church', in which he extensively treated the spiritual senses.[13] Balthasar also mentioned the spiritual senses in his monographs on Maximus the Confessor,[14] Karl Barth,[15] Romano Guardini,[16] George Bernanos,[17] and his volume on Thérèse of Lisieux and Elizabeth of the Trinity.[18] Additionally, the spiritual senses motif appeared in a number of Balthasar's well-known works, such as *Mysterium Paschale*,[19] *Love Alone*,[20] *Prayer*,[21] *The Moment*

[11] This letter is quoted in Manfred Lochbrunner, *Hans Urs von Balthasar und seine Philosophenfreunde: Fünf Doppelporträts* (Würzburg: Echter Verlag, 2005), 15.

[12] Hans Urs von Balthasar, *Origen, Spirit and Fire: A Thematic Anthology of His Writings*, trans. Robert Daly (Washington, DC: Catholic University of America Press, 1984), 218–57. See also 'Le Mysterion d'Origène', *Recherches de science religieuse* 26 (1936), 511–62 and 27 (1937), 38–64. For Balthasar's treatment of the spiritual senses, see 554–62. Later published in a single volume as *Parole et mystère chez Origène* (Paris: Éditions du Cerf, 1957). In the 1957 republication, Balthasar includes a subheading with the title 'Sens Spirituel' in the volume's table of contents.

[13] Hans Urs von Balthasar, 'Seeing, Hearing, and Reading within the Church', in *Explorations in Theology*, vol. 2: *Spouse of the Word*, trans. A. V. Littledale, A. Dru, B. McNeil, et al. (San Francisco, CA: Ignatius Press, 1991), 473–90, at 473–85.

[14] Hans Urs von Balthasar, *Cosmic Liturgy: The Universe According to Maximus the Confessor*, trans. Brian Daley, SJ (San Francisco, CA: Ignatius Press, 2003), 'spiritual eyes' (54), 'five...spiritual faculties of the soul' (304), 'spiritual senses' (305).

[15] Hans Urs von Balthasar, *The Theology of Karl Barth*, trans. Edward T. Oakes, SJ (San Francisco, CA: Ignatius Press, 1992), 'perception of God' (154), 'spiritual contact' (329), 'spiritual sense' (374).

[16] Hans Urs von Balthasar, *Romano Guardini: Reform from the Source*, trans. Albert Wimmer and D. C. Schindler (San Francisco, CA: Ignatius Press, 2010), 'spiritual eyes' (73), extra-corporeal perception (24).

[17] Hans Urs von Balthasar, *Bernanos: An Ecclesial Existence*, trans. Erasmo Leiva-Merikakis (San Francisco, CA: Ignatius Press, 1996), 'open our senses to the invisible world' (86), 'the truly real vision of invisible spiritual reality' (142), 'inner eye' (142), 'spiritual senses' (244).

[18] Hans Urs von Balthasar, *Two Sisters in the Spirit: Thérèse of Lisieux & Elizabeth of the Trinity*, trans. Dennis Martin (San Francisco, CA: Ignatius Press, 1992), 'eye of the soul' (442, 453), 'touch of the Spirit' (495), 'divine touch' (473).

[19] Hans Urs von Balthasar, *Mysterium Paschale*, trans. Aidan Nichols, OP (San Francisco, CA: Ignatius Press, 2000): 'spiritual eyes' (222), 'spiritual vision' (233), 'eyes of the heart' (228, 262).

[20] Hans Urs von Balthasar, *Love Alone is Credible*, trans. D. C. Schindler (San Francisco, CA: Ignatius Press, 2004), 'eyes of faith' (60), 'eyes...given to me only in faith' (114–15).

[21] Hans Urs von Balthasar, *Prayer*, trans. Graham Harrison (San Francisco, CA: Ignatius Press, 1986), 'spiritual senses' (269, 271), 'spiritual eye(s)' (165, 246), 'eyes of our mind' (177), 'eyes of the soul' (262), 'spiritual ear' (84), 'spiritual taste' (267).

Introduction														9

of *Christian Witness*,[22] *Science, Religion, and Christianity*,[23] *A Theology of History*,[24] *Elucidations*,[25] *Christian Meditation*,[26] *Truth is Symphonic*,[27] *Light of the Word*,[28] *New Elucidations*,[29] and of course his *Theo-Drama*[30] and *Theo-Logic*.[31]

Toward the end of his career, Balthasar made overt reference to the importance of the spiritual senses for his theological aesthetics. In an address given upon receiving an honorary doctorate from the Catholic University of America in 1980, he commented, 'My intention in the first part of my trilogy called *"Aesthetik"* was not merely to train our *spiritual eyes* to see Christ as he shows himself but, beyond that, to prove that all great and history-making theology always followed this method'.[32] This self-assessment demonstrates not only that Balthasar regarded the spiritual senses as highly significant for

---

[22] Hans Urs von Balthasar, *The Moment of Christian Witness*, trans. The Missionary Society of St Paul the Apostle in the State of New York (San Francisco, CA: Ignatius Press, 1994), '[God's] invisible nature is seen' (79).

[23] Hans Urs von Balthasar, *Science, Religion, and Christianity*, trans. Hilda Graef (London: Burns & Oates, 1958), 'ear for God' (28), 'spiritual intuition' (30).

[24] Hans Urs von Balthasar, *A Theology of History* (San Francisco, CA: Ignatius Press, 1994), 'spiritual sight' (94).

[25] Hans Urs von Balthasar, *Elucidations*, trans. by SPCK (San Francisco, CA: Ignatius Press, 1998), 'pneumatic sense' (147), 'inner ear' (147).

[26] Hans Urs von Balthasar, *Christian Meditation*, trans. Mary Skerry (San Francisco, CA: Ignatius Press, 1989), 23, 35, 53, 97.

[27] Hans Urs von Balthasar, *Truth is Symphonic: Aspects of Christian Pluralism* (San Francisco, CA: Ignatius Press, 1987), 123, 129.

[28] Hans Urs von Balthasar, *Light of the Word: Brief Reflections on the Sunday Readings* (San Francisco, CA: Ignatius Press, 1993), 'opened the disciples' eyes to perceive what really did happen in the institution of the Eucharist' (64), 'spiritual eyes' (69), 'his spirit touches the Spirit of God' (154), 'eyes of the Spirit' (295), 'spiritual vision' (317), 'as John says, they have "seen, heard, and touched the Word of eternal life"' (338).

[29] Hans Urs von Balthasar, *New Elucidations*, trans. Mary Theresilde Skerry (San Francisco, CA: Ignatius Press, 1986), 17, 42–3.

[30] *TD* II, 'spiritual ear', (73), 'spiritual gaze' (77), 'spiritual eye' (78), 'eyes of faith' (87, 89), 'eyes of the spirit' (353); *TD* III, 'inner eye' (59), 'eyes of faith' (507); *TD* IV, 'seeing God as he is' (199).

[31] *TL* I, 'a sort of vision of God in the medium of the creature (Rom. 1:20)' (235), *TL* II, 'spiritual visions' (111), *TL* III, 'by means of the power that enlightens us, we fix our eyes on the beauty of the image of the invisible God' (127), 'tasting and knowing things from within' (139), 'Christian "hearing"..."an inner feeling and tasting of the things"...and to "smell the indescribable fragrance" and "taste the boundless sweetness of the Divinity"' (195), 'it is the spirit who gives believers eyes to discern God's revelation' (203), 'ear of the heart' (372), 'spiritual feeling or tasting' (384).

[32] Hans Urs von Balthasar, 'Theology and Aesthetic', *Communio*, 8 (Spring 1981), 62–71, at 66 (emphasis added).

his own theological project, but also that he held the notion of spiritualized perception to function as a leitmotif throughout the history of Christian theology.

Most important to this study are the references to the spiritual senses that pervade Balthasar's theological aesthetics. Throughout *The Glory of the Lord* Balthasar draws from various phrases associated with the tradition, including 'spiritual senses',[33] 'spiritual perception',[34] and 'inner senses'.[35] One also finds repeated references to senses of sight, hearing, touch, taste, and smell that are described in an extra-corporeal, 'spiritual' register.[36] Of considerable import for the argument made in this study, Balthasar writes in the first volume of his aesthetics that his treatment of the human being 'culminates' in his treatment of the spiritual senses.[37]

PROGRESSION OF ARGUMENT AND CHAPTER OUTLINE

The study is organized around two sets of questions. First, why does Balthasar write what he does about the spiritual senses? Who are

---

[33] *GL* I, 249, 365–425, 461; *GL* II, 79, 260, 319–36, 333–5; *GL* IV, 359; *GL* V, 89, 298, 608.

[34] *GL* I, 153, 238, 267, 362; *GL* II, 164, *GL* IV 361.

[35] *GL* II, 318, 19, 22; *GL* IV, 353.

[36] The phrase, 'eye(s) of the soul' can be found at *GL* I, 285, 391; *GL* II, 171; *GL* III, 16; *GL* IV, 394. 'Eye(s) of the heart': *GL* II, 275; *GL* III, 180; *GL* VII, 14, 358. 'Eye(s) of the spirit': *GL* I, 200, 264; *GL* II, 291; *GL* VII, 294. 'Eye of the mind': *GL* II, 99, 107. 'Eyes of faith': *GL* I, 31, 70, 175, 190, 191, 198, 216, 236, 343, 458, 480, 487, 538, 546, 592, 643, 658; *GL* II, 325; *GL* III, 227, 233, 427; *GL* VI, 408; *GL* VII, 14, 18, 28, 89, 260, 328, 368, 493. 'Spiritual eyes': *GL* I, 30; *GL* II, 137; *GL* IV, 328. 'Spiritual sight': *GL* II, 205, 222. 'Spiritual vision': *GL* II, 142, 222. 'Spiritual seeing': *GL* II, 100, 101. 'Spiritual gaze': *GL* II, 291. 'Inner eye': *GL* I, 71, 500; *GL* II, 99; *GL* VI, 348. For references to 'seeing God' see *GL* I, 149, 248, 251, 260, 283, 327, 329, 336, 359, 368, 438, 462, 501, 606; *GL* II, 45, 46, 47, 75, 99, 108, 122, 138, 179, 204, 207; *GL* IV, 37, 66, 68; *GL* V, 82–3, 233; *GL* VI, 68, 71, 72, 92, 149, 327; *GL* VII, 14, 483, 25, 55, 287, 319, 378. For hearing, see esp. 'ear(s) of the soul': *GL* I, 285; *GL* VII, 542. 'Ear of the heart': *GL* II, 326. 'Ear of the spirit': *GL* III, 135. 'Spiritual hearing': *GL* II, 321. For hearing: *GL* I, 285, 307, 323, 362, 368, 369, 371, 376, 380, 397, 402; *GL* II, 319, 322, 324, 341; *GL* III, 112, 143, 457; *GL* IV, 359; *GL* VI, 131. Taste: *GL* I, 100, 289, 307, 425; *GL* II, 321, 347, 349; *GL* III, 257; *GL* V, 229; *GL* VII, 234, 371, 530. Smell: *GL* I, 289, 371, 386, 425; *GL* II, 218, 319, 322; *GL* IV, 359; *GL* VI, 131.

[37] *GL* I, 365.

Introduction   11

the key figures in his reading of the spiritual senses tradition, and how does he interpret those figures? In other words, the first issue this study addresses is that of influences. This will be the concern of Chapters 1–3. Second, what does Balthasar do with the idea of the spiritual senses in his own theology? How does he articulate his version of the doctrine? What place do the spiritual senses occupy in his theological aesthetics? How does the doctrine function? The second set of questions, then, is one of constructive position and systematic significance of the spiritual senses for Balthasar's own thought. This will be the concern of Chapters 4–6. A more specific account of the exact manner in which these two sets of questions are addressed now follows.

Chapter 1 examines Balthasar's reading of patristic figures on the spiritual senses. Origen receives greatest emphasis here, both because he stands at the beginning of the spiritual senses tradition (Rahner credits him with 'inventing' the doctrine), and because of his special significance for Balthasar. Broadly speaking, the most distinctive feature of Balthasar's approach to patristic writers on the spiritual senses entails the positive reading he gives to the corporeal senses to which the spiritual senses are analogous. That is, many patristic authors are ordinarily read as articulating a 'dualist' model of the doctrine whereby the spiritual senses are disjuncted from their corporeal counterparts. We shall see in Chapter 1, however, that Balthasar repeatedly interprets patristic authors as valuing the corporeal dimension to perception in addition to its spiritual correlate. As a result, Balthasar occasionally advances a somewhat hermeneutically massaged reading of patristic sources; the Church fathers whom he reads do not always actually espouse the positions he claims they advance. It will also be shown, however, that Balthasar does not push this positive reading of the body as far as might be expected, given his concern with corporeality. Additionally, we shall observe throughout the first chapter and the next the massive influence of Rahner on this aspect of Balthasar's thought. Indeed, it is first and foremost Rahner who mediates the doctrine of the spiritual senses to Balthasar, as Rahner's patristic and medieval studies extensively shape Balthasar's own examination of these figures.

Chapter 2 investigates Balthasar's reading of figures from the medieval and early modern periods. Bonaventure is most significant for Balthasar among medieval expositors of the doctrine, and Ignatius of Loyola for Balthasar's reading of the early modern period. As was true in his reading of the patristic authors, Balthasar again celebrates the material dimension to perception in the medieval and early modern figures he examines, drawing from those versions of the doctrine the most positive reading of the physical senses that he can credibly summon. In this chapter we shall also see that Balthasar finds in Bonaventure one who regards the spiritual senses as possessed of an explicitly aesthetic dimension, an attribute that has obvious affinities with Balthasar's project and his own appropriation of the doctrine.

Chapter 3 looks closely at the influence of Balthasar's contemporaries on his version of the spiritual senses, with special attention to Karl Barth, Romano Guardini, Gustav Siewerth, and Paul Claudel. Here I show that Balthasar actually evinces substantial discontentment with the versions of the doctrine articulated throughout its earlier history. Most importantly, all four of the modern figures upon whom Balthasar draws equip him with an anthropology of 'unity-in-duality' between body and soul. He then uses this anthropology to frame the doctrine of the spiritual senses such that spiritual and corporeal perception occurs in a single unified act. With modern figures as his guides, Balthasar therefore finally unites spiritual and corporeal perception, which is something that he starts—but does not finish—in his examination of traditional figures. Additionally, Balthasar draws from the 'personalism' of Barth and Siewerth to claim that the 'definitive arena' within which one receives one's spiritual senses is encounter with the neighbour.[38]

Having assessed in the first three chapters Balthasar's (often idiosyncratic) reading of various figures in the spiritual senses tradition and its modern continuations, I describe in Chapter 4 Balthasar's own version of the doctrine in his theological aesthetics. Here I cull various aspects of Balthasar's engagement with the sources outlined in the previous chapters in order to highlight key features of his constructive use of the doctrine. We will see that Balthasar advances a highly original understanding of the spiritual senses that is distinct from those models that precede him.

Chapter 5 puts forward the central claim of this study: Balthasar's theological aesthetics calls for perception of the 'form' (*Gestalt*), and that form consists of both sensory and 'supersensory' aspects

---

[38] Although Balthasar's engagement with personalism is wide-ranging, in this study I confine my examination to those versions of the idea most directly relevant to his doctrine of the spiritual senses.

(i.e., a material component and a 'spiritual' dimension, *species* and *lumen*, *forma* and *splendor*). Therefore, some account of the way in which this human perception *exceeds* the material realm is absolutely essential to the success of Balthasar's project. In other words, it is precisely because the form itself has both sensory and supersensory aspects that the *perception* of that form must be both sensory and supersensory. Balthasar's theological aesthetics thus clamours for a doctrine of the spiritual senses; in fact, one could go so far as to claim that if such a doctrine did not already exist, then for purposes of his theological aesthetics Balthasar would need to invent it.

Chapter 6 explores the far-reaching implications of the claim made in Chapter 5 by looking at Balthasar's engagement with the pressing theological issues of his day. I argue that many of Balthasar's critiques of Neo-Scholasticism, Catholic 'Modernism', Rahner, and Barth all actually have, at their core, his version of the spiritual senses. By examining topics such as the nature of faith, natural theology, apologetics, aesthetic experience, and the relationship between nature and grace, we shall see that the spiritual senses comprise an integral component of the Balthasarian solution to the problems encountered in these debates. Therefore, the treatment of the spiritual senses in this chapter offers ways of advancing theological discussion, not only for Balthasar scholarship, but, more broadly, for a recurrent set of challenges presented to modern theology.

IMPLICATIONS

In examining these aspects of Balthasar's appropriation of the spiritual senses tradition, this study contributes to scholarship at a number of different levels. First, and most obviously, it adds to a growing body of literature on the spiritual senses tradition. In particular, it demonstrates that the doctrine of the spiritual senses, long viewed as something of an oddity by many modern theologians and historians, in fact occupies an essential position in the thought of one of the most significant theologians of the twentieth century. Far from an obscure relic destined for insignificance, the spiritual senses are shown here to have an unexpected relevance for modern theology.

This book also contributes to the ongoing reception of Balthasar's *oeuvre* by observing that crucial features of his thought are illuminated by reference to the doctrine of the spiritual senses. Balthasar's use of the spiritual senses offers a corrective to those who regard him as relatively unconcerned with theological anthropology, and his use of the doctrine demonstrates a depth of epistemological concern that some scholars may find surprising. Additionally, situating Balthasar within scholarship on the spiritual senses gives his readers some idea of what to make of the dizzying array of sensory language he uses in his theological aesthetics. Indeed, placing Balthasar in the spiritual senses trajectory guards against collapsing his use of sensory language into 'merely metaphorical' descriptions of the encounter with God. Furthermore, when the spiritual senses are shown to be central to Balthasar's theological aesthetics, we see that his understanding of perception, faith, nature, and grace are all importantly inflected by his use of the doctrine.

Last, this study charts new avenues through which to appreciate previously unexamined lines of influence between Balthasar and a number of his contemporaries. Claiming that Rahner stands behind one of the most important features of Balthasar's thought underscores the fact that, despite their frequently discussed theological differences, an important commonality obtains between these two most influential Catholic theologians of the twentieth century. Additionally, to argue that Karl Barth had a hand in shaping Balthasar's model of spiritual perception is a highly counterintuitive suggestion that stands to deepen and expand our understanding of the relationship between these two seminal figures in twentieth-century theology.[39] This study therefore adds to scholarly assessments of the relationship between Balthasar and Barth by arguing that Barth is important to Balthasar not only in terms of his emphasis on revelation and his Christocentric approach to theology (as is well known), but also, and much more unexpectedly, for his theological anthropology and his claim that the human being is capable of perceiving God.

Furthermore, the spiritual senses are shown in this study to be highly relevant to contemporary thought when they are situated, as

---

[39] One would not expect that the doctrine of the spiritual senses, which has typically been used throughout the Christian tradition as a way of describing 'mystical' experience, would be so decisively shaped in Balthasar's theology by Barth, whose thoroughgoing aversion to mysticism pervades his theological works.

they should be, in the very centre of the most lively debates in modern Catholic theology: the 'Modernist' critiques of 'extrinsicism' and Neo-Scholastic ripostes to the 'immanentist' alternative, the critique of Neo-Scholastic proofs of God's existence, and the intricate descriptions of the relationship between nature and grace.

With a sense of the development of our argument now in place, we turn first to Balthasar's engagement with patristic versions of the spiritual senses.

1

'In the Spirit of Origen'

Balthasar's Exploration of Patristic Versions of the Spiritual Senses*

One of the most intriguing aspects of Balthasar's reading of the spiritual senses tradition is the extent to which he selectively chooses from among the doctrine's various patristic exponents and the way he massages his sources in accord with his theological concerns. Balthasar was not the first modern scholar to investigate the spiritual senses tradition (although he was the first major twentieth-century theologian to make explicit constructive use of the doctrine, as we shall see in Chapter 5). Among the many figures who focused on the spiritual senses in the early twentieth century, Karl Rahner provoked special interest in the topic with three articles published in the 1930s.[1] Therefore, one of the most interesting features of Balthasar's reading of the tradition is how he draws from Rahner's well-known studies while simultaneously distancing himself from Rahner's established interpretations. As we shall see, for all Balthasar's resistance to particular aspects of Rahner's interpretation of Origen and other patristic

---

* I borrow this chapter title from Werner Löser's classic study, *Im Geiste des Origenes: Hans Urs von Balthasar als Interpret der Theologie der Kirchenväter* (Frankfurt am Main: Josef Knecht, 1976).

[1] At the time of Balthasar's writing, Rahner's articles were the most frequently cited studies in scholarship on the spiritual senses, and they are still widely viewed as offering the standard treatment of the topic. See the Introduction to this study for complete bibliographical details.

figures, he in fact shows distinct signs of a deep debt to Rahner's work on the spiritual senses tradition.

Most revealingly, Balthasar adopts the same 'Origen and the rest' approach to the spiritual senses tradition first developed by Rahner, according to which the doctrine finds its definitive patristic proponent in Origen of Alexandria ($c.185$–$c.254$). Although other patristic figures pale in comparison to Origen, three others do appear in this 'standard' Rahnerian history of the doctrine: Evagrius of Pontus (345–99), Diadochus of Photice ($c.400$–$c.486$), and Pseudo-Macarius ($c.300$–90).[2] As we shall see in what follows, in spite of the fact that Balthasar differs from Rahner on some significant interpretive matters, he mirrors to a remarkable degree the level of significance that Rahner attaches to each of these figures.

With that said, Balthasar does considerably amplify the importance of two figures from their brief treatment at the hands of Rahner: Augustine of Hippo (354–430) and Maximus the Confessor ($c.580$–662). Below I demonstrate that Balthasar holds Augustine to be especially important for his notion that the spiritual senses perceive the beauty of Christ. I also show that Balthasar draws from Maximus the idea that the spiritual senses are particularly active within the liturgical setting. Both of these features of the doctrine's history are later integrated into Balthasar's constructive use of the spiritual senses in his theological aesthetics, as will be explored more thoroughly in Chapter 4.

Balthasar curiously neglects two of the most noteworthy advocates of the spiritual senses, Gregory of Nyssa ($c.335$–$c.394$) and Pseudo-Dionysius ($c.465$–$c.528$). In so doing, two points are made about his history of the doctrine. First, such odd lacunae once again accentuate the extent to which Balthasar is indebted to Rahner in his approach to the tradition, as Rahner's studies make only passing reference to Nyssen and no mention of Dionysius. Second, Balthasar's inattention to Nyssen and Dionysius demonstrates that, for all his insistence on the importance of the spiritual senses for his theological aesthetics, Balthasar is not ultimately interested in developing a more comprehensive history of the doctrine by treating figures

---

[2] Although Diadochus postdates Macarius by almost a century, Rahner places Macarius after Diadochus in his history of the spiritual senses, as does Balthasar in one of his accounts of the spiritual senses tradition. See Rahner, 'The "Spiritual Senses" According to Origen', 100–2. *GL* I, 268–82; 370.

who have been neglected in modern scholarship. Instead, I submit that Balthasar's central concern is to examine the same figures treated by Rahner (and to correct Rahner's reading of those figures, when necessary), then place those traditional exponents of the doctrine in conversation with Balthasar's modern interlocutors, as we shall see in Chapter 3 of this study.

Before turning to Balthasar's interpretation of particular patristic figures, we should acknowledge that he has been criticized for his approach to the theology of the early church. In particular, he is often regarded as allowing his own theological concerns to dictate his approach to the fathers, and many patristic scholars express a worry that he is not sufficiently attentive to the texts he examines. Brian Daley, for one, conveys his concerns as follows: 'So thoroughly has he exploited his patristic scholarship to advance his overall concerns that he often puzzles those whose interests are primarily directed towards understanding early Christian theology in its own context.'[3] In light of the potential for Balthasar to obscure the voices of the fathers with his own agenda, it will be the special concern of this chapter to determine whether or not he has inappropriately read his own theological preoccupations into the texts he examines. In some cases we will see the Balthasar that patristic scholars have come to expect; in other cases, however, I demonstrate that Balthasar actually reads those figures with greater sensitivity than one might anticipate on the basis of his reputation alone.

THE PATRISTIC IDEAL: ORIGEN OF ALEXANDRIA

In his earliest study on Origen, published in two parts in 1936 and 1937, Balthasar draws attention to the theme of the spiritual senses;[4]

---

[3] Brian Daley, SJ, 'Balthasar's Reading of the Church Fathers', in *The Cambridge Companion to Hans Urs von Balthasar* (Cambridge: Cambridge University Press, 2004), 187–206, at 187.

[4] 'Le Mysterion d'Origène', *Recherches de science religieuse* 26 (1936), 511–62, and 27 (1937), 38–64. For Balthasar's treatment of the spiritual senses, see 554–62. Later published in a single volume as *Parole et mystère chez Origène* (Paris: Èditions du Cerf, 1957). In the 1957 republication, Balthasar includes a subheading with the title 'Sens Spirituel' in the volume's table of contents.

two years later, in 1938, he publishes his anthology, *Origen: Spirit and Fire*, with a substantial section of his text specifically devoted to Origen's treatment of the topic.[5] In fact, in the latter volume Balthasar locates over 150 different passages from Origen's voluminous corpus that discuss spiritual sensation. In his own introductory comments to this assemblage of texts, Balthasar indicates both the importance of the doctrine and the significance of Origen in its history: 'Origen was the first to build up the doctrine of the spiritual senses which has remained a core element of all later mystical theology'.[6] In the first volume of his theological aesthetics, published in 1961, Balthasar again offers an account of Origen's understanding of the spiritual senses, this time in a brief reprise of the history of the doctrine that precedes his own constructive use of the idea.[7]

Although Origen's influence on Balthasar has been well documented among his commentators,[8] only Agnell Rickenmann has written an article-length study taking up Balthasar's reading of Origen's doctrine of the spiritual senses.[9] Rickenmann provides an excellent account of Origen's position and a helpful summary of

---

[5] *Origenes, Geist und Feuer: Ein Aufbau aus seinen Werken* (Salzburg: Otto Müller, 1938). Published in English as *Origen, Spirit and Fire: A Thematic Anthology of His Writings*, trans. Robert J. Daly (Washington, DC: Catholic University of America Press, 1984), hereafter *OSF*. For Balthasar's treatment of the spiritual senses, see 218–57.

[6] *OSF*, 218.   [7] *GL* I, 365–8.

[8] In an interview first published in 1976, Balthasar reflects on the significance of Origen as follows: 'Origen remains for me the most brilliant, the most encompassing interpreter and lover of the Word of God. I am nowhere more at home than with him.' 'Spirit and Fire: An Interview with Hans Urs von Balthasar', trans. Nicholas Healy, *Communio* 32 (Fall 2005), 573–93, at 593. See especially Werner Löser, *Im Geiste des Origenes: Hans Urs von Balthasar als Interpret der Theologie der Kirchenväter* (Frankfurt am Main: Josef Knecht, 1976); Elio Guerriero, 'Von Balthasar e Origene', *Rivista Internazionale di Teologia e Cultura: Communio* 116 (1991), 123–34. Francesco Franco, *La passione dell'amore: L'ermeneutica cristiana di Balthasar e Origene* (Bologna: EDB Edizioni Dehoniane Bologna, 2005); Thomas Böhm, 'Die Deutung der Kirchenväter bei Hans Urs von Balthasar—Der Fall Origenes', in *Logik der Liebe und Herrlichkeit Gottes: Hans Urs von Balthasar im Gespräch*, ed. Walter Kasper (Ostfildern: Matthias-Grünewald-Verlag, 2006), 64–75; Franz Mali, 'Origenes—Balthasars Lehrer des Endes?' in *Letzte Haltungen: Hans Urs von Balthasars 'Apokalypse der deutschen Seele' neu gelesen*, ed. Barbara Hallensleben (Fribourg: Academic Press, 2006), 280–90. Among the distinct doctrinal issues where Origen's influence is readily seen, the most notable may be Balthasar's appropriation of Origen's universalism in his eschatology. See Werner van Laak, *Allversöhnung: Die Lehre von der Apokatastasis, ihre Grundlegung durch Origenes und ihre Bewertung in der gegenwärtigen Theologie bei Karl Barth und Hans Urs von Balthasar* (Sinzig: Sankt Meinrad Verlag, 1990).

[9] Agnell Rickenmann, 'La dottrina di Origene sui sensi spirituali e la sua ricezione in Hans Urs von Balthasar', *Rivista Teologica di Lugano* 6 (2001), 155–68.

Balthasar's overall goals in his theological aesthetics. However, his actual assessment of Balthasar's appropriation of Origen on this topic is quite brief. Rickenmann notes Balthasar's general tendency to read his own theological concerns into the texts he examines,[10] but he does not offer an evaluation of specific aspects of Balthasar's interpretation of Origen's doctrine of the spiritual senses.

Below I supplement Rickenmann's scholarship by examining the most telling interpretive decisions in Balthasar's reading of Origen. Most apparently, despite some evidence to the contrary, Balthasar reads Origen's doctrine of the spiritual senses as fitting the Poulainian-Rahnerian 'definition': namely, as fivefold, 'non-metaphorical' uses of the language of sensation. Although the stakes of this interpretation may not be immediately obvious, such a reading of the spiritual senses in fact has far-reaching repercussions for Balthasar's theological aesthetics, as will be explored below. Additionally, although one finds significant variation throughout the tradition concerning what, exactly, the spiritual senses perceive, Balthasar consistently expresses interest in versions of the doctrine that hold Christ to be the object of spiritual perception. Furthermore, as will be made clear throughout this study, Balthasar shows an unswerving preoccupation with maximizing the value placed on the corporeal senses and the body in relation to their spiritual counterparts. This interest drives him to some extraordinary hermeneutical contortions when it comes to Origen's texts. Last, the spiritual senses are often understood in the patristic setting as being given to those who, through much practice, have attained the final stage of the spiritual life and been granted so-called 'mystical' experience. In his reading of Origen, however, Balthasar downplays the role of practice in acquiring one's spiritual senses, effectively repositioning the spiritual senses in the spiritual life such that they are granted not to the 'perfect', but instead to all Christians among the general gifts of grace.

No 'Mere Metaphors': Balthasar on Origen and the 'Definition' of the Spiritual Senses

Balthasar clearly reads Origen as articulating a version of the spiritual senses that is in keeping with the fivefold, 'analogical' definition of the

---

[10] Rickenmann simply indicates, 'This dogmatic interest, not without reason, has been much criticized', 167 (private translation by Lois Rankin).

doctrine advanced by Poulain and Rahner. Although this might seem like a somewhat curious issue on which to place great emphasis, it is in fact highly instructive for our investigation. As will be explored below, Balthasar gives subtle indications throughout his reading of Origen as to what is at stake for him in the spiritual senses' performing a fivefold perception of the divine.

As a brief methodological prologue, it is important to highlight the worry that lies behind scholarly discussion of analogical and metaphorical uses of sensory language in the spiritual senses tradition. Poulain and Rahner insist on the *perceptual* character of such language in order to ensure that the terms in question are not reduced to 'merely metaphorical' speech. In examining Origen's texts, for example, the reader may wonder just how seriously his talk of 'perceiving' God should be taken. Particularly vexing is the question of what 'perceiving God' could even mean, given that perception occurs on the material plane, but God is immaterial. The difficulty of the problem may tempt one to interpret Origen's language of sensation as metaphor. For example, one may be lured into holding that Origen does not actually intend to suggest that one 'sees' God with the 'eye of the mind'. Instead, one may believe that Origen is describing simply *thinking* about God. And yet, if Origen is not using sensory language figuratively, but instead holds that the human being can indeed perceive God through some set of spiritual faculties, then he is saying something theologically significant. Much depends on this distinction between analogy and metaphor, and it is largely in the interest of erecting hermeneutical blockades against the reduction of Origen's language to metaphor that Rahner adopts Poulain's criteria.

Balthasar aligns himself with Rahner in holding that the sensory language in Origen's texts is more than metaphorical. In his introduction to the topic in *Spirit and Fire*, Balthasar summarizes Origen's teaching on this matter as speaking of an 'inner "divine" faculty of perception', and, even more emphatically, 'spiritual "super-sensibility"' (*geistliche Übersinnlichkeit*).[11] Balthasar's use of these particular terms is highly significant. In rearticulating Origen's position with talk of 'inner perception' and 'super-sensibility', Balthasar demonstrates a desire to preserve the perceptual character of Origen's thought on the topic. Although he does not replicate the specific language of

[11] *OSF*, 218.

'analogy' over against 'metaphor' to speak of the relation between the spiritual and corporeal senses, it is nevertheless clear that in *Spirit and Fire* he holds that Origen uses the language of sensation in more than a metaphorical sense.

In *The Glory of the Lord*, too, Balthasar steers interpretation of the spiritual senses away from an understanding that would view them as merely metaphorical ways of speaking about the operations of the mind. For example, he explicitly insists, 'The distinguishing qualities of the "spiritual senses" are manifestly far more than mere paraphrases for the act of "spiritual" cognition.'[12] Balthasar seeks to establish that these spiritual senses should be understood as faculties of perception through which one has a multisensory encounter with the Word of God. He paraphrases Origen's *Commentary on the Song of Songs* as follows: 'Only he can see, hear, touch, taste, and smell Christ whose spiritual senses, for their part, are alive: only he, that is, who is able to perceive Christ as the true Light, as the Word of the Father, as the Bread of Life, as the fragrant spikenard of the Bridegroom who hastens to come'.[13] According to Balthasar's reading of Origen, then, the 'spiritual' is indeed perceived by the human being (as strange as it might sound), and one should resist any reduction of the language of sensation to mere paraphrases for cognition.

With that said, however, we also observe in some instances that Balthasar actually juxtaposes 'analogical' and 'metaphorical' uses of the language of sensation in Origen's texts. For example, in *Spirit and Fire* Balthasar offers a highly figurative interpretation of Origen's understanding of spiritual hearing in which, as he puts it, ' "hearing" is simply the inner readiness and "listening attitude" of the soul towards God'.[14] To speak of hearing as 'inner readiness' or a 'listening attitude', of course, does not preserve its *perceptual* character; we are no longer referring to perceiving a 'bodiless voice', as is the case elsewhere in Origen's texts. Instead, I would argue that Balthasar here slides into a figurative understanding of 'hearing' that links it to notions of openness and obedience to God's direction to the soul. To 'hear' in this sense is to ready oneself for what might be revealed by God.

And yet, in the very same passage, Balthasar also reads Origen as using sensory language 'analogically'. Specifically, he describes spiritual hearing as 'the inner dialogue that takes place without sound

---

[12] *GL* I, 369.   [13] *GL* I, 369.   [14] *OSF*, 232.

from the soul to God and from God to the soul.'[15] Fascinatingly, then, Balthasar in these passages echoes the sort of casual sliding between analogical and metaphorical uses of language actually evidenced in Origen's texts themselves.[16]

Concerning the other criterion necessary for a 'proper', Poulainian–Rahnerian doctrine of the spiritual senses: namely, that all five senses be described, Balthasar in *Spirit and Fire* arranges Origen's remarks on sensing God under subheadings of 'hearing', 'sight', 'touch', 'smell', and 'taste'.[17] For instance, Balthasar constructs a fifteen-page meditation on spiritual sight by assembling passages from Origen's *De Principiis*, *Commentary on the Song of Songs*, *Commentary on John*, and other texts. He does similar editorial work with the remaining four spiritual senses. In so doing, Balthasar substantially rearranges Origen's many comments on spiritual perception into thematically determined topics. Although Origen does indeed speak of forms of sight, hearing, touch, taste, and smell that perceive the divine, his remarks on these various forms of sensation are scattered throughout his writings, not arranged according to particular sense faculties. Balthasar's editorial hand is hard at work in this anthology, as passages from Origen's early writings, such as *De Principiis* (229–30) and the *Commentary on the Psalms* (222–5), are unceremoniously placed next to later works such as *Contra Celsum* (244–9) and the *Commentary on the Song of Songs* (249), with no mention of the fact that these items come from different periods in Origen's career.[18]

---

[15] *OSF*, 232.

[16] Balthasar similarly juxtaposes two meanings of spiritual smell in *Spirit and Fire*. On the one hand, he puts forward a highly figurative reading of the significance of spiritual smell: 'The spiritual sense of smell is what is popularly called "having a nose for", but in relation to the things of God. Those who have this sense can, from the things of this world, smell out what is Christian' (254). On the other hand, he clearly does not think that this metaphorical use of language precludes an alternative understanding of spiritual smell that allies it with perception: 'The fragrance of God flow[s] out into the world only because, in the self-emptying (kenosis) of God, the jar of nard (his body) broke open. Souls pursue this fragrance with longing until, in the mystical body, the fragrance of the creature and the Creator mysteriously mingle' (254).

[17] *OSF*, 232–57. Brian Daley has remarked that Balthasar's anthology on Origen is appropriately subtitled 'Ein Aufbau aus seinen Schriften', as the German *Aufbau* translates as 'a construction', and thus conveys the great extent to which Balthasar has organized Origen's writings into arranged topics. 'In calling the collection "ein Aufbau"—literally, "a construction"—Balthasar...emphasizes that the systematic arrangement of the excerpts in this collection is itself a central dimension of his interpretation of Origen...systematic, interpretative arrangement is clearly a central purpose of the collection.' Daley, 'Balthasar's Reading of the Church Fathers', 203–4.

[18] In dating these texts I follow Pierre Nautin, *Origène: Sa vie et son oeuvre* (Paris: Beauchesne, 1977), 366–71, 410.

Balthasar, then, clearly seeks to establish that Origen holds all five senses to function in spiritual perception, and he is happy to rearrange Origen's writings as necessary in order to make this as clear as possible. In fact, his editorial work gives an impression of greater systematicity on Origen's part than can actually be located in Origen's texts themselves.

In his theological aesthetics, Balthasar again demonstrates his interest in accentuating the fivefold nature of spiritual perception. After claiming that 'It was Origen who, so to speak, "invented" the doctrine of the "five spiritual senses" (*fünf geistlichen Sinnen*)',[19] Balthasar cites the following passage from *Contra Celsum*, which is a frequently named text in the scholarship on the spiritual senses:

> There is, as the scripture calls it, a certain generic divine sense (θείας τινὸς γενικῆς αἰσθήσεως) which only the man who is blessed finds on this earth. Thus Solomon says (Prov. 2:5), 'Thou shalt find a divine sense' (αἴσθησιν θείαν εὑρήσεις). There are many forms of this sense: a sight (ὁράσεως) which can see things superior to corporeal beings, the cherubim or seraphim being obvious instances, and a hearing which can receive impressions of sounds that have no objective existence in the air, and a taste which feeds on living bread that has come down from heaven (γεύσεως χρωμένης ἄρτῳ ζῶντι καὶ ἐξ οὐρανοῦ καταβεβηκότι) and gives life to the world (John 6:33). So also there is a sense of smell which smells spiritual things, as Paul speaks of 'a sweet savour of Christ unto God' (2 Cor. 2:15) and a sense of touch in accordance with which John says that he has handled with his hands 'of the Word of life' (1 John 1:1).[20]

Here we observe forms of sight, hearing, taste, smell, and touch that perceive 'spiritual things', and it is no surprise that Balthasar and others see it as the *locus classicus* of the spiritual senses in Origen.

Demonstrating an added level of hermeneutical sophistication, however, Balthasar also acknowledges that Origen at times refers to only one 'divine sense' (αἴσθησις θεία).[21] In his aesthetics, he contends, 'Origen constructed the doctrine that there exists "a general sense for the divine" which is subdivided into several kinds'.[22] One immediately notices here that Balthasar does not hold Origen's talk of

---

[19] *GL* I, 367.
[20] *Contra Celsum* I, 48. Original Greek text in *PG* 11, 749AB. Published in English as *Contra Celsum*, trans. Henry Chadwick (New York: Cambridge University Press, 1965), 44. *GL* I, 368.
[21] *Contra Celsum* I, 48. *PG* 11, 749AB. Chadwick, 44.   [22] *GL* I, 368.

this single sense to *exclude* a doctrine of five spiritual senses. Whereas modern scholarship on this topic has become caught up in determining whether Origen espouses *either* a doctrine of five spiritual senses *or* an understanding of one spiritual sense,[23] Balthasar simply observes that Origen discusses *both* understandings of spiritual perception in his writings.

Balthasar thus implicitly rejects two different dichotomies that had been drawn by Rahner and Poulain between, on the one hand, a single divine sense or five spiritual senses and, on the other hand, 'analogical' versus 'metaphorical' uses of sensory language. Balthasar does not engage in an extensive questioning of the scholarly apparatus that has been used to exegete Origen's comments on the spiritual senses. However, his approach to Origen's texts on this topic anticipates such critiques and remains truer to Origen's position than the alternative method, which attempts to force one into choices not well suited to Origen's actual texts.

Balthasar, then, harbours no illusions of univocity in Origen's uses of the language of sensation. He does, however, clearly exhibit greatest interest in those moments when Origen advances a fivefold model of spiritual perception. A question naturally arises: what is at stake for Balthasar in locating such a version of the spiritual senses? Why gravitate toward this reading? He addresses this question in *Spirit and Fire* as follows: 'The tremendous significance of the doctrine of the inner senses is revealed fully only by looking into the activity of the individual senses. Each sense contains a different mode of spiritual contact with the divine.'[24] Balthasar, then, holds not only that Origen does in fact espouse a doctrine of specifically five spiritual senses; he also holds that their full import involves the *distinctiveness* of the five ways in which the human being comes to know God. Each spiritual sense, on Balthasar's reading of Origen, permits a different mode of engagement with the divine.

---

[23] In addition to the work of Rahner and Poulain, Marguerite Harl has more recently posited that Origen espouses only one spiritual sense, and that his descriptions of all five spiritual senses do not actually convey his position. See Marguerite Harl, 'La "bouche" et le "coeur" de l'apôtre: Deux images bibliques du "sens divin" de l'homme (Proverbes 2, 5) chez Origène', in *Forma Futuri: Studi in onore del Cardinale Michele Pellegrino* (Turin: Erasmo, 1975), 17–42.

[24] *OSF*, 232.

In *The Glory of the Lord* Balthasar offers a fascinating glimpse into the broader significance of this reading of Origen's doctrine of the spiritual senses for his project of a theological aesthetics:

> The five individual sensory senses are but the fall and scattering into the material of an original and richly abundant capacity to perceive God and divine things. According to Origen, these divine things can never be reduced to a mystical unity without modes, but, rather, they possess a fullness and glory that far transcend the lower fullness and glory, of which material multiplicity is only a distant reflection and likeness.[25]

In a move with tremendous implications for his own theological aesthetics, Balthasar reads Origen as claiming that the perception of the divine cannot be distilled down to 'a mystical unity without modes'. Instead, it is a necessarily varied phenomenon. Why should this be the case? As Balthasar puts it, 'It is decisive that the object of the "spiritual senses" is not the *Deus nudus*, but the whole of the "upper world" (*die ganze obere Welt*) which, in Christ, has descended to earth.'[26] In other words, one of the reasons that the spiritual senses should be interpreted as fivefold is that their *object* is not the *Deus nudus*, but rather an abundant celestial sphere, made manifest through Christ, in relation to which all five spiritual senses are active in distinctive ways. If the spiritual senses are not fivefold, if they ultimately collapse into a single mode of perceiving God, then we remain aesthetically un-attuned to the richness of the 'upper world'. In short, it takes all five spiritual senses to perceive such grandeur.

It is one thing, of course, to say that the spiritual senses must be fivefold because of the nature of their objects. It is quite another to establish that Origen does in fact regard these objects as Christ and the heavenly realm. This claim will become especially important in Chapter 6, when we examine Balthasar's critique of Neo-Scholastic natural theology, in particular its attempt to prove the existence of God through reason alone by examining the natural world. Next, then, we examine this aspect of Balthasar's reading of the objects of the spiritual senses in Origen's thought.

---

[25] *GL* I, 369.   [26] *GL* I, 370.

On Perceiving Christ and the 'Upper World'

Balthasar's interpretation of the objects of the spiritual senses in Origen can be divided into three distinct, yet interrelated claims. First, Balthasar holds that, for Origen, the spiritual senses perceive Christ; second, through Christ, 'the whole of the "upper world"' is also perceived; third, these facts definitively *preclude* the possibility of the spiritual senses perceiving as their object the *Deus nudus*, as Balthasar puts it.

On the first point, Balthasar draws from a number of portions of Origen's texts that locate Christ, or the Word, as the object of the spiritual senses. He refers, for instance, to Origen's *Commentary on the Song of Songs*, which reads, 'Christ is grasped by every faculty of the soul', and then goes on to list all five spiritual senses in their application to Christ.[27] Balthasar also quotes from *Contra Celsum*, as mentioned above, in which Origen indicates that 'there is a sense of smell which smells spiritual things, as Paul speaks of "a sweet savour of Christ unto God" (2 Cor. 2:15) and a sense of touch in accordance with which John says that he has handled with his hands "of the Word of life" (1 John 1:1)'.[28]

In *Spirit and Fire*, too, an overwhelming number of quotations from Origen's texts mention Christ or the Word as the object of various forms of spiritual perception.[29] For example, we find the following from Origen's *Commentary on Luke*: 'The apostles therefore saw the Word not only because they saw Jesus in the flesh, but because they saw the Word of God.'[30] Origen's *Commentary on the Song of Songs* reads, 'Whoever has a pure sense of smell and through understanding of the divine Word can run after the fragrance of his ointments (cf.

---

[27] 'Christ is grasped by every faculty of the soul. He is called the true Light, therefore, so that the soul's eyes may have something to lighten them. He is the Word, so that her ears may have something to hear. Again, He is the Bread of life, so that the soul's palate may have something to taste. And in the same way, He is called the spikenard or ointment, that the soul's sense of smell may apprehend the fragrance of the Word. For the same reason He is said also to be able to be felt and handled, and is called the Word made flesh, so that the hand of the interior soul may touch concerning the Word of life.' *In Cant.* II, 9. Latin text in *GCS*, 8, 26–289, at 167. Published in English as *The Song of Songs: Commentary and Homilies*, trans. W. P. Lawson (Westminster: Newman Press, 1957), 162 (translation slightly emended).

[28] *Contra Celsum* I, 48. PG 11, 749AB. Chadwick, 44.   [29] *OSF*, 218–57.

[30] *OSF*, 237. *In Luc. hom.* 1. GCS 9, 7. Published in English as *Homilies on Luke, Fragments on Luke*, trans. J. T. Lienhard (Washington, DC: Catholic University of America Press, 1996). English translation in *OSF*, 237.

Cant 1:4 LXX), that person has a "nose" which is sensitive to spiritual fragrances.'[31] *Contra Celsum* indicates: 'In a manner more spiritual than physical, Jesus "touched" the leper in order to heal him, it seems to me, in two ways: not only to free him…from physical leprosy by physical touch, but also from that other leprosy by his truly divine touch.'[32] One could add to Balthasar's quotations a number of other passages from Origen's texts.[33] In short, it would be extremely difficult to contest the claim that Origen deems Christ to be the object of various forms of spiritual sensation.

On the second point, although Balthasar does not clarify the meaning of his phrase 'the whole of the "upper world"', one does find in Origen a number of instances in which it is not Christ alone but rather an entire spiritual realm that seems to be the object of the spiritual senses. In *Contra Celsum*, as mentioned above, Origen writes about 'a sight (ὁράσεως) which can see things superior to corporeal beings, the cherubim or seraphim being obvious instances, and a hearing which can receive impressions of sounds that have no objective existence in the air.'[34] Interestingly, too, in the first book of Origen's *Commentary on John*, he provides a description of those who see Wisdom, 'delighting in her highly variegated intelligible beauty, seen by intelligible eyes alone, provoking him to love who discerns her divine and heavenly charm.'[35] As Origen continues elsewhere in the same text, 'The Savior shines (ἐλλάμπων) on creatures that have intellect and sovereign reason, that their minds may see (βλέπῃ) their proper objects of vision (ὁρατὰ), and so he is the light of the intellectual world.'[36] In *De Principiis*, Origen again discusses his idea that we perceive intelligible things:

---

[31] *OSF*, 255. *In Cant. schol.* PG 17, 282D. English translation in *OSF*, 255.
[32] *OSF*, 250. *Contra Celsum* I, 48. PG 11, 749AB. Chadwick, 44.
[33] In *De Principiis*, for example, Origen writes about anointing Christ with the 'oil of gladness' and about those who 'run in the odor of his ointments'. *De Prin.* II, 6, 6. PG 11, 214C. Published in English as *On First Principles*, trans. G. W. Butterworth (Gloucester, MA: Peter Smith, 1973), 113. He also richly describes 'The only begotten Son of God…pouring (*infundens*) himself by his graces into our senses (*sensibus*), may deign to illuminate what is dark, to lay open what is concealed, and to reveal what is secret'. *De Prin.* II, 6, 6. PG 11, 214C. Butterworth, 113–14 (translation slightly emended).
[34] *Contra Celsum* I, 48. PG 11, 749AB. Chadwick, 44.
[35] 'ἐνευφραινόμενος τῷ πολυποικίλῳ νοητῷ κάλλει αὐτῆς, ὑπὸ νοητῶν ὀφθαλμῶν μόνων βλεπομένῳ.' *In Joan.* I, 11. PG 14, 40D. Published in English as *Commentary on the Gospel of John*, trans. Philip Schaff, *ANF* 9 (Edinburgh: T&T Clark, 1959), 303.
[36] *In Joan.* I, 24. PG 14, 68B. Schaff, 312.

Patristic Versions of the Spiritual Senses

A rational mind...is placed in the body, and advances from things of sense, which are bodily, to sense objects (*sensibilia*) which are incorporeal and intellectual. But in case it should appear mistaken to say as we have done that intellectual things are objects of sense (*sensibilia*), we will quote as an illustration the saying of Solomon: 'You will find also a divine sense.' By this he shows that those things which are intellectual are to be investigated not by bodily sense but by some other which he calls divine.[37]

In these passages, we find cherubim, seraphim, things superior to corporeal beings, Wisdom, 'proper objects of [the mind's] vision', and 'intellectual things' listed among the many objects of the spiritual senses. There would seem to be little reason to constrain our reading of their objects to any one spiritual entity, as Origen does indeed appear to have in mind an entire realm of spiritual objects that can be perceived by the spiritual senses.[38]

Concerning the third point, Balthasar argues that the two claims above preclude a reading of the doctrine that holds the *Deus nudus* to be their object. Although Balthasar does not develop the particular way in which he is using this term, we can reasonably presume that he

---

[37] *De Prin.* IV, 4, 10. *PG* 11, 364. Butterworth, 327–8 (translation slightly emended).

[38] One more speculative note might be made about Balthasar's reading of the 'whole upper world' as the object of the spiritual senses in Origen. It may be significant that Balthasar studied Plotinus under Hans Eibl in Vienna before beginning his formal theological education in 1929. One observes an extraordinary, extensive parallel between the reading of Origen advanced by Balthasar and Plotinus' remarks about objects of intellectual perception found in the *Enneads*. The following passage is especially relevant: 'What we have called the perceptibles of that realm [i.e., the noetic realm] enter into cognizance in a way of their own, since they are incorporeal, while sense-perception here—so distinguished as dealing with corporeal objects—is fainter than the perception belonging to that higher world, but gains a specious clarity because its objects are bodies; the man of this sphere has sense-perception because existing in a less true degree and taking only enfeebled images of things There: perceptions here are dim intellections, and intellections There are vivid perceptions.' *Enneads* 6, 7, 7. In response to this passage, John Dillon remarks, 'We have here, in Plotinus' theory, a far greater degree of "mirroring" of the noetic world by the sense-world than is traditional in Platonism. Everything here is also There, in another, more exalted, mode.' John M. Dillon, 'Aisthêsis Noêtê: A Doctrine of the Spiritual Senses in Origen and in Plotinus', in *Hellenica et Judaica*, eds., A. Caquot, M. Hadas-Lebel, and J. Riaud (Leuven and Paris: Peeters, 1986), 443–55, at 449. Given the reading of Origen offered by Balthasar, one cannot help but note that in both cases an extensive 'mirroring' is occurring between sensible and super-sensible realms. Plotinus, of course, does not advocate the Christocentrism that Balthasar claims for Origen here, but it may be worth considering that Balthasar is reading Origen through Plotinus on the spiritual senses.

resists a reading of the spiritual senses that would have them progressing beyond the two modes of spiritual perception just mentioned in order to perceive the 'naked God' who is beyond all form.[39] As we shall see in Chapter 2, Balthasar's approach here is not unlike that which he takes to Bonaventure's texts, in which he opposes the notion that the spiritual senses apply to 'the transcendent God in himself', instead privileging a reading on which their object is 'the form of God in his revelation'.[40] Balthasar's reading on this point of interpretation is well grounded, as virtually no comments are made in Origen's writings on the perception of such a 'naked', formless God. Instead, the overwhelming evidence points to the Word and other spiritual entities as the objects of spiritual perception. Simply put, Origen regards spiritual perception to be just as varied in its objects as is corporeal perception. A vast realm lies beyond the domain of sense impressions, and it is through the spiritual senses that we come to perceive this spiritually opulent world.

A Modest Rehabilitation:
Balthasar on the Value of the Corporeal Senses in Origen

The question of how Balthasar understands the disjunctive nature of Origen's doctrine of the spiritual senses provokes a complex, seemingly paradoxical response. At certain moments Balthasar reads Origen against the scholarly grain by resisting the sharp divide that is typically drawn between the spiritual and corporeal senses. At other moments, however, we observe Balthasar retreating from this particular facet of his rehabilitation of Origen and acknowledging the separation between the spiritual and bodily senses. Ultimately, we shall see that Balthasar resists 'Platonic' readings that would have Origen radically devaluing the material order,[41] but he also thinks

---

[39] In a similar vein, Balthasar directs a number of critical comments at 'naked faith' throughout the first volume of his theological aesthetics. See *GL* I, 53, 80, 121, 341, 411, 416, 420, 607.

[40] *GL* II, 321.

[41] The reader of Balthasar's works is struck by both the frequency and the vigour with which he denounces 'Platonism' throughout his theological writings. It seems that one can enter into his *oeuvre* at any point and find a comment directed against a 'Platonic' position. And yet, at many junctures his text remains unclear in regard to the precise object of its criticism. It is true that Balthasar does in a number of instances speak with considerable precision about Greek philosophy, painstakingly distinguishing between Aristotelian, Stoic, and Platonic elements in a figure's thought, or being quite deliberate about distinguishing Platonism from the Middle

Origen can get him only so far in his efforts at uniting spiritual and corporeal senses. In other words, Balthasar rescues Origen from only the most extremely negative view of Origen on the body and materiality, according to which the material order not only inhibits spiritual progress but is additionally regarded as evil. We examine this modest rehabilitation below.

First, then, let us examine the extent to which Balthasar resists the prevailing dualist paradigm according to which Origen is typically read on the spiritual senses. In *Spirit and Fire*, Balthasar insists that Origen places a high value on both corporeal vision and 'the flesh' (*das Fleisch*) that it sees. Balthasar bases this assessment on Origen's *Homilies on Luke*, which explicitly privileges physical perception in the following passage: ' "For mine eyes have seen thy salvation" (Lk 2:30). For before, said [Simeon], I believed by way of understanding, I knew through reasoning; but now I have seen with the eyes of my flesh and am thus brought to fulfilment.'[42] In this extraordinary passage, we see that, for Origen, Simeon's seeing Christ with his bodily eyes is actually superior to his previous faith based in reason. In tones that anticipate his own constructive use of the spiritual senses in his theological aesthetics, Balthasar describes Origen's conception of the vision of God as follows: 'This way [to the vision of God] does not mean a leaving behind of the incarnate Christ: rather, union with Christ is made perfect precisely through his flesh (*sein Fleisch*).'[43]

Platonism and Neo-Platonism that followed it. For example, in 'The Fathers, the Scholastics, and Ourselves', Balthasar writes, 'We should not forget how strongly Platonism and even neo-Platonism had been permeated at the time of the Fathers with Aristotelian and Stoic elements. Not only the Antiochenes, as born rivals of the Alexandrians, but even Origenist theology, is permeated with such elements. Certain tractates of Gregory of Nyssa cannot be imagined without Poseidonius, and even less can the construction of Chalcedonian theology and the *Summa* of the Damascene be understood without Aristotle.' 'The Fathers, Scholastics, and Ourselves', *Communio* 24 (Summer 1997), 347–96, at 378. However, on many other occasions Balthasar sweepingly uses the term 'Platonism' with little hesitation to encapsulate centuries of philosophical reflection under a single broad rubric. Further complicating this picture is the fact that some commentators on Balthasar's writings have actually declared him to be far too Platonist himself in his own constructive theology. See especially Noel O'Donoghue, 'Do We Get beyond Plato?: A Critical Appreciation of the Theological Aesthetics', in *The Beauty of Christ: A [sic] Introduction to the Theology of Hans Urs von Balthasar*, eds. Bede McGregor, OP, and Thomas Norris (Edinburgh: T&T Clark, 1994), 253–66.

[42] *In Luc. hom.* 15. *GCS* 9, 92–4. English translation in *OSF*, 248.
[43] *OSF*, 244.

Interestingly, however, whereas in *Spirit and Fire* Balthasar demonstrates a fairly unambiguous desire to liberate Origen from those who would read him as objectionably dualistic, in *The Glory of the Lord* we observe a much more measured, qualified assessment of this feature of Origen's thought. Here Origen's well-known passage from *Contra Celsum* plays a major role in Balthasar's reading. In that text, Origen remarks:

> Our Savior, knowing that these two kinds of eyes belong to us, says, 'For judgment came I into this world, that those who do not see may see and that those who see may become blind' (John 9:39). By those who do not see he is obscurely referring to the eyes of the soul, to which the Logos gives the power of sight, and by those who see he means the eyes of the senses. For the Logos blinds the latter, that the soul may see without any distraction that which it ought to see. Therefore, the eye of the soul of any genuine Christian is awake and that of the senses is closed. And in proportion to the degree in which the superior eye is awake and the sight of the senses is closed, the supreme God and His Son, who is the Logos and Wisdom and the other titles, are comprehended and seen by each man.[44]

Here we see a clear formulation of Origen's understanding of the relationship between the spiritual and corporeal senses. The Father and the Son are perceived by the spiritual senses only 'in proportion to the degree in which' the corporeal senses are closed. In this portion of Origen's writings we find a model of the spiritual senses in which the corporeal is not valued positively—nor is it even regarded neutrally—in its relation to spiritual things. Instead, the ordinary, corporeal senses actually detract from the cultivation of the spiritual senses, and the former must be mortified, blinded, or otherwise diminished if the spiritual senses are to develop.

In response to this passage, Balthasar asserts, 'If both sensibilities are thus, ontically as well as noetically, but different states of the one and only sensibility, it nevertheless follows that, in a Platonic sense, they cannot both be actual at the same time: Adam's spiritual eye for God is closed by his fall through sin, while at that moment his sensory eye opens'.[45] In spite of his efforts at rehabilitating Origen through his insistence that spiritual and corporeal sensation are at bottom 'one sensibility', Balthasar nevertheless acknowledges that in Origen we

[44] *Contra Celsum*, VII, 39. *PG* 11, 1476B. Chadwick, 427.   [45] *GL* I, 369.

observe a doctrine of the spiritual senses in which the development of one set of senses occurs *at the cost of* the other set of senses.[46]

Balthasar, however, still maintains that Origen had a positive regard for materiality and 'the world', more broadly understood.

> We cannot simply systematize the Christian and Biblical Origen to make him conform with the Platonic Origen. The world and matter are not evil; only the free will can be evil. For this reason, the material state as a whole remains a good likeness and an indicator for the upward-striving spirit; and in Christ, in whose flesh there is nothing evil, the lower sensibility unqualifiedly points the way to the heavenly sensibility.[47]

Balthasar, then, argues that we do see in (at least one version of) Origen a higher value placed on creation than is typically thought to be the case. And yet it is also telling that Balthasar does not in his theological aesthetics attempt to dismiss the Platonic Origen or make him out to be a betrayer of the 'real' Origen. Instead, Balthasar places the Christian Origen and Platonic Origen in a curious juxtaposition. Unexpectedly, then, the theologian who is habitually accused of being overly systematic in his approach to the church fathers leaves unresolved a tension in Origen's thought between Christianity and Platonism. Balthasar thus lets Origen speak on his own terms more than his reputation would lead one to believe, at least on this particular facet of the spiritual senses.

From a broader perspective, of course, Balthasar's reading should be considered as a comparatively modest attempt to rescue Origen from the most extreme, disjunctive version of the possible relationships between corporeal and spiritual sensation. On Balthasar's reading, Origen does not in fact succumb to viewing the physical realm in which the corporeal senses operate as categorically evil. Instead, we see in Balthasar a rereading of Origen according to which materiality is not *evil*, even though it does nevertheless detract from the functioning of spiritual sensibility. In his attempt to locate figures for whom spiritual and corporeal sensation are united with one another, Balthasar will need to look elsewhere.

---

[46] Balthasar additionally indicates in the above passage that the reason for this mutual exclusivity lies in Origen's engagement with Platonism, thus substantially qualifying the extent to which he holds Origen to have transcended its influence.
[47] *GL* I, 369.

Only for 'The Perfect'?
The Development and Place of the Spiritual Senses

Both the development of the spiritual senses in the individual human being and their position in Origen's system of thought seem to be of surprisingly little interest to Balthasar.[48] In *The Glory of the Lord* Balthasar makes no mention of Rahner's claim that the spiritual senses become active for Origen in his final stage, ἐνοπτική, where they are used only by 'the perfect' (i.e., those who have progressed through the first two stages, ἔθηκε and φυσική).[49] In fact, in his treatment of the spiritual senses Balthasar does not mention at all the three stages of the spiritual life in Origen's thought.

And yet, what little Balthasar does say in this arena actually indicates a highly significant reworking of Origen's understanding of the doctrine. In particular, it is telling that Balthasar does not examine Origen's understanding of the various *practices* that the human being must undertake in order to cultivate the spiritual senses. Instead, in his reading of Origen, Balthasar focuses almost exclusively upon the grace of God that makes such perception possible. In *Spirit and Fire*, for example, Balthasar makes clear the prominent role of grace in his

---

[48] For Origen, just as one must undertake substantial efforts in order to strengthen one's physical faculties, so too must one practise in order to develop the spiritual senses (see *In Ezech. hom.* 11 n.1. GCS 8, 319–454, at 423). This practice consists of freeing oneself from the desires of the flesh (*Contra Celsum*, VII, 39. PG 11, 1476B. Chadwick, 427), educating oneself such that one can discern the spiritual sense of scripture (*In Cant.* I, 4. GCS 8, 166. Lawson, 79), and prayer (*Contra Celsum*, VII, 44. PG 11, 1484–6. Chadwick, 431–33. See also *De Orat.*, 9, 2. GCS 2, 295–403, at 318–19. Published in English as *Prayer, Exhortation to Martyrdom*, trans. John Joseph O'Meara (Westminster: Newman Press, 1954), 39–40).

[49] As is well known, Origen divides the spiritual development of the human being into three distinct stages. The first stage, ἔθηκε (*moralis*), involves the elimination of sinful desires and the cultivation of virtue; the second stage, φυσική (*naturalis*), entails acquiring a proper attitude toward created things as having a certain purpose granted by the Creator; the third stage, ἐνοπτική (*inspectiva*), involves the contemplation of 'things divine and heavenly'. *In Cant.* Prol. 3. GCS 8, 75. Lawson, 40. There is good reason to place the operation of the spiritual senses in the enoptic stage, as this final stage explicitly entails the transcendence of corporeal vision for the purpose of beholding the divine: 'The study called inspective is that by which we go beyond things seen and contemplate somewhat of things divine and heavenly, beholding them with the mind alone, for they are beyond the range of bodily sight'. *In Cant.* Prol. 3. GCS 8, 75. Lawson, 40. Importantly, too, one reaches the enoptic stage only after having mastered both ἔθηκε and φυσική. That is to say, one observes in Origen an understanding of the 'mystical' life that entails successive progression such that the second stage is not reached without having mastered the first, and the third stage is not reached without having mastered the second.

interpretation of Origen, explaining, 'Through grace Christians have received a sensory capacity for the divine,'[50] but he makes no mention of the notion that rigorous practice has been understood to be a key constituent of Origen's rendering of the doctrine.

Balthasar, then, subtly re-reads Origen on the place of the spiritual senses by not explicitly reserving their activation for the *enoptic* stage of the spiritual life. One significant implication of this highly debatable move is that Balthasar effectively repositions the doctrine in Origen's thought. Specifically, the spiritual senses on this reading belong *not* to those few persons who have become 'perfect', but rather to the those who have received the 'gifts of grace' more generally understood.[51] In *Spirit and Fire*, he makes the case that 'one can call these senses "mystical" in the broad sense, but they are, at least initially, given along with grace itself and as such are not really mystical phenomena, still less an unveiled experience of God'.[52] In *The Glory of the Lord*, too, Balthasar is no less explicit about his resistance to a 'mystical' understanding of Origen's use of the doctrine. He writes, 'How should we interpret Origen? It will not do to go...in the mystical direction.'[53]

On this point, however, Balthasar has allowed his own theological preoccupations to dictate his reading; Origen's texts do not actually support his position on this particular topic. Instead, Rahner convincingly establishes that the spiritual senses are activated in the *enoptic* stage of the spiritual life. In *The Glory of the Lord*, Balthasar claims to have refuted Rahner's interpretation of Origen by exposing as

---

[50] *OSF*, 218.

[51] The *enoptic* stage is often thought to be the stage of the spiritual life in which 'mystical' experience takes place, for Origen. Rahner notes that Origen simply calls this final stage 'mystical' in his *Homilies on Jeremiah*, seemingly equating the two (*In Jer. Fragm.* 14. GCS 8, 241. Rahner, 'The "Spiritual Senses" According to Origen', 92). The fact that the spiritual senses are typically positioned in this stage of the spiritual life has led Origen's commentators to see in them an understanding of specifically 'mystical' experience. Rahner cites a key passage from Origen's *Commentary on the Song of Songs* that reads, 'And so those who have reached the highest degree of perfection and blessedness rejoice with all their senses in the Word of God'. *In Cant.* I, 4. GCS 8, 105. Lawson, 79. See Rahner, 'The "Spiritual Senses" According to Origen', 95. Summarizing the significance of this claim for his reader, Rahner then writes, 'This agrees exactly with Origen's conception of the "perfect", when he explains the Word of God and God himself as the object of the spiritual faculties' (95). The spiritual senses, then, are regarded as activating in the final stage of the spiritual life, for Origen, where they are employed by the individual human being in 'mystical' encounter.

[52] *OSF*, 218.   [53] *GL* I, 369.

pseudonymous certain passages from Origen's *Commentary on the Psalms*.[54] Rahner uses these passages to support his enoptic-stage reading of the spiritual senses, and therefore Balthasar believes he has undermined Rahner's reading. However, Rahner's interpretation actually relies much more heavily on Origen's *Commentary on the Song of Songs*, which unequivocally positions the spiritual senses in the final, enoptic stage.[55] For instance, in that text Origen remarks on Hebrews 5:14 (which is a classic scriptural source for the spiritual senses) as follows: 'What the Apostle says about the perfect having their senses trained to discern good and evil must not be taken carelessly and in any sense one likes.'[56] Although Balthasar makes a strong case on the topics examined above, in this instance his reading of Origen remains distanced from his primary texts and appears to reflect only his own theological concerns. Concerning this particular aspect of Balthasar's treatment of Origen's doctrine of the spiritual senses, Balthasar falls prey to the characterization of his scholarship so often levelled on him by patristics specialists.

* * *

The above discussion identified and assessed a number of telling hermeneutical decisions in Balthasar's reading of Origen on the spiritual senses. In making these interpretive moves, Balthasar simultaneously displays a deep debt to Rahner while evincing resistance to his classic approach to the spiritual senses. Rahner clearly sets the terms for Balthasar's engagement with Origen's version of the doctrine, and he is Balthasar's most regular debate partner throughout his studies. And yet Balthasar also implicitly rejects the Rahnerian paradigm, according to which Origen is presumed to advance *either* a fivefold, analogical model of the spiritual senses *or* a single, metaphorical use of the language of sensation. He also disputes Rahner's claim that the spiritual senses are given only to the 'perfect' in Origen's thought, as just seen. We shall continue to see Balthasar's debt and resistance to Rahner in the remainder of this chapter, in which other patristic versions of the spiritual senses are examined. To those figures we now turn.

---

[54] Balthasar demonstrates that these passages in fact belong to Evagrius, not Origen, in 'Die Hiera des Evagrius', *Zeitschrift für katholische Theologie* 63 (1939), 86–106, 181–206.
[55] Rahner, 'The "Spiritual Senses" According to Origen', 94.
[56] *In Cant.* I, 4. GCS 8, 105. Lawson, 79. See also GCS 8, 101–8. Lawson, 74–83.

TWO CAUTIONARY TALES: EVAGRIUS OF PONTUS AND DIADOCHUS OF PHOTICE

Although Balthasar's engagement with Origen's articulation of the spiritual senses merits thorough consideration from a number of different angles, his readings of Evagrius of Pontus and Diadochus of Photice permit a brief, straightforward analysis. Balthasar follows Rahner in holding Evagrius to be the next figure of note in the development of spiritual senses after Origen. And Balthasar, like Rahner, treats Evagrius only briefly in comparison to the robust examination that they both undertake with Origen. In fact, the handful of comments Balthasar does make indicate a dismissive stance toward the Evagrian shape that the doctrine takes in Origen's wake.[57] The points below inform not only how Balthasar understands Evagrius; they also grant us considerable insight into the portions of the spiritual senses tradition Balthasar values for his own theological aesthetics.

Balthasar reads Evagrius as compromising the fivefold understanding of the spiritual senses advanced by Origen. In his reprise of the history of the doctrine in *The Glory of the Lord*, Balthasar comments, 'In spite of an occasional mention of the spiritual organs and senses (*Cent.* 2, 80 and especially *Cent.* 3, 35), in Evagrius everything is absorbed into an inescapable mystical reduction to unity.'[58] Given the high value Balthasar places on the notion that there are indeed five spiritual senses and that Christ and the whole of the upper world are perceived through them, these comments indicate a decidedly negative evaluation of the doctrine.

Furthermore, Balthasar reads Evagrius as irredeemably dualistic in his rendering of the relationship between the spiritual senses and their corporeal counterparts. As he explains this feature of Evagrius' thought, 'Because the negation of the sensual leads to the positing

---

[57] One should not presume on this basis that Balthasar was dismissive of Evagrius' thought as a whole. In fact, Balthasar published two articles on Evagrius in 1939: 'Die Hiera des Evagrius', *Zeitschrift für katholische Theologie* 63 (1939), 86–106, 181–206; 'Metaphysik und Mystik des Evagrius Pontikus', *Zeitschrift für Askese und Mystik* (1939), 31–47. The latter has been published in English as 'The Metaphysics and Mystical Theology of Evagrius', *Monastic Studies* 3 (1965), 183–95.

[58] *GL* I, 370. It should be said that Evagrius does speak at many junctures about the five spiritual senses, and to call his mention of spiritual organs 'occasional' is a bit disingenuous. See *Cent.* II, 28, 62, 80; VII, 27, 44. Rahner, 'The "Spiritual Senses" According to Origen', 98.

of the spiritual, Evagrius can praise the sensorium (αἴσθησις) for the spiritual (*De Orat.* 28 and 41).'[59] He further says of Evagrius, 'The same spirit "perceives" or "feels" spiritually what it perceives and feels sensually in its fallen state…the spiritual act of experiencing can be contrasted with the sensual and passible act of experiencing in such a way that *they mutually exclude one another*.'[60] Whereas Balthasar goes to great lengths to defend Origen from the charge of dualism (to the extent that it is feasible), he does not similarly exert himself in attempting to rescue Evagrius in his theological aesthetics. Instead, we see in Balthasar's assessment of Evagrius a model according to which the spiritual senses can grow only at the cost of their corporeal counterparts. The sensual must be denied if the spiritual is to develop.

The last point on which Balthasar resists the Evagrian version of the spiritual senses is the decisive one, and it explains Balthasar's lack of interest in investigating counter-evidence to the first and second points just raised. Concerning Evagrius' model of the spiritual senses, Balthasar holds, 'Because the one who prays strives to go beyond all forms (*Formen*) and every definable state, he can at the same time praise "perfect *anaisthesia*", or "feelinglessness" (*De Orat.*, 120), as the highest state of prayer.'[61] It is the language of going 'beyond all forms' that is especially significant here. Specifically, the spiritual senses are ultimately irrelevant, according to Balthasar's reading of Evagrius, because as one progresses toward God all form is surpassed and one is brought into a 'higher' state of feelinglessness. The spiritual senses, then, in Evagrius' version of the idea clearly belong to an inferior, 'feeling-ful' state of relationship with God.

In sum, Balthasar regards Evagrius as significant in that he passes the theme of the spiritual senses down to later figures, but he hardly articulates a version of the doctrine that Balthasar seeks to emulate. In fact, Evagrius is instructive primarily as an example of what one should *not* do with a doctrine of the spiritual senses. Particularly significant is Balthasar's resistance to the idea that the spiritual senses are surpassed as one progresses beyond all forms, although his concern about dualism and the Evagrian collapse into a single mode of

---

[59] *GL* I, 267.   [60] *GL* I, 268 (emphasis added).
[61] *GL* I, 267. Balthasar also writes of Evagrius in a similar vein, 'For the light of God, in which we see everything that has form, is itself formless (*De Orat.* 67, 72; *Cent.* I, 35), and only he who has been wholly freed from form can behold the face of the Father (*De Orat.* 114).' *GL* I, 267.

perception are also instructive. The latter of these concerns recurs in Balthasar's treatment of Diadochus, as we shall see.

Balthasar reads the version of the spiritual senses found in Diadochus of Photice in much the same way as he does that of Evagrius: namely, as a cautionary tale of passing interest between the rich understandings of the idea advanced by Origen and by Pseudo-Macarius. In his rehearsal of the history of the spiritual senses in *The Glory of the Lord*, Balthasar simply states, 'Diadochus, too, expressly allows for only *one* spiritual sense',[62] then moves on to the version of the doctrine articulated by Pseudo-Macarius. Elsewhere in his theological aesthetics, Balthasar echoes this disapproving interpretation of Diadochus: 'The soul has but one sense of spiritual sensation which is oriented to God.'[63] This assessment of Diadochus reflects the majority view of the subject, as argued most effectively by Gabriel Horn.[64] Simply put, the brevity of Balthasar's treatment of Diadochus indicates that his interests lie in articulations of the doctrine that are fivefold, for reasons explored in his reading of Origen above. Diadochus, it would seem, has little to teach Balthasar on the matter of the spiritual senses.

PSEUDO-MACARIUS, THE SPIRITUAL SENSES, AND DEATH AND RESURRECTION

Balthasar's treatment of Pseudo-Macarius demonstrates once again the significant extent to which he relies upon Rahner's scholarship to frame his own inquiry into the spiritual senses tradition.[65] Balthasar explicitly mentions Rahner's essay in his assessment of Macarius' version of the doctrine, and he cites many of the same passages from Macarius' *Spiritual Homilies* as does Rahner. Balthasar also concurs with Rahner in his view that Macarius is more faithful to Origen's

---

[62] *GL* I, 370.   [63] *GL* I, 279.

[64] Gabriel Horn, 'Le sens de l'esprit d'après Diadoque de Photice', *Revue d'ascetique et mystique* 8 (1927), 402–19. See also Rahner, 'The "Spiritual Senses" According to Origen', 100.

[65] Balthasar treats Pseudo-Macarius in two sections of *The Glory of the Lord*, vol. 1, both of which are found within his discussion of 'The Subjective Evidence'. See *GL* I, 268–75, 370–1.

doctrine of the spiritual senses than either Evagrius or Diadochus.[66] In fact, both Rahner and Balthasar could be said to regard Macarius as the most significant figure among Greek patristic expositors of the spiritual senses after Origen.[67]

The most straightforward feature of Balthasar's reading of Macarius is his celebration of the fivefold version of the spiritual senses found in Macarius' texts. Balthasar explains, 'Origen's five senses again emerge in the Pseudo-Macarius', then he quotes portions of the *Spiritual Homilies* that unambiguously speak of five spiritual senses.[68]

Additionally, as we saw in Balthasar's treatment of Origen, with Macarius we again observe that Balthasar searches for the most positive assessment of materiality that he can possibly glean from the texts he examines. Balthasar is searching for aspects of the tradition that unite corporeal and spiritual senses, and he finds an ally in Macarius. For example, Balthasar describes the significance of the Incarnation in Macarius' understanding of the spiritual senses as follows: 'For Macarius, this event whereby God participates in the realm of the senses in Christ is the positive expression of his love: through the sensual, we are to come to know God's spiritual love.'[69] At another point in his aesthetics, Balthasar continues, 'A dualistic interpretation is impossible: for it is the same senses which first are earthly and then become heavenly through the infusion of grace. We have to do here with a "change and exchange of states (κατάστασις)" by virtue of imitating Christ.'[70] Here Balthasar finds a decidedly higher value placed on the corporeal senses than we saw in Origen's texts. Not only is the material body not evil (as some of Origen's writings claim, on Balthasar's reading), but the material body actually informs and enriches our life with God. It is precisely *through* the corporeal that we know the spiritual; the very same senses are transformed from physical to spiritual

---

[66] *GL* I, 370. Cf. Rahner, 'The "Spiritual Senses" according to Origen', 101. A key constituent to Macarius' being 'more faithful' to Origen involves the fact that he, like Origen, articulates an understanding of the spiritual senses that is once again fivefold.

[67] This claim is especially striking when one considers that Gregory of Nyssa, Pseudo-Dionysius, and Maximus the Confessor could easily be chosen for this distinction, as they all develop exceptionally rich models of the spiritual senses in their writings.

[68] *GL* I, 370. *Hom.* 4, 7. Original Greek text in *PG* 34, 450–820, at 477B. Published in English as *The Fifty Spiritual Homilies* and *The Great Letter*, trans. George Maloney (New York: Paulist Press, 1992), 53.

[69] *GL* I, 270. [70] *GL* I, 370.

perceptual faculties. Macarius thus represents a significant step forward in uniting corporeal and spiritual perception.

Concerning the role played by grace in Macarius' understanding of the spiritual senses, Balthasar disagrees with Rahner, who had insisted that the spiritual senses for Macarius are entirely natural faculties of the soul. However, Balthasar holds that they are instead dependent on divine grace for their proper operation. Strangely, Balthasar and Rahner both point to the very same passage from Macarius' fourth homily to support their respective claims. On this particular point, however, it is difficult to dispute Balthasar's interpretation, as Macarius' text clearly indicates the importance of grace:

> The five rational senses of the soul (πέντε λογικαὶ αἰσθήσεις τῆς ψυχῆς), if they have received grace from above and the sanctification of the Spirit, truly are the prudent virgins. They have received from above the wisdom of grace. But if they continue depending solely on their own nature, they class themselves with the foolish virgins and show themselves to be children of this world.[71]

One would be hard-pressed to produce a more straightforward dismissal of the idea that the spiritual senses are natural capacities, and yet Rahner inexplicably claims, 'Pseudo-Macarius regards these five spiritual senses as natural faculties, since, according to him, their operations can remain on a purely natural plane, i.e. without grace'.[72] Balthasar does not accentuate the fact that he disagrees with Rahner on this point, but he does take great pains to dismiss any interpretation of Macarius that would deny the centrality of grace. As he explains his reading, 'The man who prays has a twofold "experience": that God becomes palpable in his grace, and that there exists no relationship between man's effort and his perception of God'.[73] This insistence on the absolute gratuity of grace is a theme that we will see in Balthasar's treatment of later figures in the spiritual senses tradition, and it is a key feature of his own version of the doctrine, as will be shown in Chapter 4.

Last, and most unusually, Balthasar reads Macarius as advancing a model of the spiritual senses in which one receives one's spiritual senses only after having undergone Christ's passion with him.[74]

---

[71] *Hom.* 4, 7. *PG* 34, 477B. Maloney, 53.
[72] Rahner, 'The "Spiritual Senses" According to Origen', 101.
[73] *GL* I, 273.
[74] *GL* I, 269–75, 370–1. This aspect of Macarius' understanding of the doctrine is not discussed by Rahner.

Balthasar makes this claim on the basis of two features of Macarius' thought. First, Balthasar understands Macarius as articulating a version of the doctrine in which the senses are made 'spiritual' as a result of Christ joining himself to the human soul. Balthasar quotes a portion of Macarius' *Spiritual Homilies* that reads as follows:

> [Christ] came to change, transform, and renew our nature, to create anew and to mingle with his divine Spirit our soul, which had been laid waste by the passions following the first sin. He came to create a new *nous*, a new *psyche*, new eyes, new ears, a new spiritual tongue, in short, new men from those who believed in him.[75]

What should be noted in this account of Christ 'mingling' with the human soul, to Balthasar, is that the experience of Christ it allows is first and foremost an experience of *suffering with* Christ. As Balthasar expounds on this point, 'As probably nowhere else in all of Eastern theology, this "experience" of Christ is primarily an experience of the Passion, a lived stigmatization: "To some the sign of the Cross appeared as a splendour of light, and it impressed itself upon the interior man" (Hom. 8, 3).'[76] Christ in his grace may transform the corporeal senses, but this union and renovation come at a cost. In fact, Balthasar even goes so far as to say that the identification with Christ's suffering leads the human being to a descent into hell:

> The image of Christ's descent into hell, for instance, in order to return the lost Adam and his whole race to heaven, is applied to the individual: he himself is hell and, far from God, he experiences himself to be such. 'Your heart is a burial chamber and a grave'. The torrent of hell flows in you; you are 'submerged in the waves; you have drowned and are dead', and Christ is the diver that comes to take you up from your own depths (11, 10).[77]

In tones reminiscent of his own theology of Holy Saturday,[78] Balthasar reads Macarius as mapping Christ's descent into hell onto the individual human being, and, importantly, this pattern of death and resurrection has a direct bearing on his reading of Macarius' doctrine of the spiritual senses. Balthasar makes this connection by commenting,

---

[75] *GL* I, 371. *Hom.* 44, 1. *PG* 34, 780A. Maloney, 223.

[76] *GL* I, 271. Similarly, Balthasar also writes, 'Religious experience is the sensorium with which the soul perceives God, an instrument restored by grace and steeled by the suffering of God in Christ' (*GL* I, 272).

[77] *GL* I, 272.

[78] Hans Urs von Balthasar, *Mysterium Paschale: The Mystery of Easter*, trans. Aidan Nichols, OP (San Francisco, CA: Ignatius Press, 2000).

'It is in Christ's grace, therefore, in his dying and rising, that the "old man" is created anew and that the old fleshly senses become spiritual.'[79] The spiritual senses, then, according to Balthasar's reading of Macarius, grow in the human being through a radical *Christomimesis* in which one enters into not only Christ's suffering and passion but also his death and resurrection. It is only on the other side of death that one receives one's spiritual senses.

Thus far we have seen Balthasar replicate Rahner's history of the spiritual senses with remarkable consistency. In spite of a few differences on specific interpretive matters, Balthasar assigns a significance to Origen, Evagrius, Diadochus, and Pseudo-Macarius that precisely mirrors the importance Rahner attaches to each of these figures. Rahner sees the spiritual senses beginning with Origen, passing unremarkably to Evagrius and Diadochus, and flowering once again in Pseudo-Macarius. Balthasar views the history of the doctrine unfolding in similar fashion. We shall next examine Augustine of Hippo and Maximus the Confessor, both of whose importance Balthasar substantially amplifies in comparison to the significance given them by Rahner. After this task is complete, we shall look briefly at Balthasar's curious neglect of Gregory of Nyssa and Pseudo-Dionysius.

AUGUSTINE OF HIPPO AND THE PERCEPTION OF BEAUTY

Although Rahner makes only passing mention of Augustine's understanding of the spiritual senses in his treatment of patristic figures,[80] Balthasar devotes considerable attention to Augustine's position on the doctrine, especially in the second volume of his theological aesthetics.[81] Balthasar thus significantly augments the role of Augustine in the spiritual senses tradition in comparison to the treatment he

---

[79] *GL* I, 371.

[80] Rahner discusses briefly Augustine's significance for medieval versions of the spiritual senses in 'The Doctrine of the "Spiritual Senses" in the Middle Ages', 104–6.

[81] See *GL* II, 95–143. Balthasar published three translations of Augustine's works throughout his career: *Aurelius Augustinus, über die Psalmen* (Leipzig: Hegner, 1936); *Aurelius Augustinus, das Antlitz der Kirche* (Einsiedeln-Köln: Benzinger, 1942); *Aurelius Augustinus, Psychologie und Mystik* (Einsiedeln: Johannes Verlag, 1960).

receives from Rahner.[82] I argue below that this increased emphasis from Balthasar occurs because he finds in Augustine the particular notion that the *beauty* of the divine is perceived through the 'eye of the mind'.[83] Although other patristic figures certainly advance the notion that the spiritual senses perceive the divine, they do not discuss in so thorough a manner the notion that the spiritual senses have the capacity for appreciating God's beauty. Augustine, then, emerges as a crucial resource for Balthasar's conceptualization of the *aesthetic* abilities of the spiritual senses, which are central to his project in *The Glory of the Lord*.

In the second volume of his theological aesthetics, Balthasar offers a variety of quotations from Augustine's writings on vision and beauty, between which he intersperses his own reflections. The following passage from *The Glory of the Lord* is worth quoting at length:

> The *oculus mentis*, the *oculus interior*, is as such the *lux mentis*, and yet only a completely healthy and specially schooled eye is able to look into the eternal sun... 'Seeing the beauty of things must be left to those who as a result of a divine gift are capable of seeing it.'[84] This is true above all of seeing the beauty of God himself, access to which and passion for which will be given only to the person who, through having become himself pure and light, learns to see God's light. Such a person alone begins to have a 'taste' for God and 'an eye for the only true beauty'.[85]

---

[82] It should be said here that other scholars treat Augustine's doctrine of the spiritual senses in greater depth than Rahner. Most notably, see P. L. Landsberg, 'Les sens spirituels chez Saint Augustin', *Dieu vivant* 11 (1948), 83–105.

[83] As a terminological note, we should mention that Augustine distinguishes among three (not two) different kinds of vision: physical, spiritual, and intellectual. Importantly, however, by use of the term 'spiritual vision', Augustine does not describe the 'spiritual senses' as developed in other authors. Instead, he means a use of the imagination in 'seeing' an object that has already left one's field of physical vision. By 'intellectual' perception, by contrast, Augustine means to convey what is commonly spoken of as 'spiritual senses', since intellectual perception is the means by which one perceives the divine on Augustine's model. Augustine, then, clearly holds that the human faculty for perceiving the divine should not be confused with the acts of the human imagination. Intellectual sense perceives God, to Augustine; it does not conjure images that it wishes could be the divine. See Augustine, *De Genesi ad Litteram*, XII, 6–14, hereafter *De Gen*. Original Latin text in *PL* 34, 173–484. Published in English as *Literal Meaning of Genesis*, trans. John Hammond Taylor (New York: Newman Press, 1982), vols 41–2, at 42, 185–98.

[84] *De Libero Arbitrio*, 3, 36. Original Latin text in Jacques-Paul Migne, ed., *Patrologia Latina* (Paris: J.-P. Migne, 1844–55), vol. 32, 1221–310, at 1289. Hereafter cited as *PL*. Published in English as *On Free Choice of the Will*, trans. Thomas Williams (Indianapolis, IN: Hackett, 1993). Above translation in *GL* II, 99.

[85] *Soliloquies*, 1, 14. Original Latin text in *PL* 32, 868–903, at 876. Published in English as *Soliloquies*, and *Immortality of the Soul*, trans. Gerard Watson (Warminster: Aris and Philips, 1990). Above translation in *GL* II, 99.

that of 'the good and beautiful God, in whom and from whom and through whom everything is good and beautiful.'[86]

According to Balthasar's reading of Augustine, then, the 'eye of the mind' or 'inner eye' clearly beholds the *beauty* of God. Importantly, however, Balthasar locates in Augustine two more aspects of the aesthetic capacities of intellectual vision, both of which serve Balthasar's overarching purposes in his theological aesthetics. First, it is noteworthy that intellectual vision perceives not only God's beauty, but also the beauty of God *through* the beauty of the world. As Balthasar describes this feature of Augustine's thought:

> This training in seeing also leads, when the soul becomes pure and open, to that 'spiritual seeing' of God in his works of which Paul speaks in Romans (1, 20), *invisibilia ipsius per ea quae facta sunt intellecta conspiciuntur*. But this seeing succeeds only when the sight, leaving all finite things behind, has already reached the divine (*sempiterna ejus virtus et divinitas*) and looks back from there on what can become for it an entrance and an epiphany.[87]

In other words, once spiritual or intellectual sight has been granted the vision of God, one then 'sees' God throughout the created order. Although this particular passage emphasizes that one *first* sees God, and *then* sees God's presence in all things, Balthasar insists that 'Augustine will also ascend from the beauty and order of the world to eternal beauty,'[88] citing Augustine's *On True Religion* as support of this alternate directionality.[89] The point to bear in mind is that, much in the same way that Balthasar emphasizes the 'whole of the upper world' to be the object of the spiritual senses in Origen, so too does he focus in Augustine on the notion that spiritual seeing witnesses the divine presence throughout the creation. This point will be an important component of Balthasar's alternative to Neo-Scholastic proofs for God's existence, as will be shown in Chapter 6.

---

[86] The last quotation is taken from Augustine's *Soliloquies*, 1, 3. *PL* 32, 870. English translation and block quotation from *GL* II, 99.
[87] *GL* II, 101.   [88] *GL* II, 100.
[89] In that text Augustine explains, 'There is no lack of value or benefit in the contemplation of the beauty of the heavens...But such a consideration must not pander to a vain and passing curiosity, but must be turned into a stairway to the immortal and enduring'. *De Vera Religione* 52. Original Latin text in *PL* 34, 121–72, at 145. Published in English as *Of True Religion*, trans. Louis Mink (Chicago: H. Regnery Co., 1959). Above translation in *GL* II, 100.

It is also highly significant that, for Augustine, intellectual vision perceives not just the beauty of God, but specifically the beauty of Christ. In fact, according to Balthasar's reading of Augustine, it is *only* through acquiring spiritual sight that one can overcome Christ's physical ugliness and perceive his spiritual beauty. Balthasar notes that, for Augustine,

> A person must love Christ and have pure eyes to see his inner spiritual beauty,[90] because for those who stand at a distance, and certainly for his persecutors, he is veiled to the point of ugliness.[91] But his veiling of his beauty was not just inspired by his wish to be like us, who are ugly, in all things, but also by his desire to make the ugly beautiful by his love.[92]

In a similar vein, Balthasar also explains, 'Everything follows the path of love which leads inwards. "Christ's beauty is all the more lovable and wondrous the less it is physical beauty."'[93] Balthasar does not in his own constructive position draw the inversely proportional relationship between physical and spiritual beauty posed by Augustine here. Nevertheless, it is significant that for Augustine, as for Balthasar, spiritual vision entails not only seeing beauty but seeing in particular the beauty of Christ. In our investigation of Bonaventure in Chapter 2 we will see a similar relationship between the spiritual senses and this Christocentric aesthetic.

The surprising aspect of Balthasar's interpretation of Augustine is that whereas he is quick to dismiss the accounts of the spiritual senses in Evagrius and Diadochus on account of their reduction of the five spiritual senses to a single mode of perceiving the divine, he relaxes this standard in his treatment of Augustine. Although it is true that Augustine famously describes a fivefold inner perception in his *Confessions*,[94] the vast majority of his comments on the spiritual

---

[90] Cf. *Enarr. in Ps.* 127, 8. Original Latin text in *CCSL* 40 (Turnhout: Brepols, 1956), 1872–3. Published in English as *Expositions of the Psalms*, trans. Maria Boulding, OSB, ed. John E. Rotelle, OSA WSA III/15–20 (New York: New City Press, 2000–4).

[91] Cf. *Enarr. in Ps.* 43, 16. *CCSL* 38, 487–8. *Enarr. in Ps.* 44, 14. *CCSL* 38, 503. *Enarr. in Ps.* 103, I, 5. *CCSL* 40, 1476–8.

[92] *GL* II, 135.

[93] *GL* II, 136. *De Civ. Dei* 17, c. 16, 1. Original Latin text in *CCSL*, vol. 48, 580–1. Published in English as *City of God*, trans. John Healey (London: J. M. Dent and Co., 1967). Above English translation in *GL* II, 136.

[94] Balthasar does not miss the opportunity to quote this passage in *GL* I, 379. Augustine writes, 'But what do I love, oh God, when I love Thee? Not the beauty of a body nor the rhythm of moving time. Not the splendour of the light, which is so dear to the eyes. Not the sweet melodies in the world of sounds of all kinds. Not the fragrance of flowers, balms, and spices. Not manna and not honey; not the bodily

senses treat vision alone. In his *Literal Meaning of Genesis*, which constitutes one of his most thorough discussions of a 'sensory' encounter with God, Augustine treats exclusively vision.[95] At the heights of conceptual detail, then, spiritual senses such as hearing, smell, taste, and touch fall from Augustine's consideration.

Of course, it is not difficult to imagine that Balthasar is willing to relax the strict criteria he imposes on Evagrius and Diadochus because of Augustine's rich descriptions of the perception of God's beauty. It is nevertheless significant that, as much as Balthasar celebrates those versions of the doctrine that are fivefold, one observes a distinct privileging of sight in his understanding of the aesthetic capacities of the spiritual senses, both in his reading of Augustine above and, I would argue, in his own use of the spiritual senses, as will be examined in Chapters 5 and 6.

MAXIMUS THE CONFESSOR AND THE LITURGICAL SETTING FOR THE SPIRITUAL SENSES

In comparison with the brief treatment Maximus the Confessor receives from Rahner, Balthasar amplifies considerably his significance for the spiritual senses tradition.[96] Balthasar treats Maximus' understanding of the spiritual senses in his 1941 monograph,[97] and

members which are so treasured by carnal embrace. None of this do I love when I love my God. And yet I do love a light and a sound and a fragrance and a delicacy and an embrace, when I love my God, who is light and sound and fragrance and delicacy and embrace to my interior man. There my soul receives a radiance that no space can grasp; there something resounds which no time can take away; there something gives a fragrance which no wind can dissipate; there something is savoured which no satiety can make bitter; there something is embraced which can occasion no ennui. This is what I love when I love my God.' Augustine, *Conf.* X, 6. Original Latin text in *PL* 32, 659–867, at 782. Published in English as *Confessions*, trans. Henry Chadwick (Oxford: Oxford University Press, 1991), 183.

[95] *De Gen.*, XII, 6–14. *PL* 34, 173–484. Taylor, vol. 42, 185–98.

[96] Rahner mentions Maximus only in a footnote at the end of his essay, and even then he simply writes, 'In the 7th Century Maximus the Confessor matched the five spiritual senses with the powers of the soul which were familiar from other sources'. Cf. *Ambiguorum Liber sive de variis difficilibus locis SS. Dionysii Areopagitae et Gregorii Theologi*, in *PG* 91, 1031–417, at 1248A.

[97] *Cosmic Liturgy: The Universe According to Maximus the Confessor*, trans. Brian E. Daley (San Francisco, CA: Ignatius Press, 2003), hereafter *CL*. Originally published in

although he does not take up Maximus' thought in a sustained manner in his theological aesthetics, I nevertheless hold that Maximus has special significance for Balthasar's articulation of the spiritual senses. In particular, I argue below that Maximus is important for Balthasar's idea that the spiritual senses become active specifically in the *liturgical* setting. Before examining this aspect of Maximus' thought, however, we should observe that Balthasar locates in Maximus certain themes that we have seen elsewhere in his reading of the spiritual senses tradition.

Balthasar celebrates both the fivefold articulation of the spiritual senses found in Maximus and the high value placed on the material component of creation in Maximus' texts. Balthasar expounds on the former point as follows:

> Maximus even undertakes to work out a kind of correspondence between the five senses and the spiritual faculties of the soul by conceiving of the former as 'exemplary images' of the latter. So the organ and sensible root of the (theoretical) intellect is the eye, the organ of the (practical) reason the perceiving ear, the organ of the emotive soul the sense of smell, that of the passionate soul the sense of taste, and that of the vital principle the sense of touch.[98]

Concerning the latter point, Balthasar holds that, for Maximus, 'The soul does not contaminate itself...by its turn toward the world of sense.'[99] Balthasar quotes Maximus' *Centuries on Love* as evidence of this positive regard for the material world: 'It is not food that is evil, but our gluttony; not procreation, but fornication; not money, but avarice, not glory, but our thirst for glory. Thus there is nothing evil in things but the misuse [we make of them], which grows out of the disorder of the mind in making use of nature.'[100] These aspects of Maximus' thought are straightforward and uncontroversial, permitting us to move to the most intriguing aspect of Balthasar's reading.

Although his discussion of the point is brief, it is nevertheless instructive that Balthasar reads Maximus as holding that the spiritual

---

German as *Kosmische Liturgie. Maximus der Bekenner: Höhe und Krise des griechischen Weltbilds* (Freiburg: Herder, 1941). Later published in a second edition as *Kosmische Liturgie: Das Weltbild Maximus' des Bekenners* (Einsiedeln: Johannes Verlag, 1961). In 1941 Balthasar also published *Die Gnostischen Centurien des Maximus Confessor* (Freiburg: Herder, 1941).

[98] *CL*, 304.   [99] *CL*, 305.
[100] *Capita de Charitate*, 3, 4, in *PG* 90, 959–1082, at 1017CD. *CL*, 305.

senses have a particularly important function within liturgy. As he explains,

> Maximus speaks positively...of the 'spiritual senses': if a person has them, he 'realises' in an experiential way the mystical content of the liturgy,[101] the true meaning of Jesus' gift of himself in the Eucharist[102]...through a concurrent 'divine perception' (αἴσθησις θεῖα) that is aware [*mitwahrnimmt*] of the intelligible content *in* the symbolic ceremony.[103]

The liturgical setting is thus a key locus within which the spiritual senses are active, according to Balthasar's reading of Maximus. We shall see in Chapter 4 that there is a notable resemblance between this understanding of the operation of the spiritual senses and Balthasar's own articulation of the idea, as liturgy for him is integral to the function of spiritual perception.

CURIOUS NEGLECT: GREGORY OF NYSSA AND PSEUDO-DIONYSIUS

One of the most puzzling features of Balthasar's engagement with the patristic treatment of the spiritual senses is the lack of attention he gives to Gregory of Nyssa. This neglect on Balthasar's part is especially odd given that Balthasar has an obvious, demonstrable interest in the spiritual senses from an early date, and he was thoroughly acquainted with Nyssen's thought. In fact, Balthasar actually translated Nyssen's *Commentary on the Song of Songs* and published an article-length study of him in 1939, which was followed by an expanded monograph, *Presence and Thought*, published in 1942.[104] It is stranger still to consider that Balthasar actually studied Nyssen under Henri de Lubac

---

[101] *Mystagogia*, in *PG* 91, 658–721, at 704A. *CL*, 286.
[102] *Quaestiones ad Thalassium de Scriptura Sacra* 36, in *PG* 90, 244–785, at 381B. *CL*, 286.
[103] *Mystagogia*. *PG* 91, 700B. *CL*, 286.
[104] Hans Urs von Balthasar, *Der versiegelte Quell: Auslegung des Hohen Liedes*. Salzburg: Otto Müller Verlag, 1939; 'Présence et pensée. La philosophie religieuse de Grégoire de Nysse', in *Recherches de science religieuse* 29 (1939), 513–49; *Présence et pensée: Essai sur la philosophie religieuse de Grégoire de Nysse* (Paris: Beauchesne, 1942); published in English as *Presence and Thought: An Essay on the Religious Philosophy of Gregory of Nyssa*, trans. Mark Sebanc (San Francisco, CA: Ignatius Press, 1995).

in Fourvière alongside Jean Daniélou,[105] and Daniélou devotes a considerable portion of his renowned *Platonisme et Théologie Mystique* to Nyssen's 'doctrine of the spiritual senses'.[106] It seems highly plausible that Balthasar and Daniélou would have discussed at some point Nyssen's understanding of the spiritual senses.

And yet there is no mention of Nyssen's version of the spiritual senses in *The Glory of the Lord*, and Balthasar discusses the doctrine only once in *Presence and Thought*. In the latter text, Balthasar writes in a footnote on Nyssen's understanding of desire, 'Certainly the spiritual senses are not identical to the ordinary senses of the soul... but there is a continuity between them and not a break: thus the Song of Songs uses sensual symbols to initiate the soul into divine things.'[107] In his Maximus study, too, Balthasar indicates his awareness of Nyssen's position in the history of the tradition. There he writes, 'Origen and his disciples, of course, and later Gregory of Nyssa, Pseudo-Macarius, and Diadochus of Photike, spoke of an intellectual and spiritual brand of sensibility that was needed in order to enliven the poverty of abstract thought and bring it to full flower, through experiential contact with an intelligible or mystical object.'[108] In spite of this awareness, however, Balthasar seems not to regard Nyssen's understanding of the spiritual senses as noteworthy in *The Glory of the Lord*.

Why would this be the case? One possibility is that we see here once again the influence of Rahner's scholarship in framing Balthasar's study of the spiritual senses tradition. At the end of his examination of patristic material, Rahner mentions the 'obvious' influence of Origen in this arena, but then says of Nyssen, 'In his exposition of the Song of Songs the theory of the five spiritual faculties is explicitly presented as a teaching of the "philosophy" of the Song of Songs. Further evidence is here unnecessary.'[109] It may be the case, then, that Rahner's cursory dismissal of Nyssen's version of the doctrine led Balthasar to adopt a similar attitude to this feature of his thought.

---

[105] Concerning his period of study under de Lubac, Balthasar offers the following recollection: 'While all the others went off to play football, Daniélou, Bouillard, and I and a few others (Fessard was no longer there) got down to Origen, Gregory of Nyssa, and Maximus. I wrote a book on each of these'. In Peter Henrici, SJ, 'A Sketch of von Balthasar's Life', trans. J. Saward, in *Hans Urs von Balthasar: His Life and Work*, ed. David L. Schindler (San Francisco, CA: Ignatius Press, 1991), 7–43, at 11.

[106] Jean Daniélou, *Platonisme et théologie mystique: Essai sur la doctrine spirituelle de Saint Grégoire de Nysse* (Paris: Aubier, 1944), 235–66.

[107] *Presence and Thought*, 160.   [108] *CL*, 285.

[109] Rahner, 'The "Spiritual Senses" According to Origen', 102.

And yet Balthasar was most likely exposed to Daniélou's informed reading of Nyssen's understanding of the spiritual senses as well, and there would be no clear reason to use Rahner's study to the exclusion of others. Daniélou's *Platonisme et Théologie Mystique* was published in 1944, two years after *Presence and Thought*, and this could have delayed Balthasar's exposure to the richness of this feature of Nyssen's theology. Nevertheless, Balthasar would have had ample time to integrate Nyssen's model of the spiritual senses into *The Glory of the Lord*.

Moreover, Nyssen's articulation of the doctrine would seem to be an especially attractive option, given the extent to which Nyssen holds the bodily senses in high esteem. One of Nyssen's most significant breaks with Origen involves the high regard he has for the corporeal senses. He famously describes his *Commentary on the Song of Songs* as 'a guide for the more fleshly-minded', and in so doing opposes his work to that of Origen.[110] Such a positive assessment of the body is clearly in keeping with Balthasar's goals in his theological aesthetics, which of course makes it all the more puzzling that he does not use Nyssen's thought on the topic.

Furthermore, Balthasar's own version of the spiritual senses bears curious affinities with Nyssen's understanding of the doctrine. Specifically, as we shall see in greater depth in Chapter 4, Balthasar holds that the encounter with the neighbour is the 'decisive' arena within which one is granted one's spiritual senses. Sarah Coakley has recently shown that the spiritual senses, for Nyssen, involve the recognition of Christ in the poor.[111] Given this obvious connection, it is surprising that Balthasar is not more overtly sympathetic to Nyssen's use of the doctrine, as it would seem to serve his efforts especially well.

Balthasar's neglect of Pseudo-Dionysius similarly perplexes. He devotes a lengthy essay to Dionysius in the second volume of *The Glory of the Lord*, in which he indicates a thorough familiarity with the Areopagite's theology,[112] and Dionysius was of considerable

---

[110] *In Cant.*, Prol. Original Greek text in *GNO* 6, 4. English translation by Casimir McCambley, *Commentary on the Song of Songs* (Brookline, MA: Holy Cross, 1987), 35.

[111] Sarah Coakley, 'On the Identity of the Risen Jesus: Finding Jesus Christ in the Poor', in *Seeking the Identity of Jesus: A Pilgrimage*, eds. Beverly Roberts Gaventa and Richard B. Hays (Grand Rapids, MI, Eerdmans, 2008), 301–19; 'Gregory of Nyssa', in *The Spiritual Senses: Perceiving God in Western Christianity*, eds. Paul Gavrilyuk and Sarah Coakley (Cambridge: Cambridge University Press, 2012), 36–55.

[112] *GL* II, 144–210.

importance to the spiritual senses tradition.[113] Dionysius refers to the 'eyes of the mind' at a number of points in his writings,[114] and he even mentions a book titled *On the Objects of Spiritual and Sensible Perception*,[115] which would accord extensively with Balthasar's project in his theological aesthetics. And yet, aside from one mention of Dionysius' use of the phrase 'eye of the soul',[116] and one reference to the 'spiritual sense',[117] Balthasar ignores the theme of the spiritual senses in the Areopagite's corpus.

It may be the case that the clearly *apophatic* models of the spiritual senses in Nyssen and Dionysius dissuaded Balthasar from incorporating his version of the doctrine into the theological aesthetics. Stephen Fields has noted Balthasar's interest in a *cataphatic* understanding of the spiritual senses in his reading of Bonaventure, as will be examined in Chapter 2. If this assessment is accurate, then it stands to reason that Balthasar would shy away from the versions of the spiritual senses in Nyssen and Dionysius. Nyssen, in particular, describes in his *Commentary on the Song of Songs* the 'dark embrace' between the human being and God that does not benefit from clear vision or understanding.[118]

The likeliest reason Balthasar does not integrate Gregory of Nyssa and Pseudo-Dionysius into his reading of the history of the spiritual senses is that he is not actually terribly interested in retelling and rounding out the history of the doctrine by seeking out neglected figures in the tradition. Instead, Balthasar in *The Glory of the Lord* shows a desire to bring historical expressions of the doctrine into conversation with the thought of his contemporaries, especially Karl Barth, Romano Guardini, Gustav Siewerth, and Paul Claudel. Indeed, in his theological aesthetics itself the only figure treated at any length outside of his 'Origen and the rest' rendering of the tradition is Augustine,

---

[113] See especially Paul Gavrilyuk, 'Pseudo-Dionysius the Areopagite', in *The Spiritual Senses: Perceiving God in Western Christianity*, eds. Paul Gavrilyuk and Sarah Coakley (Cambridge: Cambridge University Press, 2012), 86–103.
[114] *Celestial Hierarchy* I. 2, 121B 4; III. 3, 165D 12; *Ecclesiastical Hierarchy* III. 12, 441D 9; IV. 6, 480D 9; *Divine Names* IV. 5, 700D 14. References in Gavrilyuk, 'Pseudo-Dionysius the Areopagite', 87.
[115] *Ecclesiastical Hierarchy* I. 2.   [116] *GL* II, 171.   [117] *GL* II, 183.
[118] *In Cant.*, VI. GNO 6, 178–83. McCambley, 130–3. It is also interesting to note that in his first homily on the Song of Songs, Nyssen emphasizes spiritual touch, taste, and smell, which are the three spiritual senses that are later in the medieval period mapped onto the will instead of the intellect. *In Cant.*, I. GNO 6, 34–42. McCambley, 43–56.

and we can easily imagine that in this one case Balthasar simply could not resist addressing Augustine's rich descriptions of aesthetic capacities of spiritual perception. Ultimately, then, as much as Balthasar is greatly influenced by patristic versions of the spiritual senses, his primary interest lies in reworking the idea of spiritual perception in a modern idiom for his theological aesthetics.

CONCLUSION

A number of themes emerge from the above treatment of Balthasar's highly selective, frequently massaged reading of patristic figures. We have seen that Balthasar is attracted to those versions of the spiritual senses that articulate a fivefold perception of the divine (Origen, Pseudo-Macarius, Maximus), and we also observed his dismissive attitude toward those models of the doctrine that collapse into a single divine sense (Evagrius, Diadochus). We also noticed Balthasar's attempts to locate Christ and the 'upper world' as the object of the spiritual senses (Origen, Pseudo-Macarius, Augustine), which has important implications for his use of the doctrine in his theological aesthetics. Additionally, we have seen Balthasar's desire to find the most positive rendering of the corporeal senses to which the spiritual senses are analogous (Origen, Pseudo-Macarius, Maximus), and we noted especially the hermeneutical acrobatics this desire elicited from Balthasar in his reading of Origen. Last, concerning the question of how one acquires one's spiritual senses, we witnessed Balthasar's downplaying of practice and his emphasis on divine grace (Origen, Pseudo-Macarius), and the correlative broadening of candidates for receiving the capacity for spiritual perception, even when this reading did not easily square with the textual evidence found in Origen's writings.

In addition to these recurrent issues, we have also seen influences on Balthasar's understanding of the spiritual senses that seem to be particular to certain figures. In Augustine we have observed an alignment between spiritual vision and the beauty of God. In Maximus we have seen the idea that the spiritual senses become active within the liturgical setting. Most intriguingly, in Pseudo-Macarius we have observed the idea that the spiritual senses become active after one has suffered Christ's passion, died, and been resurrected with him. Balthasar's own use of the doctrine appears as a veritable potpourri of intriguing features gathered from various figures in the spiritual senses tradition, as we shall see more fully in Chapter 4.

Before turning to Balthasar's engagement with his contemporary interlocutors, we shall in the next chapter examine his reading of the spiritual senses in the medieval and early modern periods.

2

Balthasar's Reading of Medieval and Early Modern Versions of the Spiritual Senses

Having put forward in Chapter 1 an account of the patristic influences on Balthasar's doctrine of the spiritual senses, this chapter treats of Balthasar's controversial yet convincing interpretation of medieval and early modern expositors of the doctrine. Here I limit my investigation to Balthasar's reading of Bonaventure (*c*.1217–74) and Ignatius of Loyola (1491–1556), as his examination of those figures exhibits once again a number of telling interpretive decisions that shed important light on his own use of the spiritual senses tradition. In his investigation of Bonaventure, Balthasar retrieves the corporeal dimension to spiritual perception, he repositions the spiritual senses such that they are not the preserve of a few 'mystical' elite, and he gives the spiritual senses an explicitly aesthetic dimension.[1] In making these hermeneutical decisions, we shall see that Balthasar resists Rahner's

---

[1] Latin quotations taken from the Quaracchi edition of Bonaventure's works: *Opera Omnia* (10 vols. Rome: Quaracchi, 1882–1902), hereafter cited as *Opera Omnia*. Unless otherwise noted, English translations of Bonaventure's works are as follows: *Itinerarium Mentis in Deum* from Bonaventure, *The Soul's Journey into God*, in *Bonaventure*, trans. Ewert Cousins (Mahwah, NJ: Paulist Press, 1978); *Breviloquium* from Bonaventure, *The Breviloquium*, in *The Works of Bonaventure*, trans. José de Vinck (Paterson, NJ: St Anthony Guild Press, 1960), vol. 2; *De Reductione Artium ad Theologiam* from Bonaventure, *On Retracing the Arts to Theology*, in *The Works of Bonaventure*, trans. José de Vinck (Paterson, NJ: St Anthony Guild Press, 1966), vol. 3, 13–32. *Soliloquy on the Four Spiritual Exercises*, in *The Works of Bonaventure*, trans. José de Vinck (Paterson, NJ: St Anthony Guild Press, 1966), vol. 3, 35–129. Abbreviations used in citations from Bonaventure's *Sentences* commentaries are understood as follows: III *Sent*. dist. 27 art. 2 q. 1: Book III of the *Sentences* commentary, *distinctio* 27, *articulus* 2, *quaestio* 1. Also, fund. = *fundamentum*, dub. = *dubium*, c. = *conclusio*.

theretofore dominant interpretation;[2] Balthasar thus works against the regnant paradigm in scholarship on the spiritual senses in order to reshape substantially modern understandings of the doctrine.

Importantly, too, as was the case in his reading of Origen and other patristic figures, with Bonaventure we once again observe Balthasar's lack of interest in discussing the various practices one may undertake in order to cultivate spiritual perception. In his reading of Ignatius, however, Balthasar offers for the first time an examination of the role that practice can play in acquiring the spiritual senses. Balthasar also finds in Ignatius one who unites the corporeal and spiritual senses to a degree not achieved in the tradition that precedes him, as will be shown below.

THE HEIGHTS OF THE TRADITION: BONAVENTURE

Balthasar follows Rahner in viewing Bonaventure as the most significant figure in the spiritual senses tradition after Origen. However, Balthasar disagrees with Rahner on a number of interpretive matters, as discussed by Stephen Fields.[3] Most importantly, Balthasar reads Bonaventure as advancing a version of the spiritual senses in which the object of spiritual perception is the 'Word in Christ', not the 'transcendent God', as Rahner would have it.[4] Balthasar's reinterpretation of the object of the spiritual senses then commands a threefold re-reading of Bonaventure's model of the doctrine. With the Word in Christ as their object, Balthasar reinterprets the spiritual senses such that they are situated in the second, 'illuminative' stage of spiritual development,[5] where they find fullest expression in a *cataphatic*

---

[2] At the time of Balthasar's writing, Rahner's studies were the most frequently cited texts in scholarship on the spiritual senses, and they have been widely regarded as offering the standard treatment of the topic.

[3] Stephen Fields, 'Balthasar and Rahner on the Spiritual Senses', *Theological Studies* 57 (1996), 224–41.

[4] *GL* II, 321.

[5] Bonaventure's three stages of the spiritual life are described as follows: the first stage is that of *purification* (the purgative way); here the individual reflects on his or her sinfulness and then turns to a different life. The second stage is that of *illumination* (the illuminative way), in which the person turns from thoughts of his or her own wretchedness and knowledge of the forgiveness of God to behold God's splendour in created things. The third stage is that of *perfection* (the unitive way), in which the

grasping of the Word, and are conjoined with the bodily senses of the human being. In sharp contrast, Rahner holds that, for Bonaventure, the spiritual senses have as their object the transcendent God, which situates them in the final, 'unitive' stage of the spiritual life, means that they are perfected in an *apophatic* 'learned ignorance', and causes them to be disjuncted from the bodily senses.[6]

We shall examine the intricacies of this debate below, but for the moment it is important to appreciate what is at stake in each of these three disputes. Balthasar uses the first point to reposition the spiritual senses such that they pertain not to 'mystical experience', as he understands it, but rather to 'Christian experience' more broadly considered. That is, by questioning Rahner's placement of the spiritual senses in the final, unitive stage of the Christian life, Balthasar recategorizes the spiritual senses such that they are fundamental features of 'ordinary Christian faith' rather than faculties that are employed only at the rare, fleeting heights of 'mystical encounter'.[7] In so doing, Balthasar recasts the spiritual senses so that they do some of the most important work in his theology, as they are employed not at the summit, so to speak, but rather at the very foundations of faith.

Balthasar uses the second point, about the *cataphatic* dimension of the spiritual senses, as a crucial pillar in his claim that they have a specifically *aesthetic* dimension. For Balthasar, the spiritual senses are not used in an *apophatic* 'dark embrace' with the transcendent God. Instead, they are used in a *cataphatic* grasping of the Word in Christ. Therefore, the spiritual senses bear witness to the glory of divine revelation as displayed throughout the created order. Furthermore, the fact that Bonaventure consistently speaks of the spiritual senses perceiving beauty—and the additional fact that he deliberates at length on the notion that beauty is a transcendental property of being—makes for a set of theological priorities that serves Balthasar's project in his theological aesthetics to a remarkable degree, as will be shown in Chapter 5.

Balthasar uses the third point about Bonaventure's view of the bodily senses as part of his ongoing effort to celebrate the role of

---

individual undertakes a 'mystical' progression toward God that seeks and ultimately finds union with the divine. See Stephen Brown's Introduction to *The Journey of the Mind into God* (Indianapolis, IN: Hackett, 1993), ix–xviii.

[6] Rahner, 'The Doctrine of the "Spiritual Senses" in the Middle Ages', 109–17, 126–8.
[7] *GL* I, 301.

the body in the perception of the divine. In reading Bonaventure against the Rahnerian, dualist paradigm, Balthasar seeks to retrieve the important role played by the corporeal senses in relation to their spiritual counterparts. Although Balthasar does not ultimately read Bonaventure as uniting bodily and spiritual sensation in as thoroughgoing a manner as modern figures, Bonaventure does nevertheless substantially improve on the value placed on corporeal sensation found in patristic figures, according to Balthasar's interpretation.

Although these points of contrast between Balthasar and Rahner will be illuminating for our treatment of the theme of the spiritual senses, other noteworthy aspects of Balthasar's appropriation of Bonaventure's thought should not be obscured. Most significantly, in Balthasar's examination of Bonaventure, he makes virtually no mention of practice in the cultivation of the spiritual senses. That is, one aspect of Bonaventure that Balthasar does *not* explicitly integrate into his own theological project is the idea that one can actively undertake various efforts to foster the growth of one's spiritual senses. Instead, as I shall discuss more thoroughly in Chapter 4 of this study, Balthasar advances a model of the spiritual senses that is deeply grace-centred.[8]

Scholarship on Bonaventure's Doctrine of the Spiritual Senses

The 1920s and 1930s witnessed a remarkable upsurge of scholarly interest in Bonaventure's doctrine of the spiritual senses.[9] Most

---

[8] Of course, every figure who articulates a doctrine of the spiritual senses throughout the history of the church ascribes an essential role to grace. However, what those figures typically do—which Balthasar does not—is speak of the manner in which practice is required in this realm.

[9] Ephrem Longpré, OFM, 'La théologie mystique de S. Bonaventure', *Archivum Franciscan Historicum* 14 (1921), 36–108, esp. 51–3; Friedrich Andres, 'Die Stufen der Contemplatio in Bonaventuras Itinerarium mentis ad Deum und in Benjamin major des Richards von St. Viktor', *Franziskanische Studien* 8 (1921), 189–200; Raoul Carton, *L'experience mystique de l'illumination interieure chez Roger Bacon* (Paris: J. Vrin, 1924), 242–5; Etienne Gilson, *La philosophie de Saint Bonaventure* (Paris: J. Vrin, 1924); Bernhard Rosenmöller, *Religiöse Erkenntnis nach Bonaventura* (Münster: Aschendorff, 1925); Dunstan John Dobbins, *Franciscan Mysticism* (New York: J. F. Wagner, 1927); J. M. Bissen, *Les degrés de la contemplation* (Paris, 1928–30); Stanislaus Grünewald, OMCap., *Franziskanische Mystik* (Munich: Naturrechts Verlag, 1932); Jean-François Bonnefoy, *Une somme bonaventurienne de théologie mystique* (Paris: Librairie Saint-François, 1934); H. Koenig, *De inhabitatione Spiritus Sancti* (Mundelein: Apud Aedes Seminarii Sanctae Mariae ad Lacum, 1934); Stanislaus Grünewald, 'Zur Mystik des hl. Bonaventura', *ZAM* 9 (1934), 124–42, 219–32; F. Beauchemin, *Le savior au*

significant among these studies is that of Jean-François Bonnefoy, whose *Le Saint-Espirit et ses dons selon Saint Bonaventure* (1929) serves as the chief point of reference for much subsequent examination of the doctrine.[10] Bonnefoy holds that Bonaventure uses the term *sensus spiritualis* equivocally throughout his writings, and he therefore concludes his examination with the claim that Bonaventure is simply inconsistent on the matter of the spiritual senses.[11] Bonnefoy's thesis thus becomes a touchstone for later investigations of the doctrine in that it accentuates the ambiguities with which any one-sided reading of Bonaventure must contend. Importantly, too, by claiming that there are irreconcilable differences in Bonaventure's texts, Bonnefoy's study represents one extreme to which the interpretation of Bonaventure's doctrine can go. In fact, Rahner uses Bonnefoy as something of a foil for his own argument for consistency in Bonaventure's doctrine of the spiritual senses. He holds that Bonnefoy's conclusions would leave one unable to derive any meaning from Bonaventure's texts on the topic. This issue and the challenges it presents will recur in our examination of Balthasar's reading below.

Perceiving the Word:
Christ as the Object of the Spiritual Senses

The most important interpretive decision Balthasar makes in his approach to Bonaventure's texts is his claim that the object of the spiritual senses is the Word in Christ. Rahner had insisted, to the contrary, that 'the spiritual senses simply have God as their primary object'.[12] Rahner attempts to support this contention by reference to

---

service de l'amour (Paris: J. Vrin, 1935); Ephrem Longpré, 'Bonaventure', *Dictionnaire de spiritualité* (Paris: 1932–95), vol. 1, 1768–1843; F. Imle, *Das geistliche Leben nach der Lehre des hl. Bonaventura* (Werl: Franziskus-Druckerei, 1939). For a contemporary treatment of these issues, see Fabio Massimo Tedoldi, *La dottrina dei cinque sensi spirituali in San Bonaventura* (Rome: Pontificium Athenaeum Antonianum, 1999).

[10] Jean-François Bonnefoy, *Le Saint-Esprit et ses dons selon Saint Bonaventure* (Paris: J. Vrin, 1929).

[11] Bonnefoy comments on the then extant scholarship on Bonaventure as follows: 'The basic error of these attempts to bring together the various statements on the subject lies in the view that all the passages in which Bonaventure speaks of "sensus spiritualis" deal with one and the same phenomenon'. Bonnefoy, *Le Saint-Esprit et ses dons selon Saint Bonaventure*, 214. Quoted in Rahner, 'The Doctrine of the "Spiritual Senses" in the Middle Ages', 110.

[12] Rahner, 'The Doctrine of the "Spiritual Senses" in the Middle Ages', 114–15.

two passages from Bonaventure's works, the first of which is taken from the *Itinerarium*. Referring to the understanding of spiritual taste described there, Rahner holds that, for Bonaventure, 'Spiritual taste consists in "suscipere ab ipso (Deo) delectationes"' ('receiving its delight from God').[13] Through this passage Rahner attempts to establish that God (*Deo*) is the object of the spiritual taste. However, an examination of the primary text shows that in this quotation Rahner has actually substituted the word *Deo* for Bonaventure's term, *Verbum incarnatum*. That is, Bonaventure's text actually reads, 'When, through charity, [the soul] embraces the *incarnate Word* by receiving delight from him and passing into him in ecstatical love, it recovers taste and touch.'[14] In direct, clear contradiction to Rahner's claim that God is the object of spiritual taste, then, Bonaventure in fact makes clear in this passage that the object of this spiritual sense (and spiritual touch, too, for that matter) is the *Verbum incarnatum*.

The second text used by Rahner to support his interpretation requires a more complex assessment. Taken from Bonaventure's *Sentences* commentary, the passage speaks of the *simplex contuitus*, which Rahner describes as the form of sight 'reserved to purity of heart, which "alone is permitted to gaze upon God"'.[15] Here Rahner claims to follow Bonnefoy in taking the *simplex contuitus* to be a simple vision of God that grants knowledge of eternal truth.[16] It is thus not Christ, according to Rahner, but rather the transcendent God who is 'seen' through this vision. The crucial question to ask, however, is whether or not it is in fact a 'spiritual sense' of which Bonaventure speaks in his description of the *simplex contuitus*. Bonnefoy, whose scholarship Rahner claims to use on this point, prefers to separate

---

[13] Rahner, 'The Doctrine of the "Spiritual Senses" in the Middle Ages', 116. Rahner leaves the passage in its original Latin. *Itin*. IV, 3. *Opera Omnia* V 306b.

[14] *Dum caritate complectitur Verbum incarnatum, ut suscipiens ab ipso delectationem et ut transiens in illud...recuperat gustum et tactum*. *Itin*. IV, 3 (emphasis added), *Opera Omnia* V 306b.

[15] Rahner, 'The Doctrine of the "Spiritual Senses" in the Middle Ages', 116. *Beatitudinis munditiae cordis, cuius est Deum videre*. III *Sent*. dist. 35 q. 3. *Opera Omnia* III 778a.

[16] He writes, 'For an account of the "simplex contuitus" we need only follow P. Bonnefoy. It involves a vision of the first truth which is immutable, and of its eternal ideas which form the ultimate principles of all creation. This "contuitus" finds its internal unity in our becoming aware of the direct operation of eternal truth upon our own spirit. Of course this simple vision of God is not a direct perception of the divine essence free of any intermediary.' Rahner, 'The Doctrine of the "Spiritual Senses" in the Middle Ages', 116.

his treatment of the spiritual senses from his examination of the *simplex contuitus*. Instead of placing the *simplex contuitus* within the section of his monograph that treats of the spiritual senses, Bonnefoy includes this examination under his treatment of 'intelligence'.[17] Much depends, of course, on how we define our terms, but it should be said that the actual words, *sensus spiritualis*, do not appear in this portion of Bonaventure's text. He does speak of *videre* as it pertains to God, but it is likely that Bonaventure intends something distinct from the *sensus spiritualis* of which he speaks at other points in his writings. This interpretation is not without its difficulties, but it does ultimately appear to be the preferable option, as the bulk of the textual evidence supports this alternate reading, as we shall see shortly.

In clear resistance to Rahner's interpretation, Balthasar insists that, for Bonaventure, 'The chief texts identify the eternal Word as the object of this experience of God through the senses, the Word in his nuptial relationship to redeemed and sanctified man'.[18] To support this claim, Balthasar alludes to two key passages from Bonaventure's texts. The first, from Bonaventure's *Breviloquium*, reflects at length on the spiritual senses in relation to Christ, and reads as follows:

> The sublime beauty of Christ the Bridegroom is seen, in so far as he is splendour; the highest harmony is heard, in so far as he is word; the greatest sweetness is tasted, in so far as he is the wisdom that contains both, word and splendour; the sublimest fragrance is smelled, in so far as he is the word inspired in the heart; the greatest delight is embraced, in so far as he is the incarnate Word.[19]

Bonaventure here gives clear indication that the spiritual senses perceive Christ, and further that they do so through five distinct forms of spiritual perception. As Balthasar comments on this passage, 'Here, the tree of the spiritual senses is related to the full height of the form of God in his revelation: not indeed to the transcendent God in

---

[17] Bonnefoy, *Le Saint-Esprit et ses dons selon Saint Bonaventure*, 176–85.
[18] *GL* II, 320.
[19] *Quibus videtur Christi sponsi summa pulchritudo sub ratione Splendoris; auditur summa harmonia sub ratione Verbi; gustatur summa dulcedo sub ratione Sapientiae comprehendentis utrumque, Verbum scilicet et Splendorem; odoratur summa fragrantia sub ratione Verbi inspirati in corde; astringitur summa suavitas sub ratione Verbi incarnati, inter nos habitantis corporaliter et reddentis se nobis palpabile, osculabile, amplexabile per ardentissimam caritatem, quae mentem nostram per ecstasim et raptum transpire facit ex hoc mundo ad Patrem. Brev.* V, 6. *Opera Omnia* V 258b. Quoted in *GL* II, 320-1 (translation slightly emended).

himself... but precisely to the three dimensions of the Word of revelation.'[20] In direct opposition to the notion that the transcendent God is the object of the spiritual senses, then, Balthasar here claims that the three aspects of the Word (i.e., *Verbum increatum, inspiratum,* and *incarnatum*) are the realities that the spiritual senses grasp.

Balthasar further supports this claim by referring to another passage from Bonaventure's corpus, this time from his *Itinerarium*:

> While she [the soul] accepts Christ, in her faith in him, as the uncreated Word, word and splendour of the Father, she recovers the spiritual hearing and sight—hearing that she may hear the address of Christ, sight that she may look on the rays of his light. When, further, she sighs in hope of receiving the inspired Word, she recovers the spiritual sense of smell through longing and inclination. When she embraces the incarnate Word in love, receiving pleasure from him and passing over to him through ecstatic love, she recovers taste and touch.[21]

In this passage, too, one finds no ambiguity concerning the object of the spiritual senses. They grasp Christ in a richly depicted, fivefold act of perception. Spiritual sight, hearing, smell, taste, and touch all perceive the Word in Christ. Based on this passage, Balthasar contends, 'the object of the senses is the same: the entire vertical extension of the revelation in the Word.'[22] We see in these two passages, then (which are frequently viewed as the main texts for Bonaventure's treatment of the spiritual senses), a notion of the spiritual senses that speaks of the fivefold perception of the Word, not the spiritualized sensation of the transcendent God.[23]

---

[20] *GL* II, 321.

[21] *Dum per fidem credit in Christum tanquam in Verbum increatum, quod est Verbum et splendor Patris, recuperat spiritualem auditum et visum, auditum ad suscipiendum Christi sermones, visum ad considerandum illius lucis splendores. Dum autem spe suspirat ad suscipiendum Verbum inspiratum, per desiderium et affectum recuperat spiritualem olfactum. Dum caritate complectitur Verbum incarnatum, ut suscipiens ab ipso delectationem et ut transiens in illud per exstaticum amorem, recuperat gustum et tactum. Itin.* IV, 3. *Opera Omnia* V 306b. Quoted in *GL* II, 321-2 (translation slightly emended).

[22] *GL* II, 322.

[23] Balthasar further directs his reader to Bonaventure's additional references to Christ as the object of the spiritual senses throughout his writings. For example, Balthasar observes that in one of his epiphany sermons, Bonaventure writes that Christ is 'lovely and refreshing to look upon in accordance with man's double power of sight: the inward sight which sees the divinity, the outward sight which sees the manhood' (*Sic oculis depuratis ab omni lippiditate peccati sit iucundum et delectabile intueri ipsum secundum dublicem visum hominis, scilicet interiorem quantum*

Medieval and Early Modern Versions 63

The two quotations Balthasar uses from Bonaventure's *Breviloquium* and *Itinerarium* are known to Rahner, and he even cites portions of them in his study.[24] Instructively for our examination, however, he writes in response to this aspect of Bonaventure's thought, 'This description of the object of the spiritual senses undeniably possesses both depth and beauty, but it must also be admitted that the attempt to discover a special object for every sense, a "ratio" through which it perceives the Word, is rather forced.'[25] Crucially, then, Rahner derives his argument against the idea that the Word in Christ is the object of the spiritual senses not from a critique of Bonaventure's thought on its own terms, but rather from Rahner's own preconceived idea that the notion of a fivefold perception of Christ is contrived. One wonders, of course, what sort of presuppositions animate Rahner's comments in regard to which of Bonaventure's ideas are credible and which are not. It is certainly surprising to witness here a moment in which the contemporary viability of Bonaventure's thought seems to be dictating Rahner's purportedly historical study.

Further betraying that his primary concern is the constructive potential of the doctrine of the spiritual senses, Rahner explains, 'Even though Bonaventure's dialectical skill and his ingenuity in drawing distinctions can cope with this difficulty, the impression remains that, despite the parallels with the physical senses and their object (*splendor, harmonia, fragrantia, dulcedo, suavitas*), a genuinely penetrating analysis of the specific character of the spiritual gifts as acts of contemplation has not been achieved.'[26] Here, then, Rahner acknowledges that Bonaventure has developed an inventive set of parallels between the spiritual and corporeal senses, yet he remains critical of

---

ad divinitatem, et exteriorem quantum ad humanitatem). *Sermo. 1, Dominica Infra Octavam Epiphaniae. Opera Omnia* IX 171b. *GL* II, 329.

[24] Rahner writes, 'A comparison between the two main passages from the *Breviloquium* and *Itinerarium* points to Christ as the reality grasped by the spiritual senses, the "verbum increatum, inspiratum, incarnatum." Spiritual hearing grasps the "verbum increatum," so that the soul hears its voice and highest harmony. Spiritual sight perceives the Word, because the soul is dazzled by its light and brilliant beauty. The spiritual sense of smell perceives the "verbum inspiratum" when the soul experiences the lofty aroma of the Word. Spiritual taste savours the "verbum increatum" when it enjoys the sublime delight of its sweetness. The spiritual sense of touch grasps the "verbum increatum" and its powerful grace'. Rahner, 'The Doctrine of the "Spiritual Senses" in the Middle Ages', 115.

[25] Rahner, 'The Doctrine of the "Spiritual Senses" in the Middle Ages', 115.

[26] Rahner, 'The Doctrine of the "Spiritual Senses" in the Middle Ages', 115.

this model because of an impression that they do not describe the contemplation of God incisively enough. Unfortunately for his reader, Rahner does not develop further the basis on which this impression has been made; he instead dismisses the texts in question and moves to his next topic.

In light of this treatment, we can see that the passages that speak most clearly about the object of the spiritual senses are those that designate the Word in Christ as their object. Although Fields' comparison of Balthasar and Rahner simply juxtaposes their readings of Bonaventure without privileging one interpretive option over the other, the textual evidence actually supports Balthasar's reading as the more viable. With this point of interpretation in place, we next turn to the implications of the spiritual senses having the Word as their object.

The Spiritual Senses and 'Archetypal Experience': A Second-Stage Reading of the Doctrine

Balthasar insists that the object of the spiritual senses dictates the stage of the spiritual life in which they should be situated. Therefore, the fact that the spiritual senses have the Word in Christ as their object—and not the transcendent God—strongly suggests that they belong in the second, illuminative stage of the spiritual life, not the third, unitive stage. Balthasar also holds that the passage from Bonaventure's *Itinerarium* quoted above points to the second stage as the proper location of the spiritual senses. To support this reading, he notes that Bonaventure includes the spiritual senses in the section of the *Itinerarium* that has to do with the contemplation of God's image in the soul of the human being, which is typically regarded as a topic treated in the second stage of the life of faith.[27] Balthasar makes this point as follows: 'Their dwelling place, in which they develop in an organic unity, is not the lowest stage, the world of mere faith, nor the highest, the ecstasy, but the wide middle area of sapiential contemplation, which has as its object the total form of revelation that is the threefold Logos.'[28]

For his part, Rahner makes the opposite point, claiming that the spiritual senses for Bonaventure do not belong among the 'gifts of the

---

[27] *GL* II, 321.   [28] *GL* II, 325.

Holy Spirit' (which are granted in the second, 'illuminative' stage), but rather among the blessings of beatitude, which are given in the final, 'unitive' stage of the spiritual life. Rahner contends, 'A closer examination of the principles of these acts, that is, of the spiritual senses, [leads to the conclusion] that the operation of the highest principles, the blessings of beatitude, is involved.'[29] However, Bonaventure himself situates the operation of the spiritual senses in the second stage of the spiritual life. Specifically, the passage from the *Itinerarium* IV, 3 quoted above troubles Rahner's interpretation yet again, as it gives his reader good reason to locate the spiritual senses in this illuminative stage. It is ordinarily understood that of the six chapters of the *Itinerarium*, chapters 1 and 2 pertain to the first stage of the spiritual life, chapters 3 and 4 to the second stage, and chapters 5 and 6 to the third stage.[30] The text in question comes from chapter 4 of the *Itinerarium*, which would situate it in this second stage of the mind's journey to God. One wonders on this point if Rahner has not imposed Origen's model of the spiritual senses, by which they become active in the final, *enoptic* stage of the spiritual life, onto Bonaventure's texts.

The spiritual senses, then, on Balthasar's reading of Bonaventure, are removed from the realm they have typically occupied throughout their history in Christian theology: namely, the 'heights', so to speak, of mystical experience. Instead, through his 'second stage' reading of Bonaventure's understanding of the spiritual senses, Balthasar locates the spiritual senses in a different portion of the Christian life. Fields puzzles at the fact that Balthasar 'shows a muted appreciation of Bonaventure's highly developed mysticism.'[31] I would suggest that the reason for Balthasar's shift in emphasis has to do with themes at the very heart of his theology of experience. Clearly, as mentioned above, Balthasar is concerned that associating the spiritual senses with 'mysticism', as the term is often understood, will allow for a notion of religious experience that takes flight from the world instead of remaining rooted within it. Additionally, Balthasar proposes his particular reading of Bonaventure in the interest of guarding against the notion that the spiritual senses are enjoyed by only a few persons in the final, perfect stage of the spiritual life. This is done in the interest of granting

---

[29] Rahner, 'The Doctrine of the "Spiritual Senses" in the Middle Ages', 112.
[30] See, for example, Stephen Brown's Introduction to the *Itinerarium* in the English translation, esp. pp. xv–xviii.
[31] Fields, 'Balthasar and Rahner on the Spiritual Senses', 240.

the spiritual senses a new degree of significance as an integral component to Balthasar's fundamental theology, as will be more thoroughly explored in Chapter 6.

Balthasar's treatment of the spiritual senses in volume 1 of *The Glory of the Lord* is instructive in this connection. Before the portion of that text formally titled 'The Spiritual Senses', Balthasar offers a highly revealing account of 'Christian experience' in which the spiritual senses figure prominently.[32] There Balthasar draws a distinction between mystical experience and what he calls 'archetypal experience' (*urbildliche Erfahrung*), claiming that the former 'is not the foundation of ordinary Christian faith'.[33] The latter, by contrast, 'is the encounter with God of the Bible, which is what lays out the foundation and the condition for all Christian experience'.[34] (As we will see in Chapter 3 in our examination of Balthasar's use of Barth, Balthasar expressly brings the spiritual senses into his discussion of this meeting between the human being and God as portrayed in the Bible.) The importance of this interpretive decision on Balthasar's part cannot be overstated, as his positioning of the spiritual senses within the realm of archetypal experience integrates them into the very foundations of Christian faith. Whereas the spiritual senses in Bonaventure have often been understood to come into play in the very last stage of the spiritual life, then, Balthasar's interpretation gives them a broad theological significance for every Christian.

Connected to this repositioning of the spiritual senses is Balthasar's curious downplaying of the role of practice in Bonaventure's understanding of the cultivation of the spiritual senses. Although Bonaventure's version of the doctrine clearly holds that the spiritual senses grow through a combination of human practice and divine grace, Balthasar does not report the role of practice to his reader in his treatment of the doctrine. Bonaventure's notion, for example, that the soul grows stronger through the three-stage process of the spiritual life in which the *habitus virtutum*, the *habitus donorum*, and the *habitus beatitudinum* are cultivated, as outlined in the *Itinerarium*, is not conveyed in Balthasar's treatment.[35] With that said, however,

---

[32] See *GL* I, 257–365.   [33] *GL* I, 301.   [34] *GL* I, 301.
[35] See Rahner, 110–11; also the Prologue of the *Itinerarium*: 'Therefore, man of God, first exercise yourself in remorse of conscience before you raise your eyes to the rays of Wisdom reflected in its mirrors, lest perhaps from gazing upon these rays you fall into a deeper pit of darkness'.

Balthasar generally has an appreciation for the idea that theology and 'holiness' must be intimately intertwined. Balthasar views theology as a discipline that is inextricable from prayer and devotion. It is all the more curious, then, that he does not represent to his reader those aspects of Bonaventure's texts that speak of the link between the cultivation of certain habits and the operation of the spiritual senses.

The Spiritual Senses and Aesthetic Attunement: A Cataphatic Reading of the Doctrine

Balthasar's handling of the *cataphatic* nature of the spiritual senses in Bonaventure's thought requires careful analysis. On this point Balthasar resists Rahner's reading of Bonaventure once again. This time, Balthasar objects to Rahner's claim that the spiritual senses reach their height in an ecstatic, *apophatic* 'learned ignorance' (*docta ignorantia*).[36] Balthasar suggests, to the contrary, that the spiritual senses may make one *ready* for ecstasy, but, crucially, they do not *continue* to function as the soul is vaulted to this ecstatic state.

The issue is complex enough to merit beginning with Rahner's scholarship on the topic before treating Balthasar's reading of Bonaventure. In his assertion that the spiritual senses reach their height in 'learned ignorance', Rahner privileges the latter of two aspects of Bonaventure's unitive stage, the *excessus ecstaticus* (which is volitional or affective), over the *simplex contuitus* (which is intellectual). Whereas the latter may constitute the greatest degree of *understanding* of God that the human being can attain, the former grants the human being the highest form of union. Rahner describes this distinction (in a rather opaque passage, it must be said) as follows: 'The "simplex contuitus," vision, is the final goal of human understanding on earth, and yet it is not the last step of mystical progress or the highest form of contemplation in this world. For "contuitus" only offers, according to Bonaventure, a "contemplatio mediocris" in contrast to "contemplatio perfecta", the "excessus ecstatici".'[37] In other words, according to Rahner, Bonaventure's affective model of union with God claims that the intellect is surpassed in the final stage of contemplation, and a form of union that is non-intellectual is then experienced.[38]

---

[36] Rahner, 'The Doctrine of the "Spiritual Senses" in the Middle Ages', 117.
[37] Rahner, 'The Doctrine of the "Spiritual Senses" in the Middle Ages', 117.
[38] The one exception to this rule is the exceedingly rare instance of *raptus*, which Rahner summarizes as follows: ' "raptus" ... is a direct, clear vision of God through the

This *excessus ecstaticus*, most often translated simply as 'ecstasy', is, in Rahner's terms, 'the experience of the will, the union with God of a more direct love'.[39]

Up to this point, Rahner's interpretation is on well-established ground. Bonaventure is frequently situated within the broad tradition of affective mysticism, which draws extensively from Pseudo-Dionysius and Thomas Gallus, among others. The controversial aspect of Rahner's interpretation involves his novel attempt to yoke together ecstasy and spiritual touch in Bonaventure's thought. Concerning the *excessus ecstaticus*, he insists, 'Its act is "spiritual touch", the highest spiritual sense. Ecstasy and spiritual touch are one and the same'.[40] Rahner claims that when Bonaventure speaks of spiritual touch in his writings, one should understand him to be speaking of an 'ecstatic' form of union characterized by a dark, obscure 'contact' with God.[41] Rahner's argument that the spiritual senses reach their height in an *apophatic*, learned ignorance, then, is based on his claim that spiritual touch should be equated with ecstasy.

However, it should be said on this point that Rahner spends very little time actually defending this portion of his argument (only one paragraph of his lengthy essay), and he summons remarkably few texts to his aid. From Bonaventure's many comments on the spiritual senses, Rahner provides only four citations.[42] And yet, even the texts that he does use do not unequivocally support his thesis that spiritual touch and ecstasy are the same. The first two passages point to Bonaventure's *Sentences* commentaries; these texts, however, simply make clear that touch is the highest spiritual sense—they do not make any mention of ecstasy.[43] Rahner also uses the portion of

---

intellect, and is a foretaste of the beatific vision as an "actus gloriae". This is a privileged and exceptional state which Bonaventure thinks, for instance, St Paul enjoyed, but not Moses' (Rahner, 'The Doctrine of the "Spiritual Senses" in the Middle Ages', 117).

[39] Rahner, 'The Doctrine of the "Spiritual Senses" in the Middle Ages', 117.
[40] Rahner, 'The Doctrine of the "Spiritual Senses" in the Middle Ages', 117.
[41] Rahner, 'The Doctrine of the "Spiritual Senses" in the Middle Ages', 117.
[42] Rahner, 'The Doctrine of the "Spiritual Senses" in the Middle Ages', 126.
[43] Rahner, 'The Doctrine of the "Spiritual Senses" in the Middle Ages', 126. The citations from Bonaventure's *Sentences* commentaries read as follows: 'In respect of an uncreated object, the mode of perception by means of touch and embrace is nobler than that by means of sight and beholding' (*respectu objecti increati nobilior est modus apprehendendi per modum tactus et amplexus quam per modum visus et intuitus*). III *Sent.* dist. 27 [sic] art. 2 q. 1. *Opera Omnia* III 604b. 'On the part of the intellect there is a twofold exercise in relation to the knowledge of any particular thing: either by its own intuition, and thus there is vision; or by an external influence or instruction, and thus there is hearing. But with respect to the affect, a threefold situation obtains: either

the *Breviloquium* quoted above in an attempt to support his notion that spiritual touch and ecstasy should be equated with one another. However, it is not at all clear that this text in fact supports his view. Rahner quotes Bonaventure as follows: ' "The supreme delightfulness [of Christ] can be touched in that He is the Incarnate Word dwelling bodily in our midst, offering Himself to our touch, our kiss, our embrace, through ardent love which makes our soul pass, by ecstatic rapture, from this world to the Father." '[44] Immediately prior to the passage used by Rahner, however, we actually see that Bonaventure speaks of all five of the spiritual senses—not just touch:

> The supreme beauty of Christ the Spouse is seen in that he is resplendence, his supreme harmony heard in that he is the Word, his supreme sweetness tasted in that he is Wisdom comprising both Word and resplendence, his supreme fragrance inhaled in that he is the Inspired Word within the heart, his supreme delightfulness touched in that he is the Incarnate Word dwelling bodily in our midst, offering himself to our touch, our kiss, our embrace, through ardent love which makes our soul pass, by ecstatic rapture, from this world to the Father.[45]

The passage does make mention of 'ecstatic rapture', of course, but the precise relationship between spiritual touch and this state remains unclear. It could be the case, for example, that all five of the spiritual senses—and not exclusively spiritual touch—function to bring the individual to ecstatic rapture. Whereas Rahner's tendency is to single out one spiritual sense as the object of his attention, Bonaventure's

---

remotely, and thus there is smell; or proximately, and thus there is taste; or in conjunction, and thus there is touch, which is the more perfect among all the senses, and it is more spiritual because it maximally unites to him who is the highest spirit' (*quia ex parte intellectus contingit dupliciter circa cognitionem alicuius exerceri: aut proprio intuitu, et sic est visus; aut aliena excitatione sive instructione, et sic auditus.—Circa affectionem vero triplicem contingit reperire statum: aut in remotione, et sic odoratus; aut in approximatione, et sic gustus; aut in unione, et sic tactus, qui est perfectior inter omnes sensus et spiritualior propter hoc, quod maxime unit ei qui est summus spiritus*). III *Sent.* dist. 13. *Opera Omnia* III 292a.

[44] Rahner, 'The Doctrine of the "Spiritual Senses" in the Middle Ages', 126. *Brev.* V, 6. *Opera Omnia* V 258b.

[45] *Quibus videtur Christi sponsi summa pulchritudo sub ratione Splendoris; auditur summa harmonia sub ratione Verbi; gustatur summa dulcedo sub ratione Sapientiae comprehendentis utrumque, Verbum scilicet et Splendorem; odoratur summa fragrantia sub ratione Verbi inspirati in corde; astringitur summa suavitas sub ratione Verbi incarnati, inter nos habitantis corporaliter et reddentis se nobis palpabile, osculabile, amplexabile per ardentissimam caritatem, quae mentem nostram per ecstasim et raptum transpire facit ex hoc mundo ad Patrem*. *Brev.* V, 6. *Opera Omnia* V 258b.

text actually describes the operation of all of the spiritual senses in relation to Christ. Rahner's decision to mention only one spiritual sense in this connection is therefore unsupported by the texts he examines. More significantly, however, it is not at all obvious from this passage that the spiritual senses are active *within* ecstatic rapture. Instead, this passage arguably suggests that the spiritual senses perform the function of making one *ready* for ecstasy, but that they do not continue to function as the soul is vaulted to an ecstatic state. Bonaventure could certainly be more straightforward about the matter, but taken in conjunction with the last passage that Rahner uses to support his thesis, the likelihood of this interpretation increases considerably. To that passage we now turn.

Rahner points to a portion of the *Itinerarium* in order to make his claim that 'ecstasy…arises from peace and this is expressly referred to spiritual touch'.[46] He quotes Bonaventure's text as saying that the soul ' "is transported to Him (the Word) in ecstatic love and recovers…touch" '.[47] However, Rahner's use of this passage misleads his reader in key ways. First, the ellipses that Rahner uses above exclude the words 'gustus ut'. That is, the passage actually reads 'is transported to Him in ecstatic love and recovers *taste and* touch (my emphasis)'.[48] If Rahner wants to use this passage to support his claim that spiritual touch should be identified with ecstasy, then he must include spiritual taste in his assessment as well. Second, and more importantly, as was true in the portion of the *Breviloquium* just examined, this passage also serves *not* to undergird the notion that spiritual touch entails an ecstatic, apophatic union with the transcendent God. Instead, it functions as the culmination of a rich description of the action of all five spiritual senses in relation to the *Verbum increatum, inspiratum*, and *incarnatum*.[49] Again, then, Rahner has taken Bonaventure's remarks

---

[46] Rahner, 'The Doctrine of the "Spiritual Senses" in the Middle Ages', 126.
[47] Ellipses in original text. Rahner leaves Bonaventure's text in its original Latin, quoting it as follows: 'ut *transiens* in illud (Verbum) per *ecstaticum* amorem recuperat…tactum.' Rahner, 'The Doctrine of the "Spiritual Senses" in the Middle Ages', 126. *Itin.* IV, 3. Opera Omnia V 306b.
[48] *ut transiens in illud per ecstaticum amorem, recuperat gustum et tactum. Itin.* IV, 3. Opera Omnia V 306b.
[49] 'When it [the soul] believes in Christ as the uncreated Word and resplendence of the Father, it recovers the spiritual senses of hearing and sight: hearing, in order to listen to the teachings of Christ; and sight, in order to behold the splendour of His light. When, through hope, it longs to breathe in the inspired Word, by this aspiration and affection it recovers spiritual olfaction. When, through charity, it embraces the

on touch out of context and given them unwarranted emphasis to the exclusion of the other spiritual senses. Last, and most significantly, the suggestion of the text seems to be that the spiritual senses are not so much active within ecstasy as they function *prior to* ecstasy. In fact, in the very same section of the *Itinerarium* as that used by Rahner, Bonaventure makes it even clearer that the spiritual senses serve this preparatory function. As Bonaventure explains, 'It is at this step, where the interior senses have been restored to see what is most beautiful, to hear what is most harmonious, to smell what is most fragrant, to taste what is most sweet, and to embrace what is most delightful, that the soul is prepared for (*disponitur*) spiritual ecstasies.'[50] Even more clearly than is stated in the *Breviloquium*, then, this passage suggests that the spiritual senses are active in a stage of preparation that is distinct from ecstasy itself, thus calling into serious question Rahner's thesis that ecstasy and spiritual touch are one and the same.

Balthasar directly responds to Rahner's use of the portion of Bonaventure's *Itinerarium* above that reads 'through this [the operation of the five spiritual senses] the soul is laid open to the intellectual ecstasies'.[51] Here Balthasar insists, 'it is the five-fold sense-experience that brings the soul into the final readiness for the ecstasy: *disponitur anima ad mentales excessus*'.[52] On Balthasar's reading, then, the spiritual senses prepare the soul for this experience of ecstasy, but they are not active within ecstasy itself. He claims, 'This chief text in no way therefore speaks of the spiritual senses as encompassing the experience of God in the ecstatic rapture (for example, as an immediate touching of the divine essence).'[53]

Balthasar is, of course, aware of Bonaventure's understanding of ecstasy, and he recognizes the use of sensory terms there.[54] The key, however, lies in the precise manner in which such language of sensation

---

incarnate Word, by receiving delight from Him and passing into Him in ecstatical love, it recovers taste and touch.'

[50] *In hoc namque gradu, reparatis sensibus interioribus ad sentiendum summe pulcrum, audiendum summe harmonicum, odorandum summe odoriferum, degustandum summe suave, apprehendendum summe delectabile, disponitur anima ad mentales excessus. Itin.* IV, 3. *Opera Omnia* V 306b.
[51] *Itin.* IV, 3. *Opera Omnia* V 306b.   [52] *GL* II, 322.   [53] *GL* II, 322.
[54] Balthasar indicates this understanding in the following quotation from Bonaventure's *Sentences* commentary: 'The sight of the eye (*oculi aspectus*) can fix itself on God, so that it looks at (*aspiciat*) nothing else, and yet does not perceive (*perspiciet*) him, nor is allowed to see the splendour of his light, but on the contrary is raised up into darkness and attains to the knowledge that Denys... calls *docta ignorantia*.' *GL* II,

is used in these portions of Bonaventure's texts. Alluding to both the *Sentences* commentary and the *Hexaemeron*, Balthasar characterizes Bonaventure's use of sensory language as follows: 'Bonaventure describes this ecstasy as that in which love surpasses all knowledge; in an extravagant [*überschwenglicher*] way (since other words are lacking) sensory experiences can be adduced to shed light on the ineffable. But in any case, it is not a "seeing" but rather a hearing of secret words, and above all a touching of one being by another.'[55] Unexpectedly, then, Balthasar actually summons more textual evidence that would aid an *apophatic*, ecstatic reading than does Rahner. And yet Balthasar holds that, in these writings, Bonaventure is using the language of sensation in an importantly different manner. Specifically, Balthasar maintains that such attempts to describe the ecstatic experience of God simply *must* appeal to sensory terms 'since other words are lacking'. That is, according to Balthasar, Bonaventure uses the language of sensation in these instances not so much out of the propriety of using such terms to describe ecstatic religious experience, but rather because of the impropriety of any other use of language for such experiences. Sensory terms, then, are the least inappropriate among a set of even more inappropriate options.

The difference highlighted by Balthasar echoes the division outlined in the introduction to this study, by which an analogous use of sensory language was distinguished from a merely metaphorical use of such terms. Balthasar does not use these distinctions by name in his analysis; however, when he insists that sensory language is used in an 'extravagant' way in Bonaventure's descriptions of ecstasy, he is arguably saying something similar to the notion that Bonaventure in these moments shifts into a *metaphorical* use of the language of sensation.

324 (translation slightly emended). Quotation from II *Sent.* dist. 23, 2 q3 ad 6. *Opera Omnia* II 546a.

[55] *GL* II, 324. Balthasar's remarks on hearing are based on Bonaventure's *Hexaemeron*: 'at the summit is the uniting of love...only the affective faculty remains awake, and imposes silence on all the other faculties, and then man is estranged from the senses and set in ecstasy, and hears secret words which a man may not utter, because they exist only in the affective sense' (*in vertice est unitio amoris...sola affectiva vigilat et silentium omnibus aliis potentiis imponit, et tunc homo alienatus est a sensibus et in ecstasi positus et audit arcana verba quae non licet homini loqui, quia tantum sunt in affectu*) *Hexaemeron* 2, 29–30. *Opera Omnia* V 341ab-342a. Translation in Balthasar, *GL* II, 324. The passages regarding touch that are used by Balthasar are taken from III *Sent.* dist. 27, art. 2 q. 1. *Opera Omnia* III 604b, and III *Sent.* dist. 13 dub. 1. *Opera Omnia* III 292a.

In other words, Balthasar can be read as taking Bonaventure to slide into a highly figurative use of sensory terms in these texts that is distinct from his use of the language of spiritual sensation in the second stage of the spiritual life. Conversely, Balthasar regards Bonaventure's use of sensory language in the second stage of the spiritual life as being of a strictly *analogous* character in that it bears a close resemblance to the corporeal senses (and it is not merely a figurative expression for the activity of the mind or soul).

With this said, however, a key question remains: on what basis does Balthasar decide that Bonaventure's 'third stage' language of sensation is 'extravagant' and arguably metaphorical, and that the 'second stage' language bears a more precise, analogical relationship to its corporeal counterpart? Could one not arbitrarily make the opposite move in reading Bonaventure's texts? Balthasar's decision in this regard is not without its interpretive difficulties, but his hermeneutic is nevertheless defensible. To begin with, in Bonaventure's use of the language of sensation, there is often a difference in terminology between those spiritual senses that pertain to a *cataphatic* grasping of the Word in Christ and those uses of sensory language that pertain to *apophatic*, ecstatic union. Specifically, the majority of instances in which the actual term *sensus spiritualis* is used pertain to the second stage of the spiritual life. Conversely, in those instances in which ecstatic union with God is discussed, 'touch', 'sight', and 'hearing' are used, but often the term *spiritualis* is not. The distinction is certainly subtle, but the general lack of the term 'spiritual' in most third-stage use of the language of sensation arguably suggests that Bonaventure has a different sort of thing in mind when he speaks of touch, sight, and hearing as they pertain to the transcendent God. We should certainly be cautious, for example, in attributing a 'doctrine of the spiritual senses' to any figure who happens to speak of the beatific vision. It is not implausible, therefore, to hold that Bonaventure uses a 'proper' doctrine of the spiritual senses only in speaking of a *cataphatic* grasping of the Word in Christ, and his other occasional uses of sensory language are indeed another sort of extravagant use that is distinct from a strict definition of the spiritual senses.[56]

---

[56] Importantly, too, Balthasar does not neglect the third stage of Bonaventure's notion of the spiritual life and its significance for the spiritual senses. The relevant point to make in this regard is that Balthasar understands the doctrine's relation to this stage very differently than Rahner does. That is, the 'darkening' of the spiritual senses is not

Furthermore, to return to our treatment of the object of the spiritual senses above, it is significant that when Bonaventure speaks of all *five* spiritual senses, he unfailingly speaks of them in their relation to the Word in Christ. Conversely, when the 'transcendent God' is discussed, touch, sight, and hearing are mentioned, but never all five senses. As outlined at the beginning of this study, one criterion by which a figure is measured in espousing a doctrine of the spiritual senses has to do with whether or not that individual has a function for all five spiritual senses.[57] The fact that all five spiritual senses for Bonaventure are used only in this cataphatic grasping of the Word in Christ would suggest, then, that a doctrine of the spiritual senses by this strict standard can be applied only to the second stage of the spiritual life.

In an important sense, then, Balthasar actually reiterates Bonnefoy's conclusions, as Balthasar also claims that the language of sensation is used in distinct ways throughout Bonaventure's texts. The difference between Balthasar and Bonnefoy, however, is that Balthasar suggests that in some of those instances Bonaventure is using a doctrine of the spiritual senses, and in other instances he simply is not. Again, the interpretive move is not without controversy, but it does present Bonaventure's reader a way of deriving meaning from his texts without being forced to attribute inconsistency to his use of the language of sensation. Significantly, too, I hold that Balthasar's method for finding resolution on this difficult matter is preferable to that of Rahner, who actually has no way of dealing with evidence that does not conform to his thesis other than claiming that it is 'forced'.

After this necessarily lengthy treatment of our topic, one may understandably wonder what is at stake in these distinctions. Could the spiritual senses for Bonaventure not perceive *both* the Word in

---

to be understood as an apophatic moment of ecstatic union with the divine, but rather for Balthasar it is the inevitable flip side of the cultivation of the spiritual senses. That is, for Balthasar the spiritual senses conform themselves to Christ, and in so doing the human being undergoes a *death* with Christ. It is the *loss* of the object of the spiritual senses and the consequent taking on of *suffering* that marks their progression, not their growth in ever-increasing degrees of ecstasy. The human being is ultimately brought to life again on Balthasar's understanding of the development of the spiritual senses, and the spiritual senses are restored, but it is not without suffering, the cross, and the grave. Thus one sees that even in his interpretation of the very same stage of the spiritual life Balthasar has a different reading of Bonaventure than does Rahner.

[57] Ironically, it is Rahner who perpetuates this definition in his study of Origen and others in the patristic milieu. See 'The "Spiritual Senses" According to Origen', 82–3.

Christ *and* the transcendent God? Why insist that they must apprehend only one reality or the other? Although the consequences of this debate may not be immediately apparent, Balthasar in fact resists Rahner's reading of Bonaventure for reasons that are at the very heart of his theological aesthetics. Specifically, Balthasar is concerned that Rahner's interpretation of Bonaventure, in celebrating the heights of ecstatic union with God, actually neglects the centrality of the *Verbum incarnatum*, and in so doing abandons the realm in which divine revelation decisively takes place. Balthasar resists any interpretation of the spiritual senses that neglects the material world through which the spiritual realities are shown.

Additionally, Balthasar's *cataphatic* reading of Bonaventure advances a version of the doctrine consonant with his project of a theological aesthetics. That is, Balthasar reads Bonaventure as one who articulates not merely a model of the spiritual senses that perceives the Word in Christ in a fivefold, *cataphatic* grasping; he also understands Bonaventure to be one for whom the spiritual senses perceive the *beauty* of the Christ form. The point may at first glance seem self-evident, but it is worth noting that many figures throughout Christian history do not necessarily align their doctrines of the spiritual senses with the perception of the beautiful.[58] In our examination of Origen, for example, we saw a florid depiction of the activity of the spiritual senses, but we did not observe in his texts the notion that the spiritual senses have an especially aesthetic configuration. By contrast, Bonaventure makes consistent reference to the idea that the spiritual senses perceive the beauty of Christ, and the significance of this fact is not lost on Balthasar.

Beauty is such a pervasive theme in Bonaventure's texts that its significance is often overlooked. For example, we have already seen that the main passages on the spiritual senses from the *Itinerarium* and the *Breviloquium* speak of the spiritual senses beholding the beauty (*pulchritudo*) and resplendence (*splendor*) of the Word in Christ.[59] We also

---

[58] More generally speaking, of course, any number of philosophers treat of 'perception' without necessarily developing an account of the perception of beauty. It is by no means a foregone conclusion, therefore, that the spiritual senses would be associated with this aesthetic dimension.

[59] 'This takes place in accordance with the spiritual senses. Then the sublime beauty of Christ the Bridegroom is seen, in so far as he is splendour; the highest harmony is heard, in so far as he is word; the greatest sweetness is tasted, in so far as he is the wisdom that contains both, word and splendour; the sublimest fragrance is smelled, in so far as he is the word inspired in the heart; the greatest delight is embraced, in so far

observed that the *Reduction of the Arts to Theology* speaks of the 'sense of the heart' seeking after what is beautiful.[60] Additionally, Bonaventure's *Soliloquy on the Four Spiritual Exercises* mentions the senses of the resurrected body perceiving what is most beautiful. In that text he simply says, 'The eye will see the most marvelous beauty.'[61] In his sermons we also see that Bonaventure regards Christ as 'lovely and refreshing to look upon in accordance with man's double power of sight: the inward sight which sees the divinity, the outward sight which sees the manhood.'[62] It is certainly interesting to note that the aesthetic capacities of corporeal sight function in a manner *opposite* to that of Augustine, as we saw in Chapter 1, for whom the physical senses perceive the ugliness of Christ and only the spiritual senses perceive Christ's beauty.

Elsewhere in his corpus, Bonaventure fascinatingly writes about the spiritual senses producing refreshing delight through the variety of their perceptions. He explains that in paradise other trees were planted around the tree of knowledge 'so that man through the alternation of the fruits, through the varieties of the beauties and tastes, might avoid the boredom which tends to ensue from attention to one single thing, and that he might have the delight that the perceptions of the spiritual senses derive from variety and renewal.'[63] In noting these passages from Bonaventure's works, Balthasar thus makes a point of conveying Bonaventure's understanding of the specifically aesthetic capacities of the spiritual senses in their perception of Christ.[64]

---

as he is the incarnate Word.' *Brev.* V, 6. *Opera Omnia* V 259b. 'At this stage, the inner senses are restored, in order to perceive what is most beautiful, to hear what sounds most lovely, to smell what is most fragrant, to taste what is most sweet, to touch what is most delightful.' *Itin.* IV, 3. *Opera Omnia* V 306b.

[60] 'The sense of our heart (*sensus cordis*) must longingly seek what is beautiful, or what sounds well, or what smells sweet, or what tastes sweet, or what is soft to touch—must find it with joy, and untiringly strive after it anew. In this way, the divine Wisdom is contained in a hidden manner in sense-knowledge, and the contemplation of the five spiritual senses is wonderful in its correspondence to the bodily senses.' *De Reductio Art.* X. *Opera Omnia* V 322b.

[61] *Solil.* IV, 20. *Opera Omnia* VIII 63a. Quoted in *GL* II, 331.

[62] *Sermo. 1, Dominica Infra Octavam Epiphaniae. Opera Omnia* IX 171b. Quoted in *GL* II, 329.

[63] *Quatenus varietate fructuum, multiformium pulcritudinum et saporum vitaret homo fastidium, quod accidere solet per conversionem ad unum, et haberet oblectamentum, quod ex varietate atque innovatione consurgit in spritualium notitia sensuum per experientiam multiformium obiectorum.* Quotation from *De plant. Par.* 9. *Opera Omnia* V 577a. Quoted in *GL* II, 333.

[64] Balthasar also picks up Bonaventure's idea that Christ is the *most* beautiful. Balthasar writes, 'As the measurement which appears and judges all things he is already

Crucially, too, Balthasar locates in Bonaventure not only a figure who has a regard for the aesthetic dimension to the spiritual senses; he finds one who also is interested in defending the notion that beauty should be regarded as a transcendental property of being. Here Balthasar is influenced by the scholarship of Emma Jane Marie Spargo and Karl Peter. Spargo's *The Category of the Aesthetic in the Philosophy of Bonaventure* demonstrates the enormous importance of beauty in Bonaventure's thought, which had been surprisingly neglected prior to her study.[65] Even more importantly, Peter's *Die Lehre von der Schönheit nach Bonaventura* offers an exposition of Bonaventure's argument for beauty as a transcendental property of being.[66] Balthasar, following Spargo and Peter, sees Bonaventure as one for whom beauty occupies an absolutely central place in the articulation of theology. Balthasar explains, 'As the sensitive study of Karl Peter has demonstrated, the beautiful can effectively be shown to be a transcendental property of all being... and this property is necessarily present in a *circumincessio* in the one, the true, and the good'.[67] In that the very justification for Balthasar undertaking a theological aesthetics in the first place rests on the notion that beauty has this status as a transcendental property of being, the importance of Bonaventure for his theological enterprise is brought into clear view.

The latter point is necessary in grasping the full significance of the former. That is, the fact that beauty is a transcendental for Bonaventure means that the spiritual senses, in perceiving the beautiful, do not witness a portion of reality that can be regarded as peripheral or ornamental. Instead, the fact that the spiritual senses perceive the beauty of Christ means that they apprehend an aspect of being that lies at

the highest beauty, *perpulchrum*: "It is this that gives all things their beauty: that he restores fair form to what has lost its shape, that he makes the beautiful more beautiful, and what is more beautiful he makes most beautiful." ' *GL* II, 331. *Hoc totum mundum pulcrificat, quia deformia facit pulcra, pulcra pulcriora et pulcriora pulcherrima.* Quotation from *Hex.* I, 34. *Opera Omnia* V 335a. For Balthasar, then, as for Bonaventure, Christ is absolute beauty; he stands at the centre of all beauty, restoring to all things the beauty they have lost.

[65] Emma Jane Marie Spargo, *The Category of the Aesthetic in the Philosophy of Saint Bonaventure* (New York: Franciscan Institute, 1953). Reference given by Balthasar in *GL* II, 260.
[66] Karl Peter, 'Die Lehre von der Schönheit nach Bonaventura' (doctoral dissertation, Basel, 1961); reference given by Balthasar in *GL* II, 260. Later published as *Die Lehre von der Schönheit nach Bonaventura* (Werl: Dietrich Coelde Verlag, 1964).
[67] *GL* II, 334.

the very heart of reality itself. Bonaventure's notion that the spiritual senses perform this act of perceiving the beauty of Christ, thereby putting the human being in contact with being, could not more closely mirror Balthasar's concerns, as Balthasar makes remarkably similar claims throughout his theological aesthetics. For him, beauty is a transcendental property of being, the beauty of Christ is absolute beauty, and the spiritual senses are capable of perceiving this absolute, transcendental beauty. In a telling passage from his aesthetics, Balthasar simply holds, 'An aesthetic element must be associated with all spiritual perception.'[68] For Balthasar, then, a necessary relationship obtains between the spiritual senses and aesthetic appreciation.

This set of concerns leads us to our fourth point of comparison, as Balthasar seeks in his interpretation of Bonaventure's doctrine of the spiritual senses to unite them with the corporeal senses such that 'spiritual perception' is inextricable from its bodily counterpart.

The 'Duplex Sensus': On the Spiritual and Bodily Senses in Bonaventure

An enormous portion of Balthasar's treatment of Bonaventure's doctrine of the spiritual senses is directed toward establishing the intimate connection between physical and spiritual perception in Bonaventure's thought. Here Balthasar emphatically resists a 'dualist' reading of Bonaventure that would separate body from soul, and he instead insists that, for Bonaventure, spiritual sensation takes place *in union with* physical sensation.[69] Balthasar writes of Bonaventure,

---

[68] *GL* I, 153.

[69] The question of 'dualism' in Rahner's reading of Bonaventure should be briefly addressed. It would seem to be more Fields—and less Rahner—who actually insists on a firm split between body and soul in the doctrine of the spiritual senses. Fields maintains, 'According to Rahner, Bonaventure conceives the spiritual senses, not as acts of the corporeal senses that have been elevated by grace, but as grace-aided acts of the intellect and the will in a soul essentially independent of the body' (235). Later in his article, Fields succinctly speaks of 'Rahner's dualist interpretation of sense' (237). It is certainly true that Rahner speaks at great length about the spiritual senses as acts of the intellect and the will, but it should also be said that he does not specify their exact relation to the body. It is also true that Rahner mentions Alexander of Hales—an important influence on Bonaventure in this arena—as articulating a system of thought in which the spiritual senses 'would only be hindered by the activity of bodily powers' (108). However, we should mention that Rahner's treatment of Bonaventure himself does not evince such a boldly put thesis regarding the body. In fact, nowhere in his examination of Bonaventure does Rahner explain the precise relation between spiritual and bodily sensation. Of course, one might assume that

'One cannot suppose that the outer and inner senses are two faculties separate from one another, perhaps indeed opposed to one another.'[70] Such a reading of the spiritual senses, however, relies upon a non-dualist anthropology, and so Balthasar first indicates aspects of Bonaventure's texts that suggest such a unified understanding of the human being.

Right from the start, Balthasar makes his goal clear. At the very beginning of his treatment of Bonaventure's anthropology, he explains, 'For Bonaventure, *man* is essentially the midpoint and summary of the world; this point must be made against anyone who would interpret his doctrine as one-sidedly spiritual, in flight from the world, ecstatic'.[71] Against any reading of Bonaventure that would regard him as devaluing the material order in the name of a 'spiritual' union with the divine (which Balthasar equates with ecstatic union), Balthasar offers numerous texts that speak of the exalted position of the body.[72] Drawing from Bonaventure's *Sentences* commentary, Balthasar writes, 'Of all material systems of organisation, the human body possesses the highest "illuminated quality (*luminositas*) and subtlety", its "harmony is greater than that of any other substance", just as "its dignity is great because of the high harmony of the proportion of its parts"'.[73] In taking a body, the soul is not compromised, according to

---

Rahner holds Bonaventure to follow Alexander in this regard, and Rahner does not offer any evidence from Bonaventure's corpus that shows resistance to Alexander's dualist scheme. Furthermore, one could argue that Rahner's extensive descriptions of the intellect and the will strongly suggest that these aspects of the soul are thought of as independent from the body. It is worth noting, however, that Rahner himself does not overtly indicate dualism in Bonaventure's worldview; neither, however, does he attempt to counter a reading of Bonaventure as dualist in his theological anthropology.

[70] *GL* II, 319.   [71] *GL* II, 315.

[72] At an even more fundamental level, Balthasar draws his reader's attention to Bonaventure's regard for matter itself, noting that 'matter has an *appetitus* towards form, and this *appetitus* gives it the capacity and disposes it for the taking-on of form. To this extent, matter is not *privatio pura*, but in its very nature has already something of beauty and light in itself.' *GL* II, 311. Balthasar here refers to *Hexaemeron* 2, 2. *Opera Omnia* V 336b, and II *Sent.* dist. 1, I, q1 ad 2. *Opera Omnia* II 17b.

[73] *GL* II, 316. Quotations from II *Sent.* dist. 17, 2, q2 c et ad 6. *Opera Omnia* II 423ab: *Ad illud quod obiicitur de ordine, dicendum, quod, etsi natura caelestis sit excelsior inter corpora simplicia secundum se considerata, non tamen excellit in gradu in comparatione ad ulteriorem formam suscipiendam; sed is est ordo, quod forma elementaris unitur animae mediante forma mixtionis, et forma mixtionis disponit ad formam complexionis. Et quia haec, cum est in aequalitate et harmonia, conformatur naturae caelesti; ideo habilis est ad susceptionem nobilissimae influentiae, scilicet vitae. Et sic in unione animae ad corpus rectus servatur ordo. Magna etiam est dignitas humani corporis propter magnam harmoniam et proportionalem coniunctionem suarum partium, ob quam in statu viatoris conformis fit naturae caelesti; in statu autem comprehensoris*

Bonaventure. In fact, Balthasar shows that Bonaventure thinks of the human soul as finding its *perfection* in its union with the human body. He again quotes the *Sentences* commentary as follows:

> The form of the composite is more perfect than any one part, because the parts are ordered towards the form of the composite. So the form of existence as man is more full and perfect than the form which the soul is by itself; since therefore the perfecting of grace and glory presupposes the perfection of nature, the whole man, not only the soul, must be transfigured (*glorificari*).[74]

For Bonaventure, then, the soul is not created so as to be isolated from the body; rather it must be embodied in order to fulfil its purpose. Human beings are the midpoint of the world, since they are the union between spirit and matter. It is for this reason that God became a human being, that Christ took a human body and did not merely appear to humanity as an angel, for the corporeal is the other half to the spiritual in creation. Balthasar summarizes Bonaventure's position on this topic as follows: 'Man in his essence must bring his body into this blessedness, and through his body the whole physical world below which is ordered towards transfiguration through man.'[75] The essence of the human being, then, is not the soul alone. Instead, the human being is a 'unity-in-duality', since the soul does not live without the body and the body does not live without the soul. In fact, the human being is perfected in the union between body and soul. Balthasar thus finds in Bonaventure an understanding of the human being as inherently united in body and soul.

This anthropology has a direct impact on the spiritual senses in Bonaventure's thought. The human being has been given a *duplex sensus*, Balthasar claims.[76] The human being has a double range of senses, one inner and one outer, but one must not understand these

---

perficietur a Deo, non tantum, ut sit conformis, sed etiam, ut supra naturam caelestem sit exaltata et sublimata, ut ei congruat potissime habitatio caeli empyrei. Cf. II Sent dist. 2 II, 1 q2. *Opera Omnia* II 73a–75b. Balthasar also writes, 'Once it is transfigured, it will be so elevated and perfected that it will most fittingly be given a place in the empyrean above the heavenly natures.' *GL* II, 316.

[74] *GL* II, 317. *Perfectior est forma compositi quam aliqua pars, quia partes ordinantur ad formam compositi: ergo completior et perfectior est forma humanitatis quam ipsa forma, quae est anima: ergo cum perfectio gratiae et gloriae praesupponat pefectionem naturae; necesse est totum hominem, non tantum animam, glorificari.* IV *Sent.* dist. 43, I, q. 1, fund. 5. *Opera Omnia* IV 883a.

[75] *GL* II, 317.   [76] *GL* II, 317.

faculties to be in any way separated from each other. In fact, precisely as the 'midpoint' of the world, human beings represent the union of these two. As Balthasar puts this point, 'The animal sees only the physical, the angel the spiritual, but, "for the sake of the perfecting of the whole", man had to "come to be, endowed with a double range of senses, so that he could read the book written on the inside and on the outside: the book of Wisdom and her works".[77] The human being is the synthesis of spiritual and physical, and this union is neither accidental nor shameful, according to Balthasar's reading of Bonaventure. Since the human being is a unity of the spiritual and the physical, so too do the perceptual faculties of the human being apprehend physical and spiritual realities in a unified act of perception.

Balthasar is able to find considerable textual support from Bonaventure's works to support his position. Most significantly, perhaps, he quotes a passage from Bonaventure's *The Reduction of the Arts to Theology* that speaks of a close relation between the spiritual and bodily senses:

> The sense of our heart (*sensus cordis*) must longingly seek what is beautiful, or what sounds well, or what smells sweet, or what tastes sweet, or what is soft to touch—must find it with joy, and untiringly strive after it anew. In this way, the divine Wisdom is contained in a hidden manner in sense-knowledge, and the contemplation of the five spiritual senses is wonderful in its correspondence to the bodily senses.[78]

This text clearly speaks to an intimate relationship between the spiritual and corporeal senses in Bonaventure's thought. The divine Wisdom is contained *within* sense knowledge, and that Wisdom is grasped in a unified act of perception in which a correspondence (*conformitatem*) obtains between the spiritual senses and the bodily senses.

In this connection Balthasar also examines Bonaventure's understanding of the human being in heaven as described in his *Soliloquies*. It is telling not only that Bonaventure speaks of all the faculties of

---

[77] GL II, 318. *Ad perfectionem universitatis debuit fieri creatura, quae hoc sensu duplici esset praedita ad cognitionem libri scripti intus et foris id est Sapientiae et sui operis.* Brev. II, 11. *Opera Omnia* V 229a.

[78] *Sensus cordis nostri sive pulchrum, sive consonum, sive odoriferum, sive dulce, sive mulcebre debet desideranter quarere, gaudenter invenire incessanter repetere. Ecce, quomodo in cognitione sensitiva continetur occulte divina sapientia, et quam mira est contemplatio quinque sensuum spiritualium secundum conformitatem ad sensus corporales.* De Reductio Art. X. *Opera Omnia* V 322b.

sense being exercised by the human being in heaven, but also that 'it is quite certain that the soul would never strive for the body to be assumed again, if the body, however transfigured it might be, were to disturb the contemplation of God in the least degree once it is assumed again.'[79] The passage then goes on to say that the soul without the body is actually at a disadvantage: 'The blessed do long for this [union with the body] because without the body their blessedness cannot reach perfection, their exultation cannot be satisfied; indeed, so great is their longing, that it actually hinders and blocks their contemplation in some measure.'[80] In the fulfilled state of the human being in heaven, according to Bonaventure, the soul is actually hindered without the body. It is, of course, a different sort of body that is being described in these passages (namely, one that is resurrected), but it is nonetheless highly significant that Bonaventure retains notions of sense perception and the intimate relation between the body and soul when he speaks of the person in heaven. Balthasar summarizes this understanding of Bonaventure's doctrine of the spiritual senses as follows: 'After reading this statement, one cannot suppose that the outer and inner senses are two faculties separate from one another, perhaps indeed opposed to one another: rather, they must have their common root in the single intellectual-material nature of man, in which the general character of seeing, hearing, tasting, and so forth is based.'[81]

Several aspects of this interpretation of Bonaventure are noteworthy for our purposes. First, whereas Balthasar in most instances places himself in thorough conversation with the extant secondary literature on the topics he examines, in his reading of the union of body and soul in Bonaventure he does not summon any allies to his cause. This likely speaks to the fact that Balthasar is charting an unusual course in his interpretation of Bonaventure's understanding of the relation between the material and the spiritual. One readily finds scholarship in this period that flatly holds Bonaventure to value the

---

[79] *Certum est enim, quod ipsa anima nunquam resumtionem corporis appeteret, si resumtum, etiam quantumcumque gloriosum, divinam contemplationem impediret.* Soliloquies IV, 21. Opera Omnia VIII 63b–64a.

[80] *Nunc autem, secundum Augustini sententiam et doctrinam, ipsae animae sanctae desiderant eius resumtionem et exspectant iteratam unionem ipsius, quia ipsarum sine eo non potest consummari felicitas nec satiari iucunditas; et adeo vehementer desiderant quod etiam aliqualiter earum contemplationem impedit et retardat.* Soliloquies IV, 21. Opera Omnia VIII 64a.

[81] GL II, 319.

spiritual over the material in his thought.[82] Balthasar thus downplays the extent to which his reading of Bonaventure's regard for the body might be a novel one.

This prevalence of dualist interpretations of Bonaventure further suggests that Balthasar would not likely come up with his reading of Bonaventure without some other, prior influence. That is to say, one certainly can locate a version of Bonaventure's anthropology that favours the body, but I would contend that one must already be looking for it if one is to sift through the multitude of passages—and secondary literature—that suggest the opposite. Fields notes that Balthasar is animated by an anthropology of unity-in-duality in his reading of Bonaventure, but he does not indicate the possible sources of this influence. In this connection it is certainly significant that Protestant theology at this cultural moment in the mid-twentieth century was rediscovering a 'Biblical anthropology' that resists 'philosophical anthropologies' by positing a radical unity between body and soul. Karl Barth, in particular, articulates such an understanding of the human being based on scriptural sources that regard the human as a psychic-corporeal totality fundamentally united in body and soul.[83] As we shall explore more thoroughly in Chapter 3, Balthasar's extensive engagement with Barth's biblical anthropology in *The Glory of the Lord* points to Barth as a likely source of the anthropology of unity-in-duality that serves as Balthasar's guide in his interpretation of Bonaventure.

* * *

Looking at the widely divergent interpretations advanced by Balthasar and Rahner, we can see that interpretive difficulties surrounding Bonaventure's doctrine of the spiritual senses remain. However, as indicated in the above analysis, it is certainly significant that whenever Bonaventure speaks of the operation of five spiritual senses, it is consistently the Word in Christ who is their object in the second stage of the spiritual life. The alternative thesis that the spiritual senses

---

[82] See, perhaps most famously, Etienne Gilson, *La philosophie de Saint Bonaventure* (Paris: J. Vrin, 1924).

[83] Barth writes, 'The statement that "man is soul" would be without meaning if we did not immediately enlarge and expound it: Soul of one body, i.e., his body. He is soul as he is a body and this is his body. Hence he is not only soul that "has" a body which perhaps it might not have, but he is bodily soul, as he is also besouled body.' Karl Barth, *Church Dogmatics* III/2: *The Doctrine of Creation*, trans. H. Knight, G. W. Bromiley, J. K. S. Reid, and R. H. Fuller (Edinburgh: T&T Clark, 1960), 350.

perceive the 'transcendent God' in the third stage of the spiritual life cannot be established with similar assurance, and in fact we saw Rahner substitute the term *Deo* for *Verbum incarnatum* in order to try to make his case. Bonaventure never discusses the operation of all five spiritual senses in relation to God (*Deo*), and the precise manner in which he uses sensory language on this particular point is unclear. If one wants to understand the manner in which the doctrine of *five* spiritual senses functions in Bonaventure's theology, then Balthasar's interpretation presents unassailable evidence that the Word in Christ is their object. This position does not definitively resolve all ambiguities in Bonaventure's understanding of the doctrine, but Rahner's interpretation certainly presents us with more misleading use of quotations, ambiguities, and special pleading than does the Balthasarian alternative.

IGNATIUS OF LOYOLA

In his reading of Ignatius' use of the spiritual senses, we once again see Balthasar's particular concerns emerge.[84] First, and most importantly,

[84] The significance of Ignatius of Loyola for Balthasar is well documented, and Ignatius' understanding of the so-called 'application of the senses' in his *Spiritual Exercises* is also widely known. However, there is at present no substantial treatment of the intersection of these two topics that would examine the importance of Ignatius' understanding of the spiritual senses for Balthasar's thought. For examinations of Balthasar's relationship with Ignatius' thought, see Werner Löser, 'Die Exerzitien des Ignatius von Loyola: Ihre Bedeutung in der Theologie Hans Urs von Balthasars', *Internationale katholische Zeitschrift Communio* 18 (1989), 333–51. Translated into English as 'The Ignatian *Exercises* in the Work of Hans Urs von Balthasar', in *Hans Urs von Balthasar: His Life and Work*, ed. David L. Schindler (San Francisco, CA: Ignatius Press, 1991), 103–20. Jacques Servais, Une theologie des 'Exercices spirituels': Hans Urs von Balthasar, interprète de saint Ignace de Loyola (Rome: Tipografia Pontificia Universitas Gregoriana, 1992). Jacques Servais, SJ, 'Au fondement d'une théologie de l'obéissance ignatienne: *Les Exercices spirituels* selon H. U. von Balthasar', *Nouvelle revue théologique* 116 (1994): 353–73. Leo O'Donovan, SJ, 'Two Sons of Ignatius: Drama and Dialectic', *Philosophy and Theology* 11 (1998), 105–25. Erhard Kunz, 'Ignatianische Spiritualität in ihrer anthropologischen Durchführung', in *Gott für die Welt: Henri de Lubac, Gustav Siewerth und Hans Urs von Balthasar in ihren Grundanliegen*, eds. Peter Reifenberg and Anton van Hooff (Mainz: Matthias-Grünewald-Verlag, 2001), 293–303. Andreas R. Batlogg, 'Hans Urs von Balthasar und Karl Rahner: Zwei Schüler des Ignatius', in *Die Kunst Gottes verstehen: Hans Urs von Balthasars theologische Provokationen*, eds. Magnus Striet and Jan-Heiner Tück (Freiburg: Herder, 2005), 410–46. Werner Löser, 'Hans Urs von Balthasar und Ignatius von Loyola', in *Logik der Liebe und Herrlichkeit Gottes: Hans Urs von Balthasar im Gespräch*, ed. Walter Kasper

whereas Balthasar's engagement with other figures in the tradition shows little interest in the practices that one may undertake in order to cultivate one's spiritual senses, his reading of Ignatius evidences a sustained concern with practice for the first time in his telling of the history of the doctrine. Second, the particular reading recommended by Balthasar indicates that he sees Ignatius as uniting spiritual and corporeal senses to an extent not previously achieved in the tradition.

Spiritual Senses without Ascent: Ignatius and Practice

Ignatius' remarks about the spiritual senses are situated within his *Spiritual Exercises*, which are of course a set of instructions for the practice of prayer.[85] There is therefore an explicit inclusion of the spiritual senses within a programme designed to encourage their growth in the individual retreatant.[86] The most important portion of these

(Ostfildern: Matthias-Grünewald-Verlag, 2006), 94–110. Werner Löser, 'Hans Urs von Balthasar und seine ignatianischen und patristischen Quellen', *Geist und Leben* 79 (2006), 194–203. For treatments of Ignatius' 'application of the senses', see Joseph Maréchal, SJ, 'Un essai de meditation orientee vers la contemplation', in *Études sur la psychologie des mystiques*, 2 vols. (Brussels, Edition Universelle, 1937), 2:362–82; 'Application des sens', in *Dictionnaire de spiritualité: ascétique et mystique* (Paris: G. Beauchesne et ses fils, 1932–95), vol. 1, 810–28. Friedrich Wulf, SJ, 'Die Bedeutung der schopferischen Phantasie für die Betrachtung nach Ignatius von Loyola', *GuL* 22 (1949), 461–7. M. Olphe-Gaillard, SJ, 'Les sens spirituels dans l'histoire de la spiritualité', in *Nos Sens det Dieu* (1954), 179–93. Hugo Rahner, 'Die Anwendung der Sinne in der Betrachtungsmethode des hl. Ignatius von Loyola', *Zeitschrift für katholische Theologie* 79 (1957), 434–56. James Walsh, 'Application of the Senses', *The Way Supplement* 27 (1976), 59–68. Etienne Lepers, 'L'Application des sens', *Christus* 21 (1980), 83–94. Sergio Rendina, 'La dottrina dei "sensi spirituali" negli Esercizi Spirituali', *Servitium* 29–30 (1983), 55–72. Philip Endean, SJ, 'The Ignatian Prayer of the Senses', *Heythrop Journal* 31 (1990), 391–418. Stephen Corder, *The Spiritual Senses in the Exercises of Ignatius of Loyola* (Berkeley, CA: Jesuit School of Theology, 2003).

[85] Ignatius of Loyola, *The Spiritual Exercises and Selected Works*, trans. George E. Ganss, *The Classics of Western Spirituality* (New York: Paulist Press, 1991), 21.

[86] It is surely significant in this connection that Balthasar decided to enter the noviatiate of the Jesuits after having completed one such retreat, and he conducted the *Exercises* again and again throughout his life. 'Almost all of us were formed by the *Spiritual Exercises*...I translated the *Exercises* into German and had the opportunity of conducting them a hundred times over: here, if anywhere, is Christian joy. Here, if anywhere, is what it means to be a Christian in its 'primordial' sense: obedience to the Word that calls and growth in freedom for the expected response.' Hans Urs von Balthasar, 'In Retrospect', in *The Analogy of Beauty: The Theology of Hans Urs von Balthasar*, ed. John Riches (Edinburgh: T&T Clark, 1986), 194–221, at 199. See also Peter Henrici, 'A Sketch of von Balthasar's Life', in *Hans Urs von Balthasar: His Life and Work*, ed. David L. Schindler (San Francisco, CA: Ignatius Press, 1991), 7–43, esp. 11–12.

instructions for our purposes, known as the 'application of the senses', occurs at the end of the first day of the second week, and reads as follows:

> It is profitable to use the imagination and to apply the five senses to the first and second contemplations [on the Incarnation and the Nativity], in the following manner. *The first point.* By the sight of my imagination I will see the persons, by meditating and contemplating in detail all the circumstances around them, and by drawing some profit from the sight. *The second point.* By my hearing I will listen to what they are saying or might be saying; and then, reflecting on myself, I will draw some profit from this. *The third point.* I will smell the fragrance and taste the infinite sweetness and charm of the Divinity, of the soul, of its virtues, and of everything there, appropriately for each of the persons who is being contemplated. Then I will reflect upon myself and draw profit from this. *The fourth point.* Using the sense of touch, I will, so to speak, embrace and kiss the places where the persons walk or sit. I shall always endeavor to draw some profit from this.[87]

Now, the reader may notice a number of ambiguities in Ignatius' text. Most significantly, his mention of the 'sight of my imagination' recalls the 'imaginative senses' of which Poulain writes. These imaginative senses, Poulain insists, are different from the spiritual senses in that they call to mind sounds, colours, etc. *without* the actual presence of those objects to the human being. The spiritual, or 'intellectual' senses, by contrast, perceive the presence of spiritual objects to the human being. A question naturally arises: is Ignatius speaking of the imaginative senses in this key passage, or does he mean to describe the operation of spiritual, 'intellectual' senses?

This question lies at the heart of a centuries-long debate on the interpretation of Ignatius. Juan de Polanco (1516–1577), who worked as Ignatius' secretary and commented on the *Spiritual Exercises* after

---

[87] Ignatius of Loyola, *Ejercicios Espirituales*, 121–5. 'Aprovecha el pasar de los cinco sentidos de la imaginación por la primera y segunda contemplación, de la manera siguiente. El primer punto es ver las personas con la vista imaginativa, meditando y contemplando en particular sus circunstancias y sacando algún provecho de la vista. El segundo: oír con el oído lo que hablan o pueden hablar; y refletiendo en sí mismo, sacar dello algún provecho. El tercero: oler y gustar con el olfato y con el gusto la infinita suavidad y dulzura de la divinidad del ánima y de sus virtudes y de todo, según fuere la persona que se contempla, refletiendo en sí mismo y sacando provecho dello. El cuarto: tocar con el tacto, asi como abrazar y besar los lugares donde las tales personas pisan y se asientan; siempre procurando de sacar provecho dello.' *Ejercicios Espirituales,* ed. Candido de Dalmases, SJ (Santander: Sal Terrae, 1987). Ganss, 60–1.

Ignatius' death, sees both interpretive options in the above passage. Instructively, however, Polanco writes that those who are *inexperienced* may regard the application of the senses as pertaining to the ordinary 'senses of the imagination', and those who are more practised in prayer can understand them as 'the spiritual senses of the higher reason'.[88] Achille Gagliardi (1537–1607) takes the second of these options in his commentary on the *Exercises*, maintaining that in the application of the senses a form of prayer is achieved in which the understanding 'is more fully enlightened by the same material [i.e., the Incarnation and Nativity], through a certain kind of intuition of it, as though it were actually present. Without any movement, or stirring of the mind, it beholds the whole matter in one moment, as if it had it there before the eyes'.[89] According to Gagliardi's reading, the 'senses' of which Ignatius speaks occur at a high level of prayer in which one experiences impressions of spiritual objects that seem to be present to the individual.[90]

However, the official 1599 *Directorium* chooses the former of the two interpretive options, by which the 'application of the senses' is read as pertaining to the corporeal and imaginative senses (which are interestingly brought together into a single interpretive option). Gil Gonzalez Davila, who had a major hand in shaping the *Directorium*, holds that the understanding advocated by Gagliardi 'is more rarefied (*curiosa*) than what should generally be given to those who are simple-minded and uninitiated (*rudibus et inexpertis*) regarding these matters'.[91] The application of the senses, then, according to this reading, is a lower form of prayer, easier than the meditation described above, and to be undertaken by the inexperienced.

The details of this debate are of less importance than Balthasar's response to it, which is, essentially, to claim that commentaries on Ignatius have become caught up in a false dichotomy. In *The Glory of*

---

[88] Juan de Polanco, *Monumenta Ignatiana*, Ser. II, (1955), 2:300–3.

[89] Achille Gagliardi, *Commentarii seu Explanationes in Exercitia spiritualia Sancti Patris Ignatii de Loyola*, ed. Constantinus van Aken (Bruges: Desclée de Brouwer, 1882), 23.

[90] It is certainly interesting to note here a reading of Ignatius that correlates extensively with Poulain's understanding of presence and the 'analogical' relationship between corporeal and spiritual senses. In fact, it may well be that Poulain is drawing from Gagliardi and other interpreters of Ignatius in formulating his criteria by which one may identify the spiritual senses.

[91] *Directoria Exercitorum Spiritualium: (1540–1599)* (Rome: Institutum Historicum Societatis Jesu, 1955), 487.

the Lord, he maintains, 'In the interpretations of Ignatius the problem emerges as an either/or between the corporeal senses and the mystical sensibility, but both of these seem to be included by Ignatius... without their mutually suppressing or jeopardising one another.'[92] Balthasar thus blurs the distinctions that had been drawn between the application of the senses undertaken by beginners (which involve the corporeal and imaginative senses) and those undertaken in later stages of prayer (which entail the spiritual, or intellectual senses).

Crucially for our examination, in viewing the imaginative application of the senses as intertwined with the use of the 'spiritual senses', Balthasar finally indicates an interest in the relationship between practice and the acquisition of the spiritual senses for the first time in his treatment of the doctrine. If using the spiritual senses is connected to using the imagination in a creative application of one's senses to the mysteries of faith, then this particular form of prayer emerges as a central arena within which the spiritual senses can develop. One 'attunes' oneself to these mysteries. As Balthasar puts this point,

> The 'attunement' of man to the mysteries of salvation plays the greatest of roles in the *Spiritual Exercises*: man's disposition is to 'correspond' and be harmonised, and this correspondence must be prayed for; however, as far as possible it must be created and acquired by man himself so that, in his spiritual-sensual totality, man may come to experience and realise the contemplated mystery by 'applying his five senses' to it.[93]

After Balthasar's lengthy neglect of the way the spiritual senses develop in the individual human being, one finally finds a resource in the notion that one receives them when one is 'attuned' to them through prayer, specifically the application of the senses to the mysteries of salvation. It is certainly striking that Balthasar here maintains that the human being can 'create' and 'acquire' the attunement necessary to perceive the mysteries of salvation, given his previous lack of attention to the role of practice.

It is also significant that, out of all the figures that Balthasar might focus upon with regard to the question of the relationship between practice and the spiritual senses, he chooses to focus on Ignatius on this issue. Werner Löser has noted the contrast between, on the one hand, ancient and medieval models of the spiritual life, which 'circled around a schema of the ladder of perfection', and, on the other hand,

---

[92] *GL* I, 378.   [93] *GL* I, 298.

the Ignatian understanding of the spiritual life, which understands 'Christian perfection completely in terms of obedient listening to God's call, completely in terms of choosing God's choice.'[94] One may question the division drawn by Löser here, but it is nevertheless noteworthy that Balthasar consistently eschews a model of the spiritual life that involves strict hierarchies and successive stages. We observe a deep reticence on Balthasar's part to reserve the spiritual senses for any sort of 'higher' prayer.

Furthermore, Balthasar seeks to establish continuity between the sensorium of 'ordinary faith' and the form of sensibility that applies to the experience of the 'Godhead itself'. Concerning Ignatius, he holds, 'We can see that in this "application of the senses" a fact is being set forth for our acceptance...that this sensibility (*Sinnlichkeit*) must become all embracing, and extend from the concreteness of the simple happenings in the Gospel to a point where the Godhead itself becomes concrete by being experienced.'[95] According to this reading, then, there is no sharp division that can be appropriately drawn between the form of perception employed at the beginnings of the life of faith and the form of perception used in the most advanced stages of prayer. Instead, the Christian life involves a form of sensibility that becomes 'all embracing'.

In one sense, then, Balthasar takes an interest in practice in the spiritual senses tradition through his engagement with Ignatius. We clearly observe an atypical emphasis on prayer and attunement to God here in comparison with his treatment of other figures in the tradition. In another sense, however, by shying away from strict hierarchies and 'ladders of ascent' in the spiritual life, Balthasar preserves the possibility of the spiritual senses befalling the individual in a moment of surprising grace such that one could receive them at any point in the spiritual life.

Bodily and Spiritual Senses in Ignatius

Our second point builds from the claims made above, and can be made with comparative brevity. In that Balthasar argues for non-exclusivity between the two interpretations of Ignatius outlined by Gagliardi and Davila, he also claims a continuity between spiritual

---

[94] Löser, 'The Ignatian *Exercises*', 107.   [95] *GL* I, 376.

and corporeal senses in the individual human being. It is telling that Balthasar renders the sixteenth-century debates about Ignatius in such a way that the imaginative senses are excluded from the relevant points of contention. As mentioned above, he claims, 'In the interpretations of Ignatius the problem emerges as an either/or between the corporeal senses and the mystical sensibility, but both of these seem to be included by Ignatius...without their mutually suppressing or jeopardising one another.'[96] Balthasar thus casts one side of the debate as endorsing the corporeal senses, even though the imaginative senses are equally prevalent in the discussion in question. Indeed, the debates initially centred around the imaginative senses and the spiritual senses, with no mention of the corporeal senses at all. Then, the 1599 *Directorium* grouped the corporeal and imaginative senses together in the lower form of prayer for beginners. In this passage we see Balthasar go a step further by discussing the corporeal senses to the exclusion of the senses of the imagination, thus demonstrating the extent to which his interests lie with uniting corporeal and spiritual perception in his reading of Ignatius. Balthasar justifies this somewhat controversial reading as follows: 'Since what must be realised is, objectively, God's worldly and corporeal form, it [must] be realised...in the encounter of the corporeal sinner who has been granted grace with the God who has corporeally become man'.[97] In short, then, Ignatius' understanding of the Incarnation demands a rethinking of the value placed on corporeal perception, according to Balthasar's reading.[98]

---

[96] *GL* I, 378. Balthasar also holds, 'Spiritual senses...presuppose devout bodily senses which are capable of undergoing Christian transformation' (*GL* I, 378).

[97] *GL* I, 376.

[98] Balthasar cites a passage from Ludolph of Saxony's *Life of Christ*, which Ignatius reports having read with great interest. 'If you wish to derive fruit from these meditations, set aside all your worries and cares. With the affections of the heart make present to yourself, in a loving and delectable way, everything the Lord Jesus said and did, just as present as if you were hearing it with your ears and seeing it with your eyes. Then all of it becomes sweet because you are thinking of it and, what is more, tasting it with longing. And even when it is related in the past tense, you should consider it all as if it were occurring today.... Go into the Holy Land, kiss with a burning spirit the soil upon which the good Jesus stood. Make present to yourself how he spoke and went about with his disciples and with sinners, how he speaks and preaches, how he walks and rests, sleeps and watches, eats and performs miracles. Inscribe into your very heart his attitudes and his actions.' Ludolph of Saxony, *Vita Jesu Christi*, ed. L. M. Rigollot (Paris: V. Palmé, 1870), 9. *GL* I, 378. Balthasar then comments on this passage as follows: 'Even though the "spiritual senses" are not explicitly mentioned, nevertheless

Elsewhere in his corpus, Balthasar offers a fascinating glimpse into not only his understanding of the relationship between spiritual and corporeal senses in Ignatius but also the way in which this reading compares with those of the two other most prominent figures in the spiritual senses tradition, Origen and Bonaventure.

The 'application of the five senses' that concludes every theme of meditation in the Ignatian Exercises does not rise above the concrete form (*Gestalt*) which is seen in the Gospels, for the text explicitly demands that we should 'see the persons with the inner eyes in recollection and meditation'; 'hear what they are saying'; with the sense of touch 'embrace and kiss the places in which the persons enter and where they remain'; and through such sense-experience come to the smelling and tasting of the 'infinite fragrance and sweetness of the Godhead.' Ignatius does not speak, therefore, (like Origen and, after him, Bonaventure) of spiritual senses that grow in the soul when the bodily senses have been laid to rest.[99]

Although these comments about Bonaventure are certainly curious in relation to the positive reading of his understanding of corporeal sensation that Balthasar outlines in the second volume of his theological aesthetics, as examined above, they are also illuminating for our investigation. It is particularly noteworthy that Balthasar ties the function of the senses to the 'concrete form' (*Gestalt*), and that the corporeality of this form requires physical perception, as will be examined in Chapter 5.

CONCLUSION

In our assessment of Balthasar's reading of traditional figures in the spiritual senses tradition, we have shown that he selectively reads the patristic, medieval, and early modern materials to advance a history of the doctrine that breaks from those of other scholars in the tradition, most notably Rahner. The clearest manifestation of this selective focus involves the often predictable way in which Balthasar

---

something spiritual is attained with the corporeal senses and the imagination, something which clearly aims at making the mystery present.' *GL* I, 378.

[99] Hans Urs von Balthasar, 'Das Schauvermögen der Christen', in *Skizzen zur Theologie V: Homo creatus est* (Einsiedeln: Johannes Verlag, 1986), 52–60, at 54–5.

pushes interpretation of any given individual toward the most positive regard for the body and materiality that can be credibly attributed to that figure. In his reading of Origen, most vividly, we observed that Balthasar locates a 'Christian and biblical' Origen who celebrates the material order, although Balthasar recognizes the limits that this particular reading must confront, and he does not press his interpretation of Origen too far. Given this general trend of often juxtaposed views, it should not be terribly surprising that Balthasar in one portion of his writings celebrates Bonaventure's regard for the body, yet in another portion criticizes Bonaventure in comparison with Ignatius.

Additionally, and pointing toward our treatment of the role played by the doctrine of the spiritual senses in Balthasar's theological aesthetics, it is certainly significant that Balthasar does not find in Bonaventure's understanding of the spiritual senses a doctrine concerning 'mystical encounter', narrowly understood. Instead he locates in Bonaventure a resource for general Christian faith. In fact, I would argue that in Balthasar's reading of Bonaventure's understanding of the spiritual senses we see a general epistemological significance not claimed in previous readings of the doctrine. This broad importance of the spiritual senses to Christian faith is integral to the central claims of Balthasar's theological aesthetics, as will be shown in the coming chapters of this study.

On a similar point, we saw in Balthasar's reading of Ignatius an understanding of the role of practice in the cultivation of the spiritual senses. Specifically, we observed an emphasis on the 'application of the senses' in the life of prayer, and we also saw a continuity between the use of the imaginative senses and the reception of the spiritual senses. Although Balthasar seeks to preserve the possibility that grace might befall the individual human being at any point in the spiritual life, he does nevertheless focus on practice in Ignatius to an extent that we do not see elsewhere in his reading of the spiritual senses tradition.

Furthermore, we can certainly say that the foremost significance of Bonaventure for Balthasar's understanding of the doctrine lies in the aesthetic attunement that Balthasar finds in Bonaventure's model of the spiritual senses. The notion that the spiritual senses possess this aesthetic capacity is of clear import to Balthasar's own constructive use of the doctrine, as will be shown more fully in Chapter 4.

As a final point on Balthasar's rendering of the history of the spiritual senses from Origen to Ignatius, we should mention again the odd lacunae in his version of the history of the doctrine. Key patristic figures, in particular, beg for more thorough treatment than they are given in Rahner's studies, but Balthasar chooses for the most part to duplicate the Rahnerian scheme, at least in terms of who is important to the tradition (if not in terms of what those figures actually say about the spiritual senses). This selectivity suggests that Balthasar is not ultimately interested in developing a more comprehensive history of the doctrine through an examination of figures who have been neglected in scholarship on the topic. This is not to say that the history of the doctrine and its classic exponents are not important for Balthasar. The spiritual senses tradition is clearly a crucial resource for his theological aesthetics, as demonstrated above. However, I submit that Balthasar's main concern in his engagement with the doctrine is to place the idea of the spiritual senses as it has been articulated throughout its history in conversation with similar ideas he finds among his modern interlocutors. To those figures we now turn.

3

The Spiritual Senses in a Modern Idiom

Balthasar's Contemporary Interlocutors

Chapters 1 and 2 outlined Balthasar's interpretation of key figures in the spiritual senses tradition. This chapter examines Balthasar's engagement with his contemporaries on this theme. In the section of his aesthetics explicitly devoted to the spiritual senses, Balthasar appeals to four modern figures: Karl Barth (1886–1968), Romano Guardini (1885–1968), Gustav Siewerth (1903–63), and Paul Claudel (1868–1955). Although Balthasar is clearly indebted to traditional versions of the spiritual senses, I argue below that he does not seek merely to repristinate the doctrine out of its patristic and scholastic instantiations. In fact, Balthasar considers the models of the doctrine that precede his own to need significant revision for his own theological project. Two predominant themes emerge from his engagement with modern figures. Most urgently, Balthasar holds that the spiritual senses must be grafted onto a 'personalist' anthropology that conceives of the human person as a 'being in encounter', and not as an individual entity who is prior to relationship. According to Balthasar's revised version of the doctrine, the interpersonal encounter with one's neighbour is the definitive arena within which one receives one's spiritual senses.

Additionally, Balthasar locates in these modern thinkers an anthropology of 'unity-in-duality' according to which corporeal and spiritual perception are inextricably intertwined with one another. Of course, we have already seen in Chapters 1 and 2 that Balthasar places a high value on corporeal sensation in his reading of the spiritual senses tradition. And yet a question has pervaded our examination thus far: given that many figures in this history are typically read in a 'dualist', 'Platonic' way concerning the negative value they attach to the physical, why would Balthasar choose the interpretation that he does? What is the deeper influence that animates his non-dualist approach? On this question, Stephen Fields has claimed that Balthasar's guide is an anthropology of 'unity-in-duality'.[1] Fields quotes from *The Glory of the Lord* in order to explain this feature of Balthasar's anthropology: 'the human person constitutes no "isolated 'soul' who must work its way to reality by inferring it from phenomena." [*GL* I, 406] ... sensation is ensouled'.[2] Somewhat curiously, however, Fields does not offer his reader any guidance in terms of influences that may have been important in this arena. As a result, a lacuna has persisted in scholarship on this topic. Balthasar himself actually aids his reader considerably on this point: the very sentence quoted by Fields in its entirety reads, '*As Barth and Siewerth stress*, man is not an isolated "soul" which must work its way to reality by inferring it from phenomena'.[3] In this chapter, then, I examine Balthasar's use of Barth and Siewerth (and, to a lesser extent, Guardini and Claudel) to articulate the anthropology of unity-in-duality on which Balthasar's model of the spiritual senses is based.

KARL BARTH

The relationship between Balthasar and Karl Barth is one of the most celebrated in studies of modern theology.[4] Balthasar took an interest

---

[1] Fields, 'Balthasar and Rahner on the Spiritual Senses', 240.
[2] Fields, 'Balthasar and Rahner on the Spiritual Senses', 227–8.
[3] Fields, 'Balthasar and Rahner on the Spiritual Senses', 227. *GL* I, 406 (emphasis added).
[4] Secondary materials abound on this topic. For the most relevant scholarship, see the following: Englebert Gutwenger, SJ, 'Natur und Übernatur: Gedanken zu Balthasars Werk über die Barthsche Theologie', *Zeitschrift für katholische Theologie* 75 (1953), 82–97, 461–4. Grover Foley, 'The Catholic Critics of Karl Barth, in Outline and Analysis', *Scottish Journal of Theology* 14 (1961), 136–55. Jérôme Hamer, OP, 'Un programme de "christologie conséquente": Le projet de Karl Barth', *Nouvelle revue théologique* 84 (1962): 1009–31. P. Corset, 'Premières rencontres de la théologie catholique avec l'oeuvre de Barth (1922–1932), III Réception de la théologie de Barth', in *Karl Barth: Genèse et réception de sa théologie* (Genève: Labor et Fides, 1987), 151–90.

in Barth at a very early point in his career: he devoted a substantial portion of his doctoral dissertation (later published as *Apokalypse der Deutschen Seele*) to Barth's theology,[5] and he also wrote a number of articles on Barth in the late 1930s and 1940s before publishing his well-known *The Theology of Karl Barth* in 1951.[6]

Scholarship on these two figures typically focuses on a number of now-familiar themes, such as Balthasar's critique of Barth's condemnation of the *analogia entis*, their revelation-centred theological

---

Werner van Laak, *Allversöhnung: Die Lehre von der Apokatastasis, Ihre Grundlegung durch Origenes und ihre Bewertung in der gegenwärtigen Theologie bei Karl Barth und Hans Urs von Balthasar* (Sinzig: Sankt Meinrad Verlag, 1990). John Thompson, 'Barth and Balthasar: An Ecumenical Dialogue', in *The Beauty of Christ*, eds. Bede McGregor, OP, and Thomas Norris (Edinburgh: T&T Clark, 1994), 171–92. Bruce McCormack, *Karl Barth's Critically Realistic Dialectical Theology: Its Genesis and Development 1909–1936* (Oxford: Oxford University Press, 1995). Roland Chia, *Revelation and Theology: The Knowledge of God in Balthasar and Barth* (Bern and New York: Peter Lang, 1999). Stephen Wigley, 'The von Balthasar Thesis: A Re-examination of von Balthasar's Study of Barth in the Light of Bruce McCormack', *Scottish Journal of Theology* 53 (2003), 345–59. John Webster, 'Balthasar and Barth', in *The Cambridge Companion to Hans Urs von Balthasar* (Cambridge, Cambridge University Press, 2004). Hans-Anton Drewes, 'Karl Barth und Hans Urs von Balthasar: Ein Basler Zwiegespräch', in *Die Kunst Gottes verstehen: Hans Urs von Balthasars Theologische Provokationen*, eds. Magnus Striet and Jan-Heiner Tück (Freiburg: Herder, 2005), 367–83. Philip McCosker, '"Blessed Tension": Barth and Von Balthasar on the Music of Mozart', *The Way: A Review of Christian Spirituality Published by the British Jesuits* 44 (2005), 81–95. Wolfgang W. Müller, ed., *Karl Barth—Hans Urs von Balthasar: Eine theologische Zwiesprache* (Zürich: Theologischer Verlag, 2006). Martin Bieler, 'Die kleine Drehung: Hans Urs von Balthasar und Karl Barth im Gespräch', in *Logik der Liebe und Herrlichkeit Gottes: Hans Urs von Balthasar im Gespräch*, ed. Walter Kasper (Ostfildern: Matthias Grünewald Verlag, 2006), 318–38. Hans Martin Kromer, 'Hans Urs von Balthasar und Karl Barth im Kontext der "Apokalypse der deutschen Seele": Der Weg zur "Umkehrung"', in *Letzte Haltungen: Hans Urs von Balthasars 'Apokalypse der deutscher Seele' neu gelesen*, ed. Barbara Hallensleben (Freiburg: Academic Press, 2006), 265–79. Stephen Wigley, *Karl Barth and Hans Urs von Balthasar: A Critical Engagement* (London: T&T Clark; Continuum, 2007).

[5] Hans Urs von Balthasar, *Apokalypse der deutschen Seele: Studien zu einer Lehre von letzten Haltungen*, 3 vols. (Salzburg: Anton Pustet, 1937–39). For Balthasar's treatment of Barth, see vol. 3, *Die Vergöttlichung des Todes*, 316–91.

[6] Hans Urs von Balthasar, 'Karl Barth und der Katholizismus', *Theologie der Zeit* 3 (1939), 126–32. 'Analogie und Dialektik: Zur Klärung der theologischen Prinzipienlehre Karl Barths', *Divus Thomas* 22 (1944), 171–216. 'Deux notes sur Karl Barth', *Recherches de science religieuse* 35 (1948), 92–111. *Karl Barth: Darstellung und Deutung seiner Theologie* (Einsiedeln: Johannes Verlag, 1951). Published in English in abridged form as *The Theology of Karl Barth* (New York: Reinhart and Winston, 1971). Complete text later published as *Karl Barth: Exposition and Interpretation*, trans. Edward T. Oakes, SJ (San Francisco, CA: Ignatius Press, 1992).

methods, and their shared Christocentrism.[7] However, a key feature of their relationship remains unexamined: namely, the significance of Barth's theological anthropology for Balthasar's highly creative rearticulation of the spiritual senses. Here I show—counterintuitively, it might seem—that it is actually Barth, of all people, who plays a key role in Balthasar's reformulation of the spiritual senses.[8] Balthasar views Barth's theological anthropology as advancing a 'personalist' understanding of the human being as necessarily 'in encounter' with an other, and also as fundamentally united in body and soul. These two features of Barth's theological anthropology shape his idea that the human being is capable of the perception (*Wahrnehmung*) of God. This claim will surprise the reader who is familiar with only Barth's early theology, as his *Epistle to the Romans* and *Church Dogmatics* I/1 give the overwhelming rhetorical impression that the *capax dei* in the human person has been so devastated by sin as to render impossible any experience of God.[9] Balthasar, however, brings to light this unexpected aspect of Barth's later work, and he draws from it for his own model of the spiritual senses, as will be shown below.

In Encounter: Balthasar on the Interpersonal Dimension of Barth's Anthropology

In the section of *The Glory of the Lord* devoted to the spiritual senses, Balthasar claims that a 'biblical' anthropology must be developed for purposes of his rehabilitation of the doctrine. The Bible—particularly, Barth's reading of the Bible—is appealing to Balthasar because it is there that he, quoting Barth, finds 'the man who meets his God and stands

---

[7] One also finds acknowledgment that Barth was significant for Balthasar's theological aesthetics in that Balthasar draws from Barth's *Church Dogmatics* II/1 for his claims concerning the 'glory' (*Herrlichkeit*) of God's revelation. See in particular *GL* I, 53–7.

[8] Especially relevant among Barth's works is his *Church Dogmatics* III/2: *The Doctrine of Creation*, trans. H. Knight, G. W. Bromiley, J. K. S. Reid, and R. H. Fuller (Edinburgh: T&T Clark, 1960), hereafter cited as *CD* III/2.

[9] Barth's early dialectical theology holds this experience to be an absolute impossibility. At the conclusion of his *Church Dogmatics* I/1, however, Barth does allow for the human being to receive divine revelation. Even here, however, he makes abundantly manifest that this is done as an act of the Holy Spirit without any agency on the part of the human being: 'The act of the Holy Spirit in revelation is the Yea to God's Word, spoken through God Himself on our behalf, yet not only to us but in us'. Karl Barth, *Church Dogmatics I/1: Doctrine of the Word of God*, trans. G. T. Thomson (Edinburgh: T&T Clark, 1936), 518.

before his God, the man who finds God and to whom God is present'.[10] Absolutely essential to this ability to meet God is the fact that he or she is not an isolable subject, but rather one who from the very start is in relationship with an other. Balthasar explains that, for Barth, the human being of the Bible 'is not examined "in himself" (*an sich*), but, from the outset, in his "vital act" and engagedness'.[11] In other words, according to Balthasar's reading of Barth, the Bible portrays the human being as one who is at his or her most fundamental level *already* in relation to others. There simply is no 'I' to speak of prior to the 'I' *in encounter*.

This must be so, to Barth, because any attempt to do the opposite, to define oneself in terms of individuality, disregards one's status as creature of the creator. That is, Barth holds that the human being is most fundamentally a creature of God who stands in relation to God. Or, to put the point another way, the human being 'is' only because he or she has been created by—and is related to—God. Therefore, the notion that one is self-subsistent is an illusion, in Barth's understanding. As he puts this idea, 'Perhaps the fundamental mistake in all erroneous thinking of man about himself is that he tries to equate himself with God and therefore to proceed on the assumption that he can regard himself as the presupposition of his own being'.[12] It is in this context that we can appreciate Balthasar's otherwise cryptic remark that 'whenever an "essence" of man is sought which is anterior to his being-with and even in opposition to it, then by this very fact one is already in the process of interchanging man and his Creator'.[13] In other words, Balthasar, with Barth, wants to ensure that theological anthropology not forget its most fundamental premise: namely, that the human being is a creature of God who does not posit his or her own existence, but rather who always 'is' in relation to the God who created him or her.

With this said, for Balthasar's anthropology we still need an account of how one is open to the fellow human being in addition to being open to God. That is, developing an understanding of how the human being is related to God along the 'vertical' axis, so to speak, does not necessarily bring anything to bear on relationships on the 'horizontal', human-to-human

---

[10] *CD* III/2, 402. *GL* I, 381.   [11] *CD* III/2, 433. *GL* I, 381.

[12] *CD* III/2, 151. We should thus hear the subtle criticism in Barth's description of the human being who asserts such autonomy: ' "I am"—this is the forceful assertion which we are all engaged in making and of which we are convinced that none can surpass it in urgency or importance; the assertion of the self in which we can neither be replaced by any nor restrained by any' (*CD* III/2, 229–30).

[13] *GL* I, 381–2.

plane. But Barth clearly does not limit the relationality of the human being to the God-human connection alone. Instead, the human being is also fundamentally open to the other human being in his or her midst. In order to account for the interpersonal dimension of Barth's anthropology, Balthasar appeals to Barth's Christology, specifically the *humanity* of Christ.

In short, Balthasar holds that the foundation for the interpersonal dimension to the human being in Barth's thought lies in the fact that in Jesus we find one who is not only 'Man for God' but also 'Man for other Men'.[14] As Barth puts this point, 'If the divinity of the man Jesus is to be described comprehensively in the statement that He is man for God, His humanity can and must be described no less succinctly in the proposition that He is man for man, for other men, His fellows'.[15] In Jesus we see one who is at his core directed towards other human beings. As Barth describes the humanity of Jesus, 'What interests Him and does so exclusively, is man, other men as such, who need Him and are referred to Him for help and deliverance'.[16] Jesus' humanity, then, cannot be considered in isolation from his fellow human beings. Since he is at core a 'man for others', we must instead think of him as always *in relation*: 'If we see Him alone, we do not see Him at all. If we see Him, we see with and around Him in ever-widening circles, His disciples, the people, His enemies and the countless millions who have not yet heard His name. We see Him as theirs, determined by them and for them, belonging to each and every one of them'.[17] To Barth, Jesus' humanity (his 'I') is determined by the Thou of his fellow human beings. Because our humanity bears *some* likeness to that of Jesus—despite the far-greater difference between our humanity and his[18]—our humanity shares in this fundamental constitution toward relation.[19]

---

[14] See *CD* III/2, §45.1 'Jesus, Man for Other Men'.   [15] *CD* III/2, 208.
[16] Karl Barth, *Church Dogmatics* II/2: *The Doctrine of God*, trans. G. W. Bromiley, J. C. Campbell, I. Wilson, J. Strathearn McNab, H. Knight, and R. A. Stewart (Edinburgh, T&T Clark, 1957), 130.
[17] *CD* III/2, 216.
[18] On Barth's understanding, one should not insist on the similarities between our humanity and the humanity of Jesus without first making abundantly clear the manifold differences. 'Christology is not anthropology. We cannot expect, therefore, to find directly in others the humanity of Jesus...On the other hand...for all the disparity between Him and us He affirms these others as beings which are not merely unlike Him in His creaturely existence and therefore His humanity, but also like Him in some basic form' (*CD* III/2, 222–3).
[19] Although Balthasar does not highlight the Trinitarian dimension to Barth's personalism, it should also be said that Barth grounds his notion of fellow humanity in his doctrine of the Trinity. That is to say, human beings may be regarded as beings in

According to Barth's anthropology, then, the human being is doubly directed toward relationality, foremost towards God and secondarily toward the neighbour. Barth puts this point memorably: ' "I am"—the true and filled "I am"—may thus be paraphrased: "I am in encounter." Nor am I in encounter before or after, incidentally, secondarily, or subsequently, while primarily and properly I am alone in an inner world in which I am not in this encounter.'[20] Barth goes on to make his point even more emphatically when he writes, 'We cannot accept any compromise or admixture with the opposite conception which would have it that at bottom—in the far depths of that abyss of an empty subject—man can be a man without the fellow-man, an I without the Thou.'[21] In Barth's anthropology, then, relationality goes all the way down. The human *qua* human is at root a being-in-encounter. This aspect of Barth's thought importantly shapes his understanding of perception, as will be examined below. For the moment, however, we investigate the second noteworthy aspect of Balthasar's reading of Barth's theological anthropology: namely, his understanding of the human being as a 'unity-in-duality'.

A Soul that Perceives:
Balthasar on Barth's Anthropology of Unity-in-Duality

In Barth, Balthasar finds an ally for his project of thoroughly uniting the spiritual senses with their corporeal counterparts. Balthasar explicitly celebrates as a 'radically anti-Platonic formula' the following passage from Barth's *Church Dogmatics* III/2: 'If the body is not organic body (*Leib*) but purely material body (*Körper*) when it is without soul, so the soul is not soul, but only the possibility of soul when it is without body.'[22] For Barth, there is no such thing as a disembodied soul, nor for that matter is there a 'de-souled' body. Rather, the soul is always embodied, and the body is always 'besouled'. The soul, then, must be regarded not merely as soul but rather always as 'soul of one's body'. As Barth puts this point, 'The statement that "man is soul"

---

relation because they are made in the *imago Dei*, and the triune God is God in relationship. In Barth's words, 'Humanity that is not fellow humanity is inhumanity...The God who is no *Deus solitarius* but *Deus triunus*, God in relationship [cannot] be mirrored in a *homo solitarius*' (*CD* III/4, 117). Relationality inheres in the Triune God, and it is on that basis, to Barth, that the human being, as the image of God, is a fundamentally relational being.

[20] *CD* III/2, 247.   [21] *CD* III/2, 247.   [22] *CD* III/2, 378. *GL* I, 386.

would be without meaning if we did not immediately enlarge and expound it: Soul of one's body, i.e., his body... Hence he is not only soul that "has" a body which perhaps it might not have, but he is bodily soul, as he is also besouled body.'[23] The soul does not dwell in the body incidentally, nor does it have any existence outside of the particular body to which it is inextricably conjoined.

Barth takes this unity of body and soul a step further than a mere Aristotelian corrective to Platonism. Specifically, Barth suggests that there is in fact a sharing of faculties between soul and body in the human being, and it is this idea that brings him within hair's breadth of actually recommending a doctrine of the spiritual senses. For Barth the notion that the soul is always 'enfleshed' and the body always 'besouled' undermines any attempt to confine 'thought' (*Denken*), to soul and 'awareness' (or 'perception'—*Wahrnehmung*), to body. Instead, Barth claims that awareness occurs not only in the body, but also in the soul. He correlatively asserts that thinking is done not only by the soul but also by the body. Balthasar explicitly draws on this aspect of Barth's thought when, quoting Barth, he writes, 'It is "certainly not only my body, but also my soul which has awareness, and it is certainly not only my soul but also my body which thinks." '[24] For Barth, then, the fundamental unity of the person means that neither thought nor perception can occur through only one of these aspects of the human being. This premise carries Barth to the conclusion that there is no realm of 'pure thought' for the human being. As he puts this point, 'I am continuously engaged in the act of becoming self-conscious... It all takes place in me and therefore in my soul. Yet it cannot be denied that this act in which my soul is at once subject and object is also wholly a corporeal act.'[25] For Barth, then, every aspect of thought has an external dimension in the body.

Just as there is no portion of the 'I' that exists anterior to relation to the 'Thou', then, for Barth there is also no aspect of the human being—not even the soul in its innermost thought—that is not directed outward toward the body and, more generally, the world. Balthasar seizes on this fundamental openness of the human being when he claims, 'The soul does not lose its sensibility even in its reflection on itself. In scholastic terms, the soul cannot attain to *reflexio completa* (or *abstractio*) without a *conversio (per phantasma) ad rem*,

---

[23] *CD* III/2, 350. [24] *GL* I, 386, *CD* III/2, 400. [25] *CD* III/2, 375.

and here the *res* is the other—God and neighbour.'[26] For Balthasar, then, as for Barth, all thought involves not only a corporeal dimension; it additionally involves an engagement with the other that takes place through the body, thus rendering such reflection unavoidably interpersonal. These two features of Balthasar's reading of Barth's anthropology lead us directly into our treatment of perception below.

Perceiving God: Balthasar's Reading of Barth on Perception

With these two key aspects of Balthasar's reading of Barth in place, we are now in a position to understand the model of perception that emerges from his anthropology. We have seen that Barth regards the human as a being-in-encounter, and we have also seen that he insists upon a fundamental unity of body and soul that opens the human being outward to the world. The human being, then, is inevitably 'driven out' into the world in a double movement, for there is no realm in which he or she is 'properly alone', nor is there an intra-psychic, purely non-corporeal aspect to his or her being. A key implication of these two premises, for Barth, is that the human being is thus necessarily a *percipient* being. That is, the twofold openness of the human being ensures against a 'self-contained self-consciousness' that would isolate him or her from the world. The human being thus necessarily perceives, and this perception is at root a spiritual-corporeal perception of the other. As Barth put this point, 'A being capable only of a purely self-contained self-consciousness (*Selbstbewusstsein*) would not be a percipient being. Man is not such a self-contained being. He is capable of self-consciousness, but he is also capable of receiving another as such into this self-consciousness of his.'[27]

For Barth, this capacity to perceive the other, to receive another into one's self-consciousness is, somewhat unexpectedly, grounded

---

[26] *GL* I, 385. Balthasar then quotes Barth at length: 'I do not exist without also being this material body.... Without having some command and making some use of them, I cannot be aware of objects different from myself. And without being aware of objects different from myself, I cannot distinguish myself from others as the object identical with myself, and cannot therefore recognise myself as a subject.... It may well be true that this act of knowledge is not seeing, hearing, or smelling or any perception communicated by my physical senses, but an inner experience of myself. Yet it is just as true that this experience.... is also external and a moment in the history of my material body' (*GL* I, 386. *CD* III/2, 375).

[27] *CD* III/2, 399.

in the capacity to perceive God. As Barth puts this surprising point, 'Man may sense and think many things, but fundamentally the perceiving man is the God-perceiving man...when the Bible speaks of perceiving man, there is nothing else which it is important or necessary for man to perceive'.[28] At root, then, the human being is a being who perceives God, and all other perception occurs with this perception of God as its foundation.

Moreover, the perception of things in the world must always be understood as having significance only inasmuch as that perception ultimately relates to God.

> Man perceives and receives into self-consciousness particular things.... But these are important and necessary for man only because God does not usually meet him immediately but mediately in His works, deeds, and ordinances, and because the history of God's traffic with him takes place in the sphere of the created world and of the world of objects distinct from God.[29]

In tones that sound remarkably similar to the natural theology Barth is known for vehemently rejecting, in this passage he claims that the human being primarily perceives God *mediately* in the created world and in history.[30] Barth thus makes clear the centrality of God in all human perception; he also gives us a more specific sense of what he has in mind when he speaks of the perception of God in the first place.

Importantly, too, this perception of God should not be regarded as in any way deficient in relation to the immediate encounter with God.

> First and last and all the time his perception has properly only one object, of which everything else gives positive or negative witness.... Thus in, behind, and over the other things which he perceives by sense and thought there always stands in one way or another the Other who through other things approaches and enters him, who wills to be sensed and thought by him, to be for and in him, not casting him off, not leaving him to himself, willing rather that man should be with Him and that He should be received and enclosed in his self-consciousness. In order that this may take place, man is percipient.[31]

---

[28] *CD* III/2, 402. *GL* I, 386.   [29] *CD* III/2, 402.

[30] Given Barth's hostility toward 'mysticism', it is unsurprising that he would prescind from claims about an immediate encounter with the divine in his account of perception (although he does, unexpectedly, suggest that such an encounter is merely unusual, and not impossible).

[31] *CD* III/2, 402–3.

For Barth, then, the 'Other' who stands behind all things seeks out the human being through those things. This gives all perception a necessarily personal dimension. No single thing is independent of the God who created and presides over all that exists, and therefore every thing gives either positive or negative witness to God. The perception that occurs between the human being and God—even when God is perceived mediately in God's works—contains no less of an interpersonal dimension than the encounter between I and Thou.

Apposite to our theme of the spiritual senses, Barth's understanding of the perception of God does not involve merely the activity of the corporeal senses. Instead, the constitution of the human being as a psychic-corporeal whole leads Barth to claim that perception must take place in a manner that reflects this totality. When this principle is applied to the perception of God, Barth comes astonishingly close to articulating a doctrine of the spiritual senses in his theological anthropology. In the portion of the *Church Dogmatics* that follows the above quotations, Barth dwells for some time on a reading of scripture that supports these claims. His exegesis culminates in his assertion, 'The Old and New Testament ideas of "hearing" and "seeing" do not merely denote external, sensuous, or bodily perception'.[32] Given Barth's previous comments about the psychic-corporeal perception described above, we can see that Barth understands the biblical witness as describing a notion of perception of God that exceeds a strictly corporeal dimension.

With all this said, however, we should reiterate the extent to which the perception of God is wholly dependent upon divine grace in Barth's theology. Indeed, one might be concerned that the above account of the perceptual capacities of the human being vis-à-vis God is so Pelagian as to distort Barth beyond all recognition. In response to these worries, we assuage the reader with a clear counterbalance to Barth's claims regarding 'the God-perceiving man'. Specifically, Barth insists that the human being perceives God only because of the continual gift of grace that allows for such perception. 'God is not in him as a matter of course. He would not be creature, but himself the Creator, if God were in him from the very outset, if it belonged to his nature to be master of God, if he did not stand continually in need of God's giving Himself to be his, of God's approaching him from

---

[32] *CD* III/2, 405. *GL* I, 388.

outside.'[33] Here we are reminded that for Barth the human being is capable of perceiving God only because God incessantly reaches out to him or her. All talk of a 'capacity' for the perception of God should be viewed in this context of the continual gift of divine grace that makes such perception possible.

In Barth, then, Balthasar finds a figure who develops an understanding of the human being as a being-in-encounter who is fundamentally united in body and soul. These aspects of the human being are so thoroughly intertwined that even the body thinks, according to Barth, and even the soul perceives. The particular notion of perception that Barth has in mind is first and foremost the perception of God as mediated through the created order. We shall bring these features of Barth's thought into conversation with Balthasar's model of the spiritual senses at the conclusion of this chapter. For now, let us turn to Balthasar's reading of Romano Guardini.

ROMANO GUARDINI

There has been surprisingly little academic attention given to the relationship between Balthasar and the well-known Catholic theologian Romano Guardini.[34] Balthasar wrote a monograph on Guardini late in his career, and he shared many of Guardini's concerns about renewing Catholic life through traditional theological resources.[35] Pertinent to our theme, Balthasar finds in Guardini an understanding of perception as a simultaneously spiritual and corporeal act, and, furthermore,

---

[33] *CD* III/2, 403.

[34] This situation is starting to be remedied, largely because of the scholarly efforts of Manfred Lochbrunner. See his 'Guardini und Balthasar: Auf der Spurensuche einer geistigen Wahlverwandtschaft', *Forum katholische Theologie* 12 (1996), 229–46; 'Romano Guardini und Hans Urs von Balthasar: Integration von Theologie und Literatur', *Internationale katholische Zeitschrift Communio* 34 (2005), 169–85; *Hans Urs von Balthasar und seine Philosophenfreunde: Fünf Doppelporträts* (Würzburg: Echter Verlag, 2005), esp. 55–89. See also Karl-Josef Kuschel, 'Literature as Challenge to Catholic Theology in the 20th Century: Balthasar, Guardini and the Tasks of Today', *Ethical Perspectives* 7 (2000), 257–68. It is certainly significant that early in his education Balthasar attended Guardini's lectures in Berlin in the 1920s.

[35] Hans Urs von Balthasar, *Romano Guardini: Reform aus dem Ursprung* (München: Kösel-Verlag, 1970). See also Hans Urs von Balthasar, 'Der Unbekannte jenseits des Wortes', in *Interpretation der Welt: Romano Guardini zum 80. Geburtstag*, ed. H. Kuhn (Würzburg: Echter Verlag, 1965), 638–45.

this model of perception is specifically configured around the notion of form (*Gestalt*). Additionally, as was the case with Barth above, with Guardini we again observe an insistence that God is perceived mediately in God's works. Guardini, however, adds to this understanding the notion that one perceives the divine with a special intensity in the liturgical setting. Furthermore, for Guardini, the ability to perceive God is given among the general gifts of grace, not as a special capacity reserved for the select few.

Perceiving Form: Balthasar on Guardini's View of Perception and Gestalt

Guardini laments the bifurcated model of perceiving and thinking that has emerged in the modern period, and Balthasar is sure to pick up on this aspect of Guardini's thought. Balthasar quotes a portion of Guardini's *Die Sinne und die religiöse Erkenntnis* that reads, 'This dislocation into abstract conceptuality and sensualistic corporeality must be overcome so that the living human reality can again emerge.'[36] The sensual and the conceptual have become split apart from one another, in Guardini's view. Thinking has been uprooted from the images out of which it arises, and perceiving has devolved into a shallow means through which to engage the world. As Balthasar summarizes this dimension of Guardini's thought, 'Seeing has become a matter of observing and verifying to which is afterwards added the activity of an abstract intellect as it orders and elaborates what is perceived.'[37] This model of seeing and thinking, according to Balthasar and Guardini, has deprived perception of its depth, and it has simultaneously robbed the intellect of its contact with the outside world.

In response to this situation, Guardini relies heavily on the notion of form (*Gestalt*) to develop an understanding of vision in which both the sensual and the spiritual are perceived by the eye in the act of seeing. As he puts this point, 'I see from the first instant "forms" (*Gestalten*) in which every element is borne, and the whole is as fundamental as the sum of the particular parts. *But such a form (Gestalt) is not only corporeal.*'[38] According to Guardini, then, the eye perceives

---

[36] Romano Guardini, *Die Sinne und die religiöse Erkenntnis: Zwei Versuche über die christliche Vergewisserung* (Würzburg: Werkbund Verlag, 1950), 73, hereafter *SRE*. *GL* I, 390.
[37] *GL* I, 389–90.   [38] *SRE*, 19 (my translation, emphasis added).

the form *as a whole*, and this whole consists of more than merely material components. In fact, 'the purely material thing does not exist; the body is from the outset determined spiritually'.[39] Importantly, too, this spiritual dimension not only determines the form, according to Guardini; it can itself be *perceived*. He claims, 'This spiritual element is not subsequently added to the sensory datum, for instance by the work of the intellect; it is grasped by the eye at once, even if indeterminately and imperfectly at first.'[40] As Balthasar summarizes this portion of Guardini's thought: 'The eye *sees* the vitality of the animal. In man, it *sees* (and does not "infer") the soul in its gestures, expressions and actions; indeed it sees the soul even before the body, and the body only in the soul.'[41]

Guardini does not deny that thinking also plays a role in the perception of form. He concedes, 'Of course I must also think. All sensory perception is continually accompanied or shot through by a process of thinking that compares, distinguishes, orders, and illumines.'[42] His question, however is 'whether the perception of every distinction is first and most fundamentally the result of thinking or a "seeing perception" (*sehender Wahrnehmung*)'.[43] In other words, Guardini wants to preserve the possibility that the perceptual faculties of the human being could pick up on aspects of form that are not strictly corporeal.

Balthasar, then, reads Guardini as resembling Barth in an important regard: both figures articulate a notion of perception that involves sensual and super-sensual aspects. Unlike Barth, however, Guardini begins phenomenologically with the notion of *Gestalt*. Whereas Barth's starting point is scripture and his method proceeds from what must be the case for the human being to have entered into a covenant with God, the starting point for Guardini's model of perception is one in which the organizing features of the form demand a notion of perception that exceeds the material realm. We have two different methods by which similar conclusions are drawn. Importantly, too, Guardini's understanding of the role of the form in spiritual perception correlates extensively with that of Balthasar, as will be explored in detail in Chapter 5.

---

[39] *SRE*, 19. *GL* I, 390–1.   [40] *SRE*, 19. *GL* I, 391.   [41] *GL* I, 391.
[42] *SRE*, 30. *GL* I, 392.   [43] *SRE*, 30 (my translation).

In the World, In the Liturgy: Balthasar on Guardini and the *Loci* within which Spiritual Perception Occurs

Although the category of *Gestalt* is central for Guardini's rehabilitation of perception, it is important to note that the human being does not see just any form through this spiritual-corporeal perception. That is to say, Guardini could develop a model of perception that did not necessarily involve seeing specifically religious forms. Guardini, however, actually positions himself in the spiritual senses tradition in order to specify the *loci* within which spiritual perception occurs. He claims, in the first place, that God is perceived through God's works in the world and, in the second place that Christ is perceived in the liturgical setting.

Concerning the first claim, Guardini makes a number of allusions to Augustine's 'eye of the soul',[44] and in fact the first half of his book is an extended meditation on Romans 1:19–21, to which Augustine refers in his statements on spiritual vision, as seen in Chapter 1.[45] Interestingly, in one of his quotations of the Romans passage, Guardini even goes so far as to insert the term 'the eye' into the text such that it reads, 'For from the creation of the world his invisible things are seen with the eye of reason (*mit [dem Auge] der Vernunft*) in his works' (bracketed text in original).[46] The Greek text itself does not mention an 'eye', and the 'seeing' (καθορᾶται)[47] of which Paul speaks is not typically taken to modify 'being understood' (νοούμενα).[48] For instance, the NRSV translation of the passage simply reads, 'Since the creation of the world his eternal power and divine nature, invisible though they are, have been understood and seen through the things he has made.' Guardini, then, actually inserts the term 'the eye' into the text so as to yoke together 'seeing' and 'understanding'. The two terms are then translated together as the 'eye of reason'.

---

[44] 'The eye...moves from the corporeal form all the way to that height to which Augustine refers when he speaks of the "eye of the soul"'. *SRE*, 53.
[45] *Die Sinne und die religiöse Erkenntnis* is divided into two parts, the former of which is titled 'Das Auge und die religiöse Erkenntnis: Philosophische Erwägungen zu Römerbrief 1, 19–21'.
[46] 'Denn das [an sich] Unsichtbare von Ihm wird von Erschaffung der Welt her an seinen Werken mit [dem Auge] der Vernunft gesehen, nämlich seine ewige Macht sowohl als seine Göttlichkeit'. *SRE*, 27.
[47] Or, more accurately, 'is clearly seen'.
[48] The Greek text reads as follows: τὰ γὰρ ἀόρατα αὐτοῦ ἀπὸ κτίσεως κόσμου τοῖς ποιήμασιν νοούμενα καθορᾶται ἥ τε ἀΐδιος αὐτοῦ δύναμις καὶ θειότης.

More interesting still, Guardini openly acknowledges his creative emendation of the text, and he even offers a rationale for his editorial decision:

> 'Nooumena kathoratai'. This vision through the 'nous', the higher reason, is not merely an analysis...but rather really a 'seeing'. It is possible that Hellenistic epistemology plays a part in the Pauline expression, whereby it is actually perceived not with sensory perception (*Wahrnehmung*), but with the pure perception (*Anschauung*) of the mind—in any case it deals with an 'eye', not with abstract reason.[49]

Guardini thus goes to significant lengths to insist that Paul does not intend an 'abstract reason' with his use of the term νοούμενα, and that he instead in this passage speaks of a form of vision, an 'eye' that perceives invisible things. It is highly debatable that the point can be supported exegetically, but Guardini's altering of the text certainly indicates a clear desire to ensure that the 'seeing' of which Paul speaks is not taken in a metaphorical sense. Invisible things are in fact 'seen' by the human being, albeit by the 'eye of reason'.

Guardini relies on this interpretation of Romans 1:20 for his claim that the eye of reason sees the creator through God's works. As he puts this point, 'Things bear witness to themselves as "works"; indeed as works of divine power.... That power expresses itself in the manner in which things exist. This "manner" is "seen"—but with the "eye of reason" (*Auge der Vernunft*).... The eye cannot see God in himself, but in his deeds.'[50] The object of the spiritual senses, then, is God the creator, who is seen through the things of the world.

Balthasar picks up this feature of Guardini's thought, and he summarizes it as follows: 'Now we can understand how, by referring to Rom. 1:18f., Guardini can demand of the eye and the senses that they see and perceive God. It is not God's unmediated essence that he means, but God's eternal power and glory, which are expressed in his works.'[51] As was the case with Barth, then, so too in Balthasar's reading of Guardini do we observe that the perception of God occurs mediately, in God's works. It is certainly significant that Balthasar has drawn out from both Barth and Guardini a notion of perception that apprehends the divine in the midst of creation, remaining rooted, so

---

[49] *SRE*, 27 (my translation).   [50] *SRE*, 32 (my translation).
[51] *GL* I, 392.

to speak, in the things of the world without leaving them behind in the perception of God.

Unlike Barth, however, Guardini adds another dimension to spiritual perception in his claim that these senses are operative in liturgy. In fact, his reflections on the senses and religious knowledge culminate in the treatment of liturgy found in the latter portion of his book. Guardini holds that the epiphany that takes place in liturgy has a particularly notable intensity and concreteness to it. This is the case, to Guardini, because 'the liturgy…does not have to do with abstract teachings and rules, but rather everything is the gazed-upon form (*anschaubare Gestalt*).'[52] In liturgy, the glory of God has become visible. As Guardini expresses this idea, 'The "Lord of Glory" (*Herr der Herrlichkeit*) can, if his grace desires, allow this glory to be visible as a liturgical symbol, so that we "will be enlightened through the knowledge of the glory of God in the face of Christ" (2 Cor. 4:6).'[53] In liturgy, God's glory becomes apparent in a manner that is at once material and spiritual.[54] As Balthasar summarizes this aspect of Guardini's thought, 'Christ expects that in its [liturgy's] signs—bread and wine, the water of baptism, and others—we should recognise his presence.'[55] It is Christ, then, who is present through the signs or symbols of the liturgy, giving himself to be perceived in an act that is at once sensory and super-sensory.

For All: Balthasar on Guardini and the Place of the Spiritual Senses in the Christian Life

As our final point about Balthasar's reading of Guardini, it is worth noting that he regards the spiritual perception of which Guardini speaks to be among the general gifts of grace, not a special perception reserved for a few at the heights of 'mystical' experience. As Balthasar remarks on Guardini's discussion of perceiving God, 'What we are dealing with here is…"normal" in a Christian sense, while our fall into rationalistic cerebralism and monotony can in a Christian sense by no means be considered normal.'[56] As was true in his reading of

---

[52] *SRE*, 63 (my translation). [53] *SRE*, 60 (my translation).
[54] Guardini echoes this sentiment: 'It is a free decision of the Lord of the liturgy that the "sign" should be not only an indication, but also a revelation'. *SRE*, 59. *GL* I, 393.
[55] *GL* I, 392–3.   [56] *GL* I, 393.

Origen, Bonaventure, and Ignatius, with Guardini again Balthasar focuses on the way in which the spiritual senses are given to the human being as a normal aspect of Christian life. One need not have passed through extensive stages of spiritual development to receive them, nor are they active in 'mystical' experience alone. Instead, the spiritual senses are included among the general gifts of grace.

In Guardini, then, Balthasar finds a notion of perception that is simultaneously spiritual and corporeal. Additionally, Guardini's understanding of the form presenting both sensory and super-sensory aspects to the human being in the act of perception mirrors Balthasar's own understanding of the spiritual senses to a remarkable extent, as does Guardini's notion of the spiritual senses perceiving the creator in God's works and Christ in the liturgical setting.

GUSTAV SIEWERTH

To the extent that academic treatments of Balthasar engage with Gustav Siewerth, they typically focus on Balthasar's use of Siewerth's reading of Thomas Aquinas and Martin Heidegger.[57] As a result, Siewerth's importance for Balthasar's rearticulation of the spiritual senses remains almost entirely unexplored. And yet Balthasar holds Siewerth to be a key modern figure who emphasizes the human being as both 'in encounter' with an other and united in body and soul. As mentioned in our treatment of Barth above, Balthasar summarizes the importance of these two features of Siewerth's (and Barth's) thought as follows: 'As Barth and Siewerth stress, man is not an isolated "soul" which must work its way to reality by inferring it from phenomena. Man always finds himself within the real, and the most real reality is

---

[57] Manfred Lochbrunner, 'Gustav Siewerth im Spiegel von Hans Urs von Balthasar', in *Im Ringen um die Wahrheit: Festschrift der Gustav-Siewerth-Akademie zum 70. Geburtstag ihrer Gründerin und Leiterin Prof. Dr. Alma von Stockhausen*, eds. Remigius Bäumer, J. Hans Bernischke, and Tadeusz Guz (Weilheim-Bierbronnen: Gustav-Siewerth-Akademie, 1997), 257–72. Peter Reifenberg and Anton van Hooff, eds., *Gott für die Welt: Henri de Lubac, Gustav Siewerth und Hans Urs von Balthasar in ihren Grundanliegen* (Mainz: Matthias-Grünewald-Verlag, 2001). Manfred Lochbrunner, *Hans Urs von Balthasar und seine Philosophenfreunde: Fünf Doppelporträts* (Würzburg: Echter Verlag, 2005), esp. 143–88. Andrzej Wiercinski, *Between Friends—A Bilingual Edition: The Hans Urs von Balthasar and Gustav Siewerth Correspondence, 1954–1963* (Konstanz: Verlag Gustav Siewerth-Gesellschaft, 2005).

the Thou—his fellow-man and the God who created him and who is calling him.[58] Somewhat strangely, however, Balthasar's brief exposition of Siewerth's thought as it is found in the first volume of *The Glory of the Lord* does not support the second of these claims in any further depth than that just mentioned. That is to say, the account of Siewerth that Balthasar offers in his theological aesthetics does not actually discuss Siewerth's 'personalist' views. We shall therefore refer to other portions of Balthasar's corpus in examining his use of Siewerth's thought on this topic. For now, however, we investigate Balthasar's reading of Siewerth's non-dualist anthropology and its importance for perception.

Senses Open to the World: Balthasar on Siewerth's Anthropology of Unity-in-Duality

Balthasar begins his exposition of Siewerth's thought with the idea of the 'openness' (*Offenheit*) of the senses. Siewerth understands the senses as 'roads' or 'ways' (from the Old German word, *sin*) to their objects.[59] As Siewerth puts this point in *Die Sinne und das Wort* (*The Senses and the Word*):

> Openness is the essence of the senses... Therefore, what the senses perceive or see does not prompt them to a renewed exercise of their own awareness, because in their openness they are always alert and expecting some manifestation. Forms and sounds do not therefore awaken sight and hearing,... but rather emerge as colours and tones within the open landscape of the eye, where sight is always seeing, and in the open sphere of hearing, where the ear is always hearing.[60]

Siewerth here emphasizes the fact that, when the senses perceive, they do not arouse consciousness of their actions in the perceiver. Rather, they make one aware of their *objects*; they open out onto the world. Whereas many treatments of perception may focus on the various ways in which the senses can be unreliable, Siewerth concentrates his attention on the extent to which the senses are effective in bringing the 'forms and sounds' of objects to the human being. As Balthasar succinctly summarizes this feature of Siewerth's thought, 'The eye does

---

[58] *GL* I, 406.   [59] *GL* I, 394.
[60] Gustav Siewerth, *Die Sinne und das Wort* (Düsseldorf: Schwann-Verlag, 1956), 8–9, hereafter *SW*. Quoted in *GL* I, 394. Translation slightly emended.

not see its own seeing, but only the things themselves.'[61] The senses do not focus on their perceptual acts themselves but rather on that which is *other*, outside of the human being in the world. Although Balthasar does not mention Siewerth by name in his *Epilogue* to his trilogy, one detects Siewerth's influence in the description of the openness of the senses found there: 'The human senses are gates that are constantly open…letting the appearing and self-giving entities enter into the senses and helping them to unfold through the senses. The eye does not learn to see; it has always been seeing.'[62] For both Balthasar and Siewerth, this effortless manner in which the senses are used gestures toward the fundamental openness of the human being to the world.

The openness of the senses leads to two further claims that are of interest for our investigation. First, for Siewerth this openness does not stop at the level of the senses. Rather, the *whole person* is open to the world. In *Wort und Bild* (*Word and Image*), Siewerth claims, 'Our senses are essentially the open heart of man (*das geöffnete Herz des Menschen*); they are the paths on which the heart's willing love (*mögende Liebe*) confronts things and beings and thus comes to power and riches, that is, to an actualised capacity (*Vermögen*).'[63] The senses serve as the avenues through which the inner aspect of the human being—here referred to as 'heart'—comes into contact with the world. In a similar fashion to Barth's model of a soul that perceives, Siewerth advances the idea of a heart that senses. And, as is true for Barth, for Siewerth this inner aspect of the human being adds another dimension to perception. It is not merely the bodily senses that perceive, but rather the entire human being as a unity-in-duality, senses and heart.

Second, our open senses pick up on the fact that objects in the world are not reducible to their surface appearance. Although Siewerth does not refer to the particular notion of *Gestalt* upon which Guardini relies, he invokes a similar idea. As Balthasar summarizes his view: 'Essential forms (*Wesensformen*) shape themselves from and in the receptive foundation of matter; they develop and, as a formed image, have their existence in matter. As such they "emerge", "re-present themselves" and "appear".'[64] The depths of things are shown through their concrete appearance, and,

---

[61] *GL* I, 394.   [62] *Ep.*, 78.
[63] Gustav Siewerth, *Wort und Bild* (Düsseldorf: Schwann-Verlag, 1952), 25, hereafter *WB*. *GL* I, 395.
[64] *SW*, 19–22. *GL* I, 395.

as is true for Siewerth's anthropology above, for things in the world they exist as a unity-in-duality.

Another way to put this point about the depth of things presenting themselves is to say that, for Siewerth, there is an interpenetration of 'objective' and 'subjective' dimensions to the act of perception. As Siewerth puts this point, 'The seeing is always at the same time the object seen.... "*Anschauung*" (perception) is both the act of seeing and the objectivity of what is perceived.... A sensation is both my feeling and what is offered to me in feeling.'[65] Siewerth, then, draws a distinction between the experience of the perceiver and the object that the perceiver is experiencing, and he insists that the latter is not reducible to the former. This is so, according to Siewerth, because in the act of perception the human being does not remain within him or herself. As Siewerth puts this point, 'Vision (sensory knowledge) has in itself moved out to the open and, thus, into that which is other. Awakened to itself by the light, vision has strayed from its origins and become "lost" in the other and, hence, in the exteriority of spatial extension.'[66] According to Siewerth, perception involves becoming 'lost' in that which lies beyond the self. At the very same time that objects in the world are being received by the human being, the human being is also transcending him or herself, proceeding outward into the world. As Siewerth further reflects on this double movement, 'To take something into oneself therefore does not mean to make it "subjective," but rather to concentrate one's vision on the depth of Being manifesting itself in the image. It means, in other words, to empty oneself out more deeply to the stream of light of the real.'[67] Human beings, then, according to Siewerth, are capable of a movement beyond the self. In this self-emptying they come into contact with the 'depth of Being' that is shown through objects in the world.

All of this leads up to a set of claims about Siewerth's understanding of the perceptual capacities of the interior aspect of the human being, to which he refers in the following passage as 'reason' rather than 'heart':

> Reason perceives Being (*die Vernunft vernimmt das Sein*)...Just as the senses see, hear, and feel in the openness of the world and the things in it, so, too, reason sees, hears, and feels in the foundation of Being, which

---

[65] *SW*, 10. Balthasar comments on this passage, 'This combination of subjective and objective aspects of perception holds...for the senses'. *GL* I, 394.
[66] *WB*, 13. *GL* I, 395–6.   [67] *SW*, 15. *GL* I, 396.

rules, weaves, and breathes life. But reason's synthesising perception is not something alongside the senses.[68]

Remarkably, then, although Siewerth does not espouse a doctrine of the spiritual senses per se, he does advance an understanding of reason as capable of seeing, hearing, and feeling the depths of being.

Although Siewerth's treatment may raise a number of further questions from a philosophical standpoint, we can see in the above examination a number of now familiar themes. The human being is a unity-in-duality, and he or she is capable of a form of perception that exceeds the physical realm.

The Mother's Smile: Balthasar's Use of Siewerth's 'Personalism'

Whereas the above treatment of Balthasar's reading of Siewerth's anthropology draws extensively from the first volume of *The Glory of the Lord*, in examining Balthasar's use of Siewerth's personalism we must appeal to other aspects of his work. The best starting point on this topic is Balthasar's account of the mother's smile, which he adopts from Siewerth and describes in detail in his 1967 essay 'Movement toward God'.[69] In this piece Balthasar describes the birth of consciousness in the human being, which he sees as inextricably tied to the encounter with one's mother. To Balthasar, 'The little child awakens to self-consciousness through being addressed by the love of his mother.... The interpretation of the mother's smile and of her whole gift of self is the answer, awakened by her, of love to love, when the "I" is addressed by the "Thou".'[70] According to Balthasar, the smile of the mother functions as the stimulus that brings the child to self-consciousness. Critically, too, such self-awareness cannot be achieved by remaining 'within' the self, so to speak. Instead, consciousness is founded on a movement beyond the self that occurs at the initiation of the other. As Balthasar develops this point, 'The event in which the spirit awoke to its being as "I" was the interpersonal experience of the "Thou" in the sheltering sphere of common human

---

[68] *SW*, 36. *GL* I, 396.

[69] Hans Urs von Balthasar, 'Movement toward God', in *ET* 3: *Creator Spirit*, trans. Brian McNeil, CRV (San Francisco, CA: Ignatius Press, 1993), 15–55. See also Gustav Siewerth, *Metaphysik der Kindheit* (Einsiedeln: Johannes Verlag, 1957).

[70] 'Movement toward God', 15.

nature, indeed, more intimately still, in the sphere of the common flesh of mother and child.'[71] It is certainly significant that the specific arena within which the child is awakened to self-consciousness is that which is given by his or her mother.[72] In the fifth volume of his theological aesthetics, Balthasar makes the fundamental importance of this particular relationship even more explicit. He holds, 'There is no encounter—with a friend or an enemy or with myriad passers-by—which could add anything to the encounter with the first-comprehended smile of the mother.'[73] The human being, according to Balthasar's use of Siewerth's thought, cannot come into self-awareness without the encounter with another human being, rendered here specifically as the mother. In a similar fashion to Barth, then, there is no 'I' prior to the relationship with the 'Thou'.[74]

As in his reading of Barth, then, Balthasar finds in Siewerth the notion that the human being is a being-in-encounter who is fundamentally united in body and soul. Siewerth puts his own particular stamp on these ideas through his understanding of the encounter with the smile of the mother and the openness of the senses. We now turn to the last figure we will examine in our assessment of the many influences on Balthasar's doctrine of the spiritual senses: Paul Claudel.

PAUL CLAUDEL

Early in his career Balthasar was intensely occupied with the writings of the French poet Paul Claudel, and he continued to translate Claudel's works throughout his life.[75] Curiously, however, little work

[71] 'Movement toward God', 21–2.
[72] Balthasar further reflects on this relationship as follows: 'In the beginning was the word with which a loving "Thou" summons forth the "I": in the act of hearing lies directly, antecedent to all reflection, the fact that one has been given the gift of the reply; the little child does not "consider" whether it will reply with love or nonlove to its mother's inviting smile, for just as the sun entices forth green growth, so does love awaken love; it is in the movement toward the "Thou" that the "I" becomes aware of itself'. 'Movement toward God', 15–16.
[73] *GL* V, 617.
[74] Of course, differences remain; Barth purports to derive his inter-personal understanding of the human being from a biblical, not philosophical method, and his 'other' is the neighbour, not the mother.
[75] Hans Urs von Balthasar, 'Auch die Sünde: Zum Erosproblem bei Charles Morgan und Paul Claudel', *Stimmen der Zeit* 69 (1939), 222–37. Balthasar translated

has been done on the relationship between these two figures,[76] and the value of Claudel's writings for Balthasar's rearticulation of the spiritual senses remains largely unexplored at present. In his exposition of Claudel's thought, Balthasar emphasizes two motifs, the first of which we have come to expect: Balthasar reads Claudel as advancing an understanding of the human being as united in body and soul, for whom perception is simultaneously spiritual and corporeal. Balthasar also finds in Claudel an understanding of the spiritual senses as particularly active in the Eucharist, in which Christ continues to make himself known 'flesh to flesh'.

The Body as the Work of the Soul: Balthasar on Claudel's Anthropology

In the portion of *The Glory of the Lord* that deals with the spiritual senses, Balthasar focuses his attention on Claudel's essay 'La Sensation du Divin'.[77] Balthasar begins with the claim that, for Claudel, 'the body is a work of the soul, its expression and its extension in matter. Through the body the soul experiences the world and has a shaping effect upon the world.'[78] In a refrain now familiar to us, Balthasar reads Claudel's anthropology as positing an interpenetration between body and soul. For Claudel, the senses only exist in the first place because of the *need* for the soul to engage with the outside world. As Claudel

---

the following works into German: Paul Claudel, *Fünf große Oden* (Freiburg: Herder, 1939). *Der seidene Schuh* (Salzburg: Otto Müller Verlag, 1939). 'Verse der Verbannung', *Rundschau* 40 (1940), 406–13. *Gedichte* (Basel: Sammlung Klosterberg, 1940). *Der Kreuzweg* (Luzern: Josef Stocker, 1940). *Mariä Verkündigung* (Luzern: Josef Stocker, 1946). *Strahlende Gesichter* (Einsiedeln: Johannes Verlag, 1957). *Der Gnadenkranz* (Eindiedeln: Johannes Verlag, 1957). 'Der Architekt', *Hochland* 51 (1959), 217–23. 'Paul Verlaine', *Hochland* 51 (1959), 251–3. *Gesammelte Werke* (Einsiedeln-Zürich-Köln: Benziger, 1963). *Corona Benignitatis Anni Dei* (Einsiedeln: Johannes Verlag, 1965). *Antlitz in Glorie und vermischte Gedichte* (Einsiedeln: Johannes Verlag, 1965). *Heiligenblätter* (Einsiedeln: Johannes Verlag, 1965). *Singspiel für drei Stimmen* (Einsiedeln: Johannes Verlag, 1965). *Die Messe des Verbannten* (Einsiedeln: Johannes Verlag, 1981).

[76] Edward Block, 'Hans Urs von Balthasar as Reader of *Le Soulier de Satin*', in *Claudel Studies* 24 (1997), 35–44. Manfred Lochbrunner, *Hans Urs von Balthasar als Autor, Herausgeber, und Verleger: Fünf Studien zu seinen Sammlungen (1942–1967)* (Würzburg: Echter Verlag, 2002). Manfred Lochbrunner, *Hans Urs von Balthasar und seine Literatenfreunde: Neun Korrespondenzen* (Würzburg: Echter, 2007).

[77] Paul Claudel, 'La Sensation du Divin', in *Présence et prophétie* (Fribourg en Suisse, Éditions de la librairie de l'Université, 1942), 49–126, hereafter SD.

[78] *GL* I, 402.

puts this point, 'The senses are a product and the external form of our interior faculties and of that need which shapes the depths of our being in conformity to something outside us in order that we might perceive it and receive its impress.'[79] For Claudel, then, the senses arise out of a longing in the innermost parts of human beings to conform with that which is beyond themselves.

Because the senses bear witness to the desires of the soul, Claudel suggests that we may acquire knowledge of the soul *through* those senses. He holds that 'the correct way of coming to know the soul, therefore, is to consider the body and, from the external organs of perception, to draw conclusions as to the internally operating forces which use the senses and direct them after they have created them for themselves'.[80] With the senses as our starting point, we can actually reason our way to understanding the soul. They are reliable guides.

According to Balthasar, this implies that the soul is equipped with a set of interior senses that parallel our exterior senses. As he summarizes this feature of Claudel's thought, 'Philosophically, what was said was that it is the spirit-soul which hears, sees, and tastes…it creates for itself the material organs necessary for perception.'[81] In other words, the senses are products of the longing of our souls, and, given that we possess five discrete senses, the evidence suggests that our souls themselves have interior senses that have produced analogates in the external body.[82] In Claudel, then, we see yet another method by which the notion of the spiritual senses is developed. As one point of distinction, we note the primacy of the soul in Balthasar's reading of Claudel. That is, whereas the other modern figures Balthasar examines do not so clearly emphasize a hierarchy between soul and body, according to Claudel the senses exist in the first place only because the soul longs to bring them into being. They may ultimately be unified with one another, but the soul clearly dictates their configuration in the human being.

When it comes to the theological import of this model of exterior and interior senses, however, the directionality is actually reversed, according to Balthasar's reading of Claudel. That is, Balthasar holds

---

[79] SD, 60. *GL* I, 402.   [80] SD, 60. *GL* I, 402.   [81] *GL* I, 403.

[82] Claudel indeed develops an understanding of five distinct interior senses in the human being. For sight, see SD, 84–97; for hearing, SD, esp. 71; also 'Non impedias musicam', in *Les aventures de Sophie* (Paris: Gallimard, 1937), 211; for touch, see SD, esp. 116; for smell, see *La cantate à trois voix* (Paris, 1943), *Conversations dans le Loir-et-Cher* (Paris, 1957); for taste, see SD, esp. 124–6. Citations in *GL* I, 403–5.

that, for Claudel, 'the God who became man begins with the external senses and moves back to the interior senses, awakening in the world that deep sensorium for himself, the non-worldly one, which had been dulled by sin.'[83] God stirs us out of sinfulness by appealing to our corporeal senses through the Incarnation. After commenting on the fact that the incarnate Word made himself known to our bodily senses, Claudel expounds on the function of Christ vis-à-vis the spiritual senses: 'Likewise, he willed in his compassion to do the very same for our interior senses, to make himself available to their grasp and hold himself in readiness for them.... He turns to our senses, that is, to the different forms of our interior sensibility (*sens intime*).'[84] Inner perception follows from the outer, according to this understanding of the relationship between God and the human being.[85] Balthasar takes this to mean that 'through the correct use of the external senses, we can encounter God in everything in the world. It presupposes this even as it integrates it into the higher dimension that it seeks to demonstrate. Claudel, in fact, is not thinking (as is Bonaventure, in Rahner's interpretation) of a naked mystical sense, so to speak.'[86] Although he arrives at this conclusion through a slightly different method, Balthasar once again finds a notion of spiritual sensing that encounters the divine in physical things in the world, remaining rooted in the material creation at the very same time that one is perceiving God.

Balthasar on the Importance of the Eucharist for Claudel

Balthasar reads Claudel as grounding the perception of God not only in the Incarnation, as treated above, but also in the Eucharist. To Balthasar, 'He [Claudel] is thinking of a supernatural and, at the same time, sensory perceptive faculty that can sense the specific quality

---

[83] *GL* I, 403.   [84] SD, 62. *GL* I, 402.

[85] It is striking that Claudel, like Guardini and Origen, indulges in a creative misinterpretation of scripture in developing his notion of the spiritual senses. Whereas Origen's favourite text is Proverbs 2:5 and Guardini's is Romans 1:20, Claudel's is 1 Corinthians 2:16, which he renders as speaking of the 'sense (*sens*) of Christ' through which is placed in us the 'sense (*sens*) for God' (SD, 60). However, 1 Corinthians 2:16 does not in fact mention a 'sense' of Christ or God, but rather the 'mind of Christ' (νοῦς Χριστοῦ) and the 'mind of the Lord' (νοῦς κυρίου). Claudel, then, like Origen and Guardini, has altered the biblical text in order to accentuate the sensory character of our knowledge of God.

[86] *GL* I, 403.

of the divine Essence because it is founded upon God's Incarnation and upon the Eucharist.'[87] In fact, for Claudel, the Eucharist offers us the means by which we can, after the resurrection and ascension of Christ, *continue* to perceive the incarnate God. As Claudel puts this point, 'He [Christ] willed to become flesh not only for a short time and for a few men, but for all epochs and all men.'[88] Balthasar picks up on this special importance of the Eucharist, noting that, for Claudel,

> The Eucharist, in particular, is the adaptation of our being to God by the descent of the Word into the senses.... Not only does Spirit speak to spirit, but Flesh speaks to flesh.... It must, like it or not, learn to taste, to taste how God tastes—God himself, our means of sustenance, who has now become 'accessible to our bodily organs'.[89]

Crucially, too, in his discussion of the Eucharist Claudel explicitly resists a dualism that could endure if he were only to speak of interior senses *mirroring* the exterior senses. In this portion of his text, Claudel unambiguously holds: 'Our flesh has ceased being an obstacle; it has become a means and a mediation. It has ceased being a veil to become a perception.' The Eucharist, then, is the primary arena within which spiritual perception occurs, and in it one finds the union of the spiritual and the corporeal par excellence.

CONCLUSION

In this final chapter examining the various influences on Balthasar's model of the spiritual senses, we have observed that his contemporary interlocutors provide him two key ideas. Most importantly, in our examination of Barth and Siewerth above, we observed two figures who articulate 'personalist' views of the human being as a 'being in encounter'. As we shall see in Chapter 4, Balthasar most clearly breaks from previous articulations of the doctrine of the spiritual senses when he, drawing on the notion of the human being as a being-in-encounter, integrates this interpersonal dimension into his own doctrine of the spiritual senses. Through this anthropology, Balthasar claims to supply the necessary corrective to interpretations of the spiritual senses that have, according to him, isolated the human being as an individual

---

[87] *GL* I, 403.   [88] SD, 61. *GL* I, 402.   [89] *GL* I, 401–2.

entity prior to encounter. Balthasar insists, to the contrary, that the encounter with the Thou is an inextricable component of his doctrine of the spiritual senses.

We also have seen that all four figures above oppose an anthropology that would divide body from soul, and they similarly resist notions of perception that would separate the corporeal senses from their spiritual counterparts. As Balthasar summarizes their views, 'In his own way, each of them conceives man as a sensory-spiritual totality and understands man's two distinctive functions from the standpoint of a common centre in which the living person stands in a relationship of contact and interchange with the real, living God.'[90] What we have in these figures, then, is a thoroughgoing attempt to ground Christian life in the particularity of the senses. Although each of them reaches his conclusions by a different method, their collective effort at unifying body and soul in the human being exerts a profound influence on Balthasar's own rearticulation of the doctrine.

In terms of influences specific to each figure, one is struck by the extensive parallel between Guardini's notion of *Gestalt* and Balthasar's use of the same term in his own constructive use of the doctrine. Siewerth's model of the birth of consciousness in the human being is of tremendous import for Balthasar as well, as will be demonstrated in Chapter 6. Claudel's understanding of the importance of the Eucharist for the spiritual senses permeates Balthasar's thought, as will be indicated in our upcoming treatment of his own use of the doctrine. Concerning Barth, one cannot help but notice that for Balthasar it is specifically the encounter with the neighbour—about which Barth speaks at length—in which one receives one's spiritual senses. With our assessment of the many influences on Balthasar's understanding of the spiritual senses, we now turn to the noteworthy features of his constructive use of the doctrine in his theological aesthetics.

[90] *GL* I, 405.

4

Balthasar's Distinctive Rearticulation of the Doctrine of the Spiritual Senses

The previous chapters developed an appreciation for the wide array of influences (both traditional and modern) on Balthasar's understanding of the spiritual senses. This chapter describes Balthasar's own version of the doctrine as deployed in his theological aesthetics. Gathering the most significant aspects of our earlier examination, a number of points emerge concerning Balthasar's constructive use of the spiritual senses tradition. Most distinctively, Balthasar maps the spiritual senses onto a personalist anthropology of 'being-in-relation'. According to this reconfigured understanding of the doctrine, the interpersonal encounter with the neighbour functions as the paradigmatic arena within which one receives his or her spiritual senses. Additionally, drawing on the anthropology of 'unity-in-duality' between body and soul that he finds among his contemporary interlocutors (Barth, Guardini, Siewerth, and Claudel), Balthasar interweaves spiritual and corporeal perception with each other such that spiritual perceiving simply cannot occur without its bodily counterpart. On this rendering, there is no inner vision of Christ that occurs through the 'eye of the soul'. Instead, all spiritual perceiving occurs outwardly, in the very midst of the physical world. Furthermore, whereas the spiritual senses have traditionally been interpreted as pertaining to a 'mystical' encounter with God reserved for a few, Balthasar repositions the doctrine such that the spiritual senses are granted to all Christians among the general gifts of grace. Last, and most importantly for Balthasar's overall goals in his theological aesthetics, he gives the spiritual senses an explicitly aesthetic dimension such that they are capable of perceiving and appreciating the splendour of the form.

In highlighting the distinguishing characteristics of Balthasar's rendering of the spiritual senses, I do not claim that his rearticulation of the doctrine is wholly unique. Balthasar certainly displays noteworthy lines of continuity between his own model of the spiritual senses and those that came before him. Nevertheless, it is important to observe that Balthasar weaves strands of this tradition together in a particular configuration that does not simply replicate the thought of his patristic and scholastic forebears. Moreover, drawing attention to the ways in which Balthasar's own articulation of the doctrine differs from those that have preceded him helps us to see more clearly the particular use to which Balthasar puts the doctrine in his own theology, which will aid our investigation in Chapter 5 of this study.

THE 'PERSONALIST' DIMENSION TO BALTHASAR'S DOCTRINE OF THE SPIRITUAL SENSES

The most innovative feature of Balthasar's version of the spiritual senses involves the way in which he integrates 'personalist' thought into his understanding of the doctrine. The notion that the human being receives his or her spiritual senses in the encounter with an 'other' is not evident in the various strains of the tradition that precede him. Balthasar certainly sees this feature of his thought as breaking with that of his patristic and scholastic forebears. For example, Balthasar appropriates Barth's understanding of the human being as a 'being-in-encounter' in order to claim, 'With Barth, then, we must profoundly deplore the fact that the Patristic and scholastic anthropology strayed from this first of all Biblical premises concerning human reality [pertaining to the interpersonal dimension to the human being] and let itself be inspired by an abstract Greek concept of essence'.[1] What Balthasar objects to in these patristic and scholastic anthropologies is the notion that the human being can first be considered a discrete, isolable entity who exists *prior to* encounter. Instead, the human person is always already 'in relation' to an other. As Balthasar puts this point, 'Man always finds himself within the

---

[1] *GL* I, 382.

real, and the most real reality is the Thou—his fellow-man and the God who created him and is calling him.'[2] Coming into contact with reality involves a meeting between subjectivities. Reality at its most fundamental level has a distinctly personal aspect.

Balthasar explicitly brings this personalist anthropology to bear on the spiritual senses in the portion of *The Glory of the Lord* devoted to his constructive position. In this section of his text he insists on the significance of the neighbour for his project: 'There is *one* image… which stands wholly by itself and which is like no other image… this is the image of the fellow-man we encounter.'[3] This unique image of the fellow-man, to Balthasar, confronts the human being and places a demand on him or her. 'In you faith compels me to see, to respect, and to anticipate in action the supremely real image which the triune God has of you. In our neighbour faith is at each instant tested through the senses, and, if it is authenticated as faith, it immediately receives its sensory corroboration.'[4] The encounter with the neighbour, then, is the arena where faith is examined, and Balthasar emphasizes the fact that this testing occurs through the senses. These remarks culminate in Balthasar's extraordinary and unprecedented claim, 'In his love for his neighbour, the Christian definitively receives his Christian [or, spiritual] senses, which of course, are none "other" than his bodily senses, but these senses in so far as they have been formed according to the form of Christ.'[5] Balthasar thus gestures toward a deeply ethical aspect of his doctrine of the spiritual senses, and he sees this personalist anthropology through to its logical conclusion: if human beings are fundamentally constituted in an interpersonal act, and if they are able to experience God, then the experience of God must also occur as an encounter with the other human being.

The further implications of this interpersonal rendering of the spiritual senses will be explored below in the observation that the neighbour shows forth *Christ* in the midst of this encounter. For the moment, however, the point to be made is that this model, according to which love of neighbour is integral to receiving one's spiritual senses, is not found in the versions of the doctrine that precede Balthasar, and that it constitutes a highly distinctive reworking of the spiritual senses in his theological aesthetics.

---

[2] *GL* I, 406.   [3] *GL* I, 423.   [4] *GL* I, 423.   [5] *GL* I, 424.

THE UNITY OF SPIRITUAL AND CORPOREAL PERCEPTION IN BALTHASAR'S THOUGHT

Throughout Balthasar's various treatments of figures in the spiritual senses tradition, we have seen that he consistently reads those persons as valuing corporeal perception to a greater extent than is typically thought to be the case among commentators on their texts. This comes as no great surprise, as one of the most apparent motifs within Balthasar's theological aesthetics is his repeated emphasis on the importance of sense perception for the theological task. In *The Glory of the Lord* he undertakes a tireless campaign against the 'spiritualization' and 'demythologization' of the Christian faith into a 'Platonizing' flight from the concrete, material world.[6] Furthermore, as we observed in Chapter 3, Balthasar demonstrates a clear attraction to those anthropologies that consider the human being to be a 'unity-in-duality', fundamentally united in body and soul.

This non-dualist anthropology serves as the foundation on which Balthasar's reformulation of the spiritual senses rests. In his constructive rearticulation of the doctrine, Balthasar takes great pains to conjoin the spiritual senses in as thoroughgoing a manner as possible with the bodily senses to which they are analogous. He explains, 'Perception, as a fully human act of encounter, necessarily had not only to include the senses, but to emphasise them...The centre of this act of encounter must, therefore, lie where the profane human senses, making possible the act of faith, become "spiritual", and where faith becomes "sensory" in order to be human.'[7] For Balthasar, then, it is actually the corporeal senses *themselves* that become spiritual. The spiritual senses grow out of the bodily senses. There is therefore no parallel set of spiritual sense faculties that must be brought together with the corporeal senses. Instead, the spiritual senses are transformed versions of the ordinary perceptual faculties of the body.

This move sharply breaks with the articulation of the doctrine of the spiritual senses found in Origen and some other patristic figures, for whom the spiritual and bodily senses are deeply disjuncted from one another.[8] For Balthasar, by contrast, the spiritual senses are

---

[6] See, for instance, *GL* I, 51–7.   [7] *GL* I, 365.

[8] The reader will recall from Chapter 1 that for Origen the 'spiritual eye' of the human being opens only to the extent that the 'physical eye' closes. The clear indication from Origen is not only that there is a radical disjunct between spiritual and corporeal senses, but also that the development of one set of faculties is inversely

thoroughly conjoined. As he describes this unity, 'What is at stake is always man as a spiritual-corporeal reality...If he thinks as he ought then he allows to come into him also the God who, through perception, had announced himself to be there for him. Both things—sensory perception and spiritual thinking—are constantly considered in their unity.'[9] Later in his aesthetics, he adds, 'It is with both body and soul that the living human being experiences the world and, consequently, also God.'[10] Thus the reader sees the 'spiritual-corporeal' unity of the human being on Balthasar's model, and he or she also observes the key fact that—as a direct result of this anthropology of unity-in-duality—perception occurs as an act that is simultaneously corporeal and spiritual.

One implication of this view is that spiritual perception for Balthasar is always rooted in the concrete, material world. Or, to put the point more strongly, one never perceives spiritually without also perceiving corporeally. According to Balthasar's reformulation of the spiritual senses, then, there is no internal vision of God that is presented to the 'eye of the soul'. To Balthasar, the spiritual senses do not perceive immaterial presences, as they have been thought to do by previous expositors of the doctrine. Instead, when one perceives spiritually, one also *necessarily* perceives with the bodily senses, and what one perceives is an object that is both material and spiritual.

Intimately connected to this concern about the corporeality of spiritual perception is a set of claims about the *object* of the spiritual senses in Balthasar's thought. Indeed, one of the reasons Balthasar so emphatically resists any trace of dualism in his rendering of the spiritual senses is that the object of spiritual-corporeal perception is the Incarnate Word, according to his version of the doctrine. Given that the Word has taken on flesh, the material order has been given a capacity to bear God's presence.

Of course, the claim that Christ is the object of the spiritual senses, taken by itself, would not necessarily distinguish Balthasar's doctrine of the spiritual senses from those of his predecessors. However, Balthasar's rearticulation is dissimilar from previous versions of the doctrine in its insistence that the spiritual senses absolutely do not perceive the *Deus nudus*, as Balthasar puts it. We certainly observed

---

proportional to that of the other. The spiritual senses grow at the cost of their corporeal counterparts.

[9] *GL* I, 384, 387.   [10] *GL* I, 406.

models of the spiritual senses that describe the encounter with Christ in figures such as Origen, Augustine, Pseudo-Macarius, and Bonaventure. And yet, we did not observe among those figures such emphatic resistance to the possibility that they could perceive the 'transcendent God' as well. In fact, the very reason Balthasar must exert such hermeneutical effort in his interpretation of the object of the spiritual senses is that there is substantial ambiguity on this aspect of the doctrine in certain figures in the tradition. Balthasar's own constructive rearticulation of the doctrine, by contrast, is unambiguous in its resistance to the possibility of a 'mysticism without modes', to borrow a phrase from his reading of Origen. On this point, he similarly claims, 'A mysticism of radical union is necessarily alien to the "spiritual senses", but it is likewise alien to the Christian way as such.'[11] Whereas one certainly finds other versions of the spiritual senses that emphasize Christ as their object, then, one is hard-pressed to locate such forceful expression of the idea that the 'transcendent God' absolutely *cannot* be the object of the spiritual senses.

This perception of Christ occurs within four particular arenas in Balthasar's thought: Christ is present in the world, the Church, liturgy, and the neighbour. Concerning the claim that one perceives Christ in the world, Balthasar's position echoes the reading of Origen, Augustine, Barth, and Guardini that we saw in the first and third chapters of this study. Balthasar, however, lends an even more explicitly Christocentric emphasis to the notion that 'the whole upper world' is the object of the spiritual senses, and that we perceive God mediately, in God's works. As Balthasar expounds on this notion of Christ's presence in the cosmos: 'If Christ is the image of all images, it is impossible that he should not affect all the world's images by his presence, arranging them around himself.'[12] In other words, according to Balthasar, every image in the world has been imprinted with the Christ-form, in whom everything is in fact based. For this reason, the human being encounters Christ in all objects throughout the world. Balthasar describes this aspect of the experience of the human being as follows:

> This his sensory environment, in which he lives and with which he is apparently wholly familiar, is through and through determined by the central image and event of Christ, so that, by a thousand open and

[11] *GL* I, 378. [12] *GL* I, 419.

hidden paths, his wholly real and corporeal sense-experiences bring him into contact with that central point…he stands in the world which has been determined and established by the appearance of God and which is oriented to that appearance. The reality of creation as a whole has become a monstrance of God's real presence.[13]

In no uncertain terms, then, Balthasar here holds that the human being encounters Christ through all things. The creation bears the presence of Christ, and this fact is made manifest to human beings through his appearing in the world.

Balthasar also holds that Christ is perceived in the Church. In fact, he claims that the Church has a special capacity for showing forth Christ's presence: 'The Church is the more immediate space in which his form shines. Not only is the Church illuminated by him like the images of the world; rather, suffused by his light, the Church actively radiates him onto the world.'[14] In describing this active function, Balthasar endorses the notion that the Church has a particularly important role in relation to the spiritual senses. As he puts this point, 'The Church, as a spiritual and sensory reality, mediates really between the believer's spiritual senses and the form of Christ'.[15] The Christ-form, then, is shown to the spiritual senses through the Church, and it is a part of the Church's mission to do so to all believers.

Balthasar's reflections on the significance of the Church lead him into a consideration of the liturgy, in particular, as a primary arena within which the spiritual senses are operative. He speaks of the connection between these two things as follows: 'Within the space of the Mother-Church, the features and gestures of Christ reach all believing generations as the sensory gestures of the liturgy.'[16] In tones reminiscent of his reading of Maximus, Guardini, and Claudel, as we have seen in Chapters 1 and 3, Balthasar also writes of 'the continual offer of Christ's presentation in the Mass, of his grace in the Sacraments, of his effective action in the preached word'.[17] In response to this continually condescending grace, liturgy 'enhances' with incense, vestments, and music. In so doing, Balthasar holds that 'the Church moulds the κόσμος αἰσθητός in conformity to the κόσμος νοητός of the reality of faith'.[18]

As our last point on the different arenas within which Christ is made manifest to the spiritual senses, we turn once again to the neighbour.

---

[13] *GL* I, 419–20.   [14] *GL* I, 420.   [15] *GL* I, 420.   [16] *GL* I, 422.
[17] *GL* I, 418.   [18] *GL* I, 423.

After discussing the image of Christ in the world, Church, and liturgy, Balthasar singles out the neighbour as an image of Christ that is especially relevant to the spiritual senses. As mentioned above, he holds, 'There is *one* image, however, which stands wholly by itself and which is like no other image...this is the image of the fellow-man.'[19] What we did not address previously is Balthasar's notion that '[o]ur fellow-man as we encounter him is in every case our neighbour, and this neighbour of man's is Christ'.[20] In the encounter with the neighbour, then, with whom one is necessarily in relation, one sees Christ. As Balthasar further reflects on this idea, 'In his neighbour man encounters his Redeemer with all his bodily senses, in just as concrete, unprecedented, and archetypal a manner as the Apostles when they "found the Messiah" (Jn 1:41)'.[21] Given these comments, we can now better appreciate the reasoning behind Balthasar's claim above, that the spiritual senses become particularly active in the encounter with the neighbour. In the neighbour, it is specifically Christ whom we see.

Of course, the idea that Christ is found in the neighbour is hardly new to Christian theology. What is unusual, however, is Balthasar's notion that the spiritual senses are especially active in this encounter. Furthermore, what is wholly unprecedented in the history of the spiritual senses is the specific idea that the relationship with the neighbour is one in which the human being finds him- or herself in an I-Thou encounter permeated by spiritual-corporeal perception.

BALTHASAR ON THE PLACE OF THE SPIRITUAL SENSES IN THE LIFE OF FAITH

One of the most significant features of Balthasar's reformulation of the spiritual senses involves his repositioning the doctrine such that one receives the spiritual senses in 'ordinary' Christian experience, as he calls it, among the general gifts of grace. In locating the spiritual senses in this place within the life of faith, Balthasar resists those models that situate the doctrine in the final stage of the spiritual life (for Origen, the 'enoptic' stage; for Bonaventure, the 'unitive').

---

[19] *GL* I, 423.   [20] *GL* I, 423.   [21] *GL* I, 423.

According to Balthasar, the spiritual senses are not exclusively offered to the few who have achieved the heights of so-called 'mystical' experience. Instead, they are made available to all. In the portion of his theological aesthetics devoted to his constructive position on the topic, Balthasar claims, 'If Christ is God's epiphany in the world, then by the very nature of that epiphany, provision has been made to insure that this emergence of the divine glory does not occur only before a few chosen ones...but precisely, really and truly, before the whole world.'[22] Balthasar thus demonstrates his unequivocal opposition to the view that the spiritual senses are given to a select group of believers.

In this connection, Balthasar discusses the spiritual senses in a section of his aesthetics titled 'Christian Experience'.[23] There Balthasar accounts for and opposes the distinction that has been drawn in the modern period between the ordinary experience of faith and 'mystical' experience. He claims, 'The delimitation of a mode of experience which is "mystical" in the narrower sense over against the experience of "ordinary" faith...did not happen until modern times.'[24] Balthasar holds that previous generations saw greater continuity between so-called 'mystical' experience and 'normal' Christian experience,[25] and he uses this blurred distinction to read the spiritual senses into a more broadly applicable form of Christian life. The importance of this interpretive decision on Balthasar's part cannot be overstated, as his positioning of the spiritual senses within the realm of ordinary Christian experience integrates them into the very foundations of Christian faith. Whereas the spiritual senses in Origen and Bonaventure have often been understood to come into play in

---

[22] *GL* I, 419.

[23] This portion of his theological aesthetics immediately precedes his formal treatment of the spiritual senses. See *GL* I, 257–365. For examinations of Balthasar's understanding of experience, see the following: Markus Engelhard, *Gotteserfahrung im Werk Hans Urs von Balthasars* (St Ottilien: EOS Verlag, 1998); Peter Casarella, 'Experience as a Theological Category: Hans Urs von Balthasar on the Christian Encounter with God's Image', *Communio* 20 (Spring 1993), 118–28; Christophe Potworowski, 'Christian Experience in Hans Urs von Balthasar', *Communio* 20 (1993), 107–17; Raymond Gawronski, *Word and Silence: Hans Urs von Balthasar and the Spiritual Encounter between East and West* (Edinburgh: T&T Clark, 1995).

[24] *GL* I, 297.

[25] 'The late Middle Ages and even Baroque spirituality still think from an undivided centre. What, in a more modern sense, is called "mystical" experience, at that time was still viewed as a particular unfolding of the general and, so to speak, "normal" experience of the Christian who is seriously seeking to live faith' (*GL* I, 297).

the very last stage of the spiritual life, then, Balthasar's interpretation gives them a broader theological significance.

These claims are closely related to another theme we have seen throughout our investigation: namely, Balthasar's lack of interest in the role of practice in patristic and medieval articulations of the spiritual senses. As we saw in Chapter 2, the only figure mentioned by Balthasar on the question of the role practice might play in cultivating one's spiritual senses is Ignatius of Loyola. Given the above analysis, we can see why Balthasar would gravitate toward Ignatius on this topic. Balthasar holds, 'Ignatius of Loyola, who, speaking out of what undoubtedly was a most intimate mystical experience...sets up his "rules for the discernment of spirits" as criteria for every Christian who is ardently seeking for God's will.'[26] In other words, Balthasar finds in Ignatius one who understands the continuity between mystical experience and the experience of 'every Christian'. According to Balthasar's understanding, Ignatius' *Spiritual Exercises* are not tools for cultivating 'mystical' experience in the narrow sense of the term. Instead, one uses them in ordinary faith to become attuned to God.

In specific regard to our theme, we saw in Chapter 2 that the 'application of the senses' pertains to a wide range of possibilities within Christian experience. Concerning this feature of Ignatius' thought, Balthasar explains, 'We can see that in this "application of the senses" a fact is being set forth for our acceptance...that this sensibility (*Sinnlichkeit*) must become all embracing, and extend from the concreteness of the simple happenings in the Gospel to a point where the Godhead itself becomes concrete by being experienced.'[27] The Christian life involves a form of sensibility that becomes 'all embracing'. In shying away from strict hierarchies or successions of stages in the spiritual life, Balthasar preserves the possibility that the spiritual senses will befall the individual in a moment of surprising grace such that one could receive them at any point in the life of faith.

Balthasar's campaign against achievement-oriented notions of mystical progress reflects his Ignatian inheritance. Indeed, some of Balthasar's most sharply critical comments in his theological aesthetics are directed against the notion that one might improve in the ability to perceive God: 'No achievement, no amount of training, no prescribed attitude can force God to come to us!'[28] Balthasar thus

---

[26] *GL* I, 297.   [27] *GL* I, 376.   [28] *GL* I, 418.

emphasizes the great extent to which God is free in the decision to become present to human beings.

For Balthasar, then, the spiritual senses are reconfigured such that they enable only the self-emptying necessary for the glory of the Lord to be shown in its fullness. As he describes this process, 'To be a recipient of revelation means...the act of renunciation which gives God the space in which to become incarnate and to offer himself as he will. Only in this way is the sphere of the "spiritual senses" given its proper place.'[29] The cultivation of the spiritual senses involves simply *making room* for God, not striving toward greater knowledge and understanding. As Balthasar puts the point, 'This purification of subjective attitudes is the way in which he is to encounter the real Lord and God in a fully human manner and with less and less dangers. God will enter precisely by the door which allows him full freedom of action.'[30] The role of the human being is only to wait patiently and cultivate 'indifference' such that he or she can go wherever God's call might lead.

THE AESTHETIC DIMENSION TO SPIRITUAL PERCEPTION

It may at first seem obvious that the spiritual senses would have a distinctly aesthetic dimension. However, just as any number of theories of ordinary sense perception make no particular reference to beauty, so too does one find models of the spiritual senses that do not dwell at any length on this aspect of spiritual perception. Balthasar, drawing on Augustine and Bonaventure, as we have seen in Chapters 1 and 2, does understand the spiritual senses as having an aesthetic dimension. As he succinctly expresses this point, 'An aesthetic element must be associated with all spiritual perception as with all spiritual striving.'[31] Furthermore, for Balthasar, as discussed in our treatment of Bonaventure above, beauty is a transcendental property of being, the beauty of Christ is absolute beauty, and the spiritual senses are capable of perceiving this absolute beauty of Christ. A necessary relationship therefore ties the spiritual senses to aesthetic appreciation. This feature of Balthasar's rendering of the doctrine is by no means

---

[29] *GL* I, 418.   [30] *GL* I, 418.   [31] *GL* I, 153.

unique, as Bonaventure serves as a notable precedent in the history of the spiritual senses. It is, however, a crucial aspect of Balthasar's theological aesthetics. Just exactly what it means for the spiritual senses to perceive the absolute beauty of the Christ-form will be demonstrated in Chapter 5 of this study.

CONCLUSION

In this chapter we have picked up various threads from Balthasar's reading of the spiritual senses tradition in order to illuminate his own distinctive rendering of the doctrine in his theological aesthetics. A number of noteworthy features of Balthasar's highly creative rearticulation of the spiritual senses have been observed. We have seen that Balthasar presses the spiritual senses onto a 'personalist' anthropology according to which the encounter with the neighbour emerges as a key *locus* within which the spiritual senses are bestowed upon the human being. We noted that Balthasar thoroughly conjoins spiritual and corporeal perception such that the two occur together in a single unified act, and we also saw that this spiritual-corporeal perception (which is ultimately of Christ) occurs within the four arenas of world, Church, liturgy, and neighbour. The spiritual senses do not afford an opportunity for flight from this world. Instead, the spiritual senses grant one a deeper mode of encounter with the very world in which we live. Additionally, whereas the spiritual senses have frequently been interpreted as pertaining to a 'mystical' encounter with God reserved for a few, Balthasar repositions the doctrine such that the spiritual senses are granted among the general gifts of grace in 'ordinary' Christian experience. Last, and most importantly for Balthasar's overall goals in his theological aesthetics, he gives the spiritual senses an explicitly aesthetic dimension such that they are capable of apprehending and appreciating the beauty of the form of Christ. It is to this aesthetic capacity of the spiritual senses that we now turn in our examination of the crucial role of the spiritual senses in Balthasar's theological aesthetics.

5

Perceiving Splendour

The Role of the Spiritual Senses in Balthasar's Theological Aesthetics

The previous chapter argued for the distinctiveness of Balthasar's rearticulation of the spiritual senses in relation to the versions of the doctrine that precede his own. In this chapter the central claim of this study can finally be advanced: namely, that the spiritual senses, when reconfigured according to Balthasar's modifications, function as the anthropological structure through which the beauty of the form (*Gestalt*) is perceived. At the heart of Balthasar's theological aesthetics stands the task of perceiving (*wahr-nehmen*)[1] the form through which God is revealed to human beings. Although Balthasar's commentators agree that revelation, beauty, and form are key categories for his aesthetics, what remains curiously neglected is Balthasar's model of the perceptual faculties through which the form is seen. I demonstrate below that Balthasar draws upon the tradition of the spiritual senses in order to develop the anthropological correlate to divine revelation. Or, to use Balthasarian terminology, it is through the spiritual

---

[1] Balthasar deliberately hyphenates the word for 'perceiving' in the German original of this theological aesthetics in an effort to expose its suggestive etymology, making clear that for him perceiving (*wahr-nehmen*) is literally 'to take to be true', or, to further emphasize the point, it is a taking (*nehmen*) of that which is true (*Wahr*) into oneself. See Erasmo Leiva-Merikakis' translator's note in *GL* I, Foreword.

senses that one performs the epistemologically central task of 'seeing the form'.

The stakes of this claim should be made clear: to say that the spiritual senses perform this sort of work is to say that they are integral to the fulfilment of Balthasar's goals in his theological aesthetics. Because Balthasar's aesthetics requires the perception of the form—which has both a sensory and a supersensory aspect, as will be examined below—some account of the way in which this human perception exceeds the corporeal register is absolutely essential for the success of his project. In other words, it is precisely because the form itself has both sensory and supersensory aspects that the *perception* of that form must be both sensory and supersensory. Balthasar's theological aesthetics thus requires a doctrine of the spiritual senses. In fact, if such a doctrine did not already exist, then for purposes of his aesthetics Balthasar would need to invent it.

I will proceed by examining three claims central to Balthasar's project. Balthasar stresses that the sort of beauty on which his aesthetics is based is not superficial or ornamental; instead (in a somewhat contentious reading of the history of metaphysics), Balthasar insists that beauty is a transcendental property of being. 'The beautiful', therefore, does not pertain to mere surface appearance, nor is it a subjective determination. Rather, it lies at the very roots of reality. Balthasar also holds that the beauty of being is shown to the human observer through concrete, particular forms (*Gestalten*). When beauty appears, it necessarily does so through the form. Finally, Balthasar asserts that this form must be perceived by the human being in order for God's revelation to be received. Succinctly summarized, beauty appears as the depths of being in a form that is perceived. After these features of Balthasar's aesthetics have been treated, the role of the spiritual senses will come into view, and the centrality of the doctrine for his project will be established.

AT THE ROOTS OF REALITY: BEAUTY AS A TRANSCENDENTAL PROPERTY OF BEING

We moderns have lost sight of the beauty of God's revelation, or so Balthasar contends in *The Glory of the Lord*. Balthasar describes his project as an 'attempt to develop a Christian theology in the light of the third transcendental, that is to say: to complement the vision of the true and the good with that of the beautiful'.[2] He undertakes this rehabilitation of beauty in response to what he regards as the widespread impoverishment of theology in the modern period. Balthasar holds that modern theology has let itself be shaped too much by rationalism and the exact sciences, and that resuscitating 'the beautiful' (τὸ καλόν, *pulchritudo*) as a theologically significant category signals an overdue return to celebrating the glory (*Herrlichkeit*) of God's revelation. Balthasar is aware of the derision that may be directed toward such a retrieval of beauty. However, he insists that such cursory dismissal comes at a cost: 'We can be sure that whoever sneers at her [beauty's] name as if she were the ornament of a bourgeois past— whether he admits it or not—can no longer pray and soon will no longer be able to love.'[3]

As intimated in this portion of his text (and as seen in our examination of Bonaventure in Chapter 2), the sort of beauty of which Balthasar speaks in his theological aesthetics is not merely decorative. Talk of 'the beautiful' does not pertain to inconsequential embellishment. Rather, Balthasar draws on the medieval (and ancient, although in a less rigorously defined way) notion that beauty is a transcendental property of being. As such, beauty permeates all of reality, as do the other transcendentals, truth and goodness. In witnessing beauty, therefore, one comes into contact with the shimmering depth of being as it shines forth to the human person.

Now, it is somewhat unexpected for Balthasar to begin his theology with this sort of reference to transcendental properties of being, for two reasons. In the first place, philosophy since Kant has become accustomed to using the term 'transcendental' in an entirely different sense from that employed by Balthasar: namely, as applying to universal structures of the human mind that function as the conditions for the possibility of experience. 'Transcendental', according to this understanding, does not have to do with attributes of being, or with

---

[2] *GL* I, Foreword. Balthasar regards his theological aesthetics as necessarily accompanied by his extended meditations on 'the good' (which he writes as his *Theo-Drama*) and 'the true' (which he writes as his *Theo-Logic*). It is for this reason that, for Balthasar, a theological aesthetics cannot stand alone. In fact, it is precisely when goodness and truth are not upheld along with beauty that the spectre of 'mere aestheticism' rears its head, as beauty can thereby be severed from goodness and truth all the more easily.

[3] *GL* I, 18.

any thing 'out there' in the world, for that matter, but instead with the constitution of the human subject.[4] Moreover, embedded within this modern usage is a criticism of the very notion that one can come into direct 'contact', so to speak, with objects in the world at all. Balthasar, then, begins his theology with a more historically established, but perhaps less widely known, understanding of the term 'transcendental' and in so doing indicates a commitment to metaphysical realism to which some moderns may object.

The second reason it is a bit provocative for Balthasar to begin his theological aesthetics by discussing beauty, goodness, and truth as transcendental properties of being is that he gives little indication, at least at the beginning of his aesthetics, of the disagreement among medieval figures concerning which properties can rightly be thought of as having full 'transcendental' status. Indeed, although goodness, truth, and unity are consistently mentioned among scholastics as transcendentals, beauty frequently does not qualify.[5] Balthasar's seeming lack of acknowledgement of these difficulties has led some to accuse him of unconcern with the highly debatable question of whether 'the beautiful' in fact remains a transcendental throughout the medieval period.[6] What, then, are the transcendentals, how does Balthasar defend his position on this matter, and what is at stake in his doing so? We shall see that the particular way in which Balthasar defends beauty as a transcendental actually determines that the spiritual senses will be necessary for his reading to be viable.

---

[4] At the outset of his *Critique of Pure Reason*, for example, Kant explains, 'I call all cognition *transcendental* that is occupied not so much with objects but rather with our *a priori* concepts of objects in general' (A11/B25). Immanuel Kant, *Critique of Pure Reason*, trans. Paul Guyer and Allen W. Wood (Cambridge: Cambridge University Press, 1998), 133.

[5] Philip the Chancellor, who is typically credited with first developing a definition of the transcendentals during the medieval period, includes in his list only being, oneness, truth, and goodness. See Henri Pouillon, 'Le premier traité des propriétés transcendentales, La "Summa de bono" du Chancelier Philippe', *Revue néoscolastique de philosophie* 42 (1939), 40–77. Alexander of Hales counts 'the divine unity, goodness, and truth' as transcendentals. Alexander of Hales, *Summa Theologica*, vol. IV: *Prolegomena* (ed. Collegii S. Bonaventurae, Quaracchi, 1948). See Jan A. Aertsen, *Medieval Philosophy and the Transcendentals: The Case of Thomas Aquinas* (Leiden, New York, and Köln: Brill, 1996), 41.

[6] Stephan van Erp, for example, laments, 'Instead of arguing for interpreting beauty as a transcendental, he merely states that the church fathers as well the medieval scholastics granted beauty the status of a transcendental'. *The Art of Theology: Hans Urs von Balthasar's Theological Aesthetics and the Foundations of Faith* (Leuven, Paris, and Dudley, MA: Peeters, 2004), 138.

We may take as our starting point the standard definition of the transcendentals as properties that are 'co-extensive' or 'convertible' with being, by which is meant that these properties transcend particular things in the world; they are instead attributes of *all* things that exist.[7] For instance, 'goodness' is a transcendental property of being because, on this understanding, everything that exists is good. Goodness is not confined to a limited set of things or categories. Instead, goodness obtains across all existents. It is 'cross-categorical'. Simply put, 'to be' is 'to be good'.[8]

Although they are convertible with being, the transcendentals must nevertheless describe different *aspects* of being if they are to be non-redundant,[9] and it is on this issue that a relatively unknown aspect of Balthasar's theological aesthetics focuses. In other words, although all things are good, to describe a thing as good is to say something distinct from describing, for example, that thing as true. And yet, a unique challenge presents itself concerning the transcendentals in that any further specification of being cannot *add* anything to being. Being is all-inclusive. Therefore, goodness and beauty cannot add to being in the sense that they supplement being with something that had not already been a part of being. Being already includes everything. How could the transcendentals add to it?

A frequent response to this question among medieval figures is to claim that the transcendentals do not add any *reality* to being; instead they only add to being 'notionally' or 'conceptually' (*in ratione*). The *ratio* of the good, for instance, according to Thomas Aquinas is that it 'expresses the correspondence of being to the appetitive power'.[10]

---

[7] One first finds the notion that unity and being are 'convertible' (ἀντιστρέφει) with one another in Aristotle's *Metaphysics* XI. 3 (1061a 15–18), trans. Hugh Tredennick (Cambridge, MA: Harvard University Press, 1935), 67.

[8] Pouillon intriguingly argues that the development of goodness as a transcendental in the medieval period was catalysed by the need to resist a renewed form of Manichaeism under the Cathari in the mid-twelfth century. See his 'Le premier traité des propriétés transcendentales', 74.

[9] Kant famously rejects the transcendentals because, in his estimation, use of them has 'yielded merely tautological propositions' (B113). *Critique of Pure Reason*, 216. To this characterisation Aertsen issues a noteworthy riposte: 'Kant radically misunderstood "The Transcendental Philosophy of the Ancients" by suggesting in his *Critique of Pure Reason* (B 113) that the Scholastic thesis: *quodlibet ens est unum, verum, bonum* is tautological. Again and again the thinkers of the thirteenth century emphasize that it is no *nugatio*, no useless repetition of the same, to say that being is one, true, and good'. Aertsen, *Medieval Philosophy and the Transcendentals*, 97.

[10] *De Ver.* 1.1.

Human beings desire the good, and the good is convertible with being. Therefore, one may say that goodness adds to being in the sense that it makes explicit something that may otherwise remain implicit. To speak of 'being' alone does not convey the *desirability* of that which is. Our question is thus: does beauty have a distinct *ratio*? Does beauty describe an aspect of being that is distinguishable from other transcendentals such as goodness and truth? Although the beauty of being had certainly been a theme in ancient philosophy and patristic theology,[11] the question of the precise *ratio* of the beautiful was not rigorously posed until the medieval period.

Balthasar certainly feels the weight of this issue, despite assessments of his thought that would suggest otherwise. During his examination of Bonaventure, Balthasar insists, 'We must ask what the *ratio pulchri* is, over against the other fundamental properties of Being.'[12] In addressing the question he draws primarily from an interpretation of Bonaventure advanced by Karl Peter, whose mid-century study of Bonaventure's aesthetics gave scholarly attention to this theme.[13] According to Balthasar, Peter's study establishes the transcendental status of beauty for Bonaventure 'inductively through its presence in all categories of being and deductively from some occasional remarks'.[14] Especially significant among these 'occasional remarks' is Bonaventure's *Itinerarium*, in which he holds, 'All things are beautiful and in some manner delightful.'[15] In his *Sentences* commentary, too,

---

[11] Most significant for medieval figures is Pseudo-Dionysius the Areopagite, who speaks of the beauty of all things emanating from a beauty beyond being: 'The Superessential Beautiful is called "Beauty" because of that quality which It imparts to all things severally according to their nature, and because It is the Cause of the harmony and splendour in all things, flashing forth upon them all, like light, the beautifying communications of Its originating ray'. *The Divine Names*, trans. C. E. Holt (London, 1920), 95–6. Plato and Plotinus were also highly influential for this development (Plato's *Timaeus* speaks of 'the grandeur, goodness, beauty, and perfection' of this world. Plato, *Timaeus*, trans. A. E. Taylor (London: Methuen, 1929), 100. See also *Symposium* 211A–B. For Plotinus, *Enneads*, I, 6, 2). Another line of influence begins in the Book of Wisdom 11:21 ('But thou hast ordered all things in measure, and number, and weight'), and is developed by Augustine in his ideas of *modus, forma,* and *ordo* (dimension, form, and order), which are then used in medieval discussions of beauty. See Umberto Eco, *The Aesthetics of Thomas Aquinas*, trans. Hugh Bredin (Cambridge, MA: Harvard University Press, 1988), 23.

[12] *GL* II, 334.

[13] Karl Peter, 'Die Lehre von der Schönheit nach Bonaventura' (doctoral dissertation, Basel, 1961). Later published as *Die Lehre von der Schönheit nach Bonaventura* (Werl: Dietrich Coelde Verlag, 1964).

[14] *GL* II, 334.   [15] *Itin.* II, 10. *Opera Omnia* V, 302b. *GL* II, 334.

Bonaventure indicates that beauty pervades all being: 'Whatever has being has form, and whatever has form has beauty.'[16] To Balthasar, these passages and others mentioned in Peter's study amount to a notion of the beautiful that lies at the very roots of reality, permeating all of being.[17]

It is one thing, of course, to locate texts in which Bonaventure indicates that beauty pervades all being. It is another thing to develop a distinct *ratio* of what the beautiful *adds* to being. Balthasar responds to this problem by claiming that the distinct *ratio* of the beautiful is that it *appears*. After discussing Bonaventure's understanding of unity, truth, and goodness, Balthasar ventures the following: 'If one wished to deduce a corresponding formula for the beautiful from what Bonaventure elsewhere says about it, then (following [Karl] Peter) this would have to run somewhat as follows: the beautiful is the basis of its physical appearing, because what is is not separated from being.'[18] In other words, the distinctive *ratio* of the beautiful, according to Balthasar's reading of Bonaventure, is that the beautiful *is shown*. Returning to our original question of what the beautiful adds to being, we now see that, according to Balthasar, beauty makes being known to the senses.[19]

---

[16] *Omne quod est ens, habet aliquam formam; omne autem quod habet aliquam formam, habet pulcritudinem.* II Sent. dist. 34, art. 2, q. 3, 6. Opera Omnia II, 814. GL II, 334.

[17] In an unexpectedly cautious moment, Balthasar refrains from basing his argument for the transcendentality of beauty on a manuscript, presumed by many to have been written by Bonaventure, in which the author explicitly mentions beauty as a fourth transcendental attribute of being. The author of that text holds that there are 'four conditions of a being, namely that it be one, true, good, and beautiful' (quoted in Spargo, *The Category of the Aesthetic in the Philosophy of Saint Bonaventure*, (New York: Franciscan Institute, 1953), 36). This overt mention of beauty alongside the one, true, and good is exceptional among medieval figures, and such an unambiguous classification of beauty as a transcendental has justifiably elicited comment from scholars. Balthasar, however, believes the author of the manuscript should be regarded as anonymous, and he indicates only that it *may* have been written by Bonaventure in his youth (GL II, 260, 334; GL IV, 383).

[18] GL II, 335.

[19] It should be said that Balthasar discusses the transcendentality of beauty in other ways than that described here. In some of his most memorable moments he speaks of beauty as 'dancing' between the good and the true. 'Beauty…dances in an uncontained splendour around the double constellation of the true and the good and their inseparable relation to one another'. GL I, 18. For the distinct *ratio* of the beautiful, however, Balthasar's notion that beauty appears is most helpful.

Now, at one level, this interpretation is obvious. Beauty is evident to the senses. And yet, at another level, the issue is complexified enormously by the fact that it is not simply *a being* that appears, according to Balthasar. Instead, *being* appears. The senses, then, as faculties that actually perceive the whole of being, are asked to do more 'heavy lifting' in Balthasar's aesthetics than is required of them by the scholastic figures he examines. Balthasar acknowledges that in this formulation he and Peter are actually extending the ideas of Bonaventure, not simply interpreting Bonaventure's texts: 'Naturally such a formula could be achieved "at a price which Bonaventure was not willing to pay... that of the elevation of sense-perception into the rank of irreducible being".[20] And yet, such a reassessment of sense perception is precisely what Balthasar has in mind for his theological aesthetics. 'If one were to take "sense-perception" as "a direct act of permitting to appear" at all levels... then one might step beyond the general scholastic manner of thinking and speaking and speak of a "transcendental sense-perception".'[21] Being appears, then, only if there are senses that can perceive it. Human sense perception must therefore operate at a 'transcendental' level. We shall examine further this highly suggestive 'transcendental sense-perception' of which Balthasar speaks in our treatment of the spiritual senses below, and we shall pick up his idea that beauty necessarily appears in a moment when we examine Balthasar's theory of form (*Gestalt*). At present, however, we touch on one final point concerning beauty: namely, the relationship Balthasar envisions between philosophical and theological aesthetics.

Although Balthasar goes to great lengths to defend beauty as a transcendental property of being, he wants to make unambiguously clear that the beauty of the world must never be taken to be identical with the glory of God. Instead, Balthasar maintains that an analogous relation obtains between worldly beauty and divine glory. Therefore, although there may be some similarity between the beauty that is manifested in the world and the absolute glory of God, the dissimilarity between these two far outweighs any notion of sameness. Balthasar's project indeed finds aesthetics at its centre, but it should be noted that his concern is with aesthetics of a certain kind. He writes of his particular enterprise as follows: 'We mean a theology which does not primarily work with the extra-theological categories

[20] *GL* II, 335. [21] *GL* II, 335.

of a worldly philosophical aesthetics (above all poetry), but which develops its theory of beauty from the data of revelation itself with genuinely theological methods.'[22] For all his celebration of the aesthetic dimension to theology, then, it must be said that Balthasar's is a 'theological aesthetics', not an 'aesthetic theology'.

One key implication of this idea is that the standard for beauty is not found in any worldly aesthetic, but rather always finds its source in God. Talk of 'beauty' for Balthasar frequently pertains to that which is of the world, whereas the aesthetic dimension to the divine is most precisely referred to in Balthasarian idiom as 'glory'.[23] More to the point, however, one must understand that in the very moment that Balthasar exalts beauty and its relation to the divine, he repeatedly reminds his reader to guard against imposing an 'inner-worldly aesthetic' onto God's self-revelation.

Concerning Balthasar's understanding of 'the beautiful', we have seen his insistence on its transcendental status, his innovative interpretation of the *ratio pulchri* as that aspect of being that appears, and his distinction between theological and philosophical aesthetics. Ultimately, it is most accurate to say that Balthasar's interests in engaging this discussion are synthetic and constructive, not primarily historical. As a result, his treatment of the transcendentality of beauty is not so much a faithful representation of medieval thought, but rather a creative appropriation of tradition. With that said, it should be emphasized that, unlike some of the moments of interpretive licence that we witnessed in Chapters 1 and 2, Balthasar here overtly indicates the points at which he extends certain premises beyond the scope of the texts he examines. This transparency on Balthasar's part helps us to see easily the distinctiveness of his own approach to the question

---

[22] *GL* I, 117. Balthasar makes a similar point in one of his summaries of his work from late in his career: 'The "glorious" corresponds on the theological plane to what the transcendental "beautiful" is on the philosophical plane'. Hans Urs von Balthasar, 'In Retrospect', trans. Kenneth Batinovich, NSM, in *The Analogy of Beauty: The Theology of Hans Urs von Balthasar*, ed. John Riches (Edinburgh: T&T Clark, 1986), 213. Adapted from *Rechenschaft 1965* (Einsiedeln: Johannes Verlag, 1965).

[23] Balthasar actually does allow this distinction (which he so rigorously maintains in some portions of his writings) to become blurred at many points in his theological aesthetics. Importantly, however, this elision occurs only in his use of the term 'beauty' to speak of God, and never in the opposite possibility that he use the term 'glory' to speak of things in the world. Furthermore, one should understand that when Balthasar does use beauty as an attribute of God, he regards God as *absolute* beauty, to which all other beauty is relative.

of the *ratio* of the beautiful, which in turn prepares us well for the next feature of Balthasar's argument. If being appears, it must take a form.

BEING APPEARS: BALTHASAR ON FORM (*GESTALT*)

We saw above that Balthasar develops a distinct *ratio* of the beautiful as that aspect of being that appears. This claim that beauty is always concretely manifested leads to the notion that beauty must take a form (*Gestalt*). Balthasar develops this idea in an important section of *The Glory of the Lord* titled 'Transcendentality and Form', in which he explains, 'No metaphysics of being qua being and of its transcendental determinations is separable from concrete experience, which is always sensuous…Here, where it is always the totality of being that presents itself…the concept of *form* is appropriate.'[24] Being is made available to the senses as beauty. And yet, when beauty appears, it does not do so as a disorderly mass. Instead, a key principle of beauty is that it appears in an organized fashion in a distinct form.

This principle of organization receives extensive attention from Balthasar. He holds that, in witnessing the form, one is always beholding something more than the outward visage alone. The form also exhibits an inner coherence that makes it a discrete entity. Form, then, has two distinct components in Balthasar's aesthetics: the materially manifested form, which is visible and concrete, and that which is doing the form-ing, so to speak, which is 'invisible'.[25]

Michael Waldstein has observed that Balthasar develops this understanding of form through a creative appropriation of ideas from Goethe, Aristotle, and the scholastic tradition.[26] Goethe plays something of a heroic role to Balthasar for his resistance to the mechanistic view of nature ascendant in the eighteenth century, as had been championed by Newton and was being perpetuated by Kant.[27] This mechanistic view, to

---

[24] *GL* IV, 28–9.   [25] *GL* I, 151.

[26] Michael Waldstein, 'Expression and Form: Principles of a Philosophical Aesthetics according to Hans Urs von Balthasar' (doctoral dissertation, University of Dallas, 1981); 'An Introduction to von Balthasar's *The Glory of the Lord*', *Communio* 14 (Spring 1987), 12–33.

[27] *GL* V, 363. Balthasar devotes a substantial portion of his aesthetics to Goethe (*GL* V, 339–408), and his debt to Goethe is well known. In a frequently cited interview from late in his career, Balthasar famously contrasts his theology to that of Rahner,

Goethe, misses the fact that living forms are constituted such that they are more than the aggregate of their components. Goethe criticizes such an 'analytic' understanding as follows: 'These analytic attempts…result also in a defect. The living can be divided into elements, but one cannot compose and enliven it again from them.'[28] Living forms, then, possess a unity that resists any attempt to divide those forms into their individual ingredients. With division would come the death of the living form. As Goethe further develops this idea:

> I can certainly put together the individual parts of a machine made of separate pieces and in the case of such an object I can speak of composition. But I cannot speak of composition when I am thinking about the single parts of an organic whole which form themselves in living fashion and are permeated by one soul.[29]

Goethe's morphology, then, could be said to recognize the significance of a *whole*, of a productive unity in the form that transcends its components. According to Waldstein, Goethe's understanding of form 'is able to see a principle of unity that is *interior*. It is able to see a principle of unity that does not lie in the same plane, so to speak, as the parts which it unites, but is superior to them in dominating them from within.'[30]

This understanding of form has obvious affinities with Balthasar's concept of form as described briefly above. In fact, after explicitly referring to Goethe in the section of his aesthetics previously mentioned ('Transcendentality and Form'),[31] Balthasar describes form as having a 'transcendent centre' that unites its different components, joining them in a distinct whole.[32] This centre is something more than

---

and he uses Goethe's notion of form as the key point of distinction within his own approach: 'Rahner has chosen Kant, or, if you prefer, Fichte: the transcendental starting point. And I—as a Germanist—have chosen Goethe, [who stressed] the form (*Gestalt*), the indissolubly unique, organic, developing form (*Gestalt*)—I am thinking of Goethe's poem *Die Metamorphose der Pflanzen*—this form (*Gestalt*) [is] something that Kant, even in his aesthetics, never really dealt with'. Hans Urs von Balthasar, 'Geist und Feuer', *Herder Korrespondenz* 30 (1976), 75. English translation in Edward T. Oakes, SJ, *Pattern of Redemption* (New York: Continuum, 1994), 72–3.

[28] Johann Wolfgang von Goethe, 'Die Absicht eingeleitet', in Ferdinand Weinhandl, *Das Vermächtnis des Wanderers* (Klosterneuberg: Stifterbibliothek, 1956), 19. Waldstein, 'Expression and Form', 81.

[29] Johann Wolfgang von Goethe, *Gespräche mit Eckerman* (Berlin: Knaur, 1924), Part III, June 20, 1831, 513. Waldstein, 'Expression and Form', 82.

[30] Waldstein, 'Expression and Form', 81–2.   [31] *GL* IV, 30.
[32] *GL* IV, 30.

the individual parts. And, although this 'more' is not obviously visible to the (bodily) senses, the centre is nevertheless fully a part of the form. Indeed, without it, one would not have a form in the first place. Waldstein further explains that, for Goethe, this principle of unity actually dominates to varying degrees depending on the quality of the form in question. On this point Goethe maintains, 'The subordination of parts points to a more perfect creature.'[33] In other words, the greater the degree of dominance, the 'higher' the form. A stone (to use one of the examples Waldstein mentions to illustrate this point) does not exhibit a terribly high degree of organization or subordination of its parts. Its shape is simply imposed from without, and it has no noteworthy inner principle of unity.[34] The stone is therefore relegated to a low position in the hierarchy of forms. The stone need not be shaped in any particular way. A plant, by contrast, 'has a form that is governed from within. It puts forth members, keeps them in a certain order of function with each other, and moves them all in harmonious fashion.'[35] Animals are governed even more thoroughly from within, as a greater diversity of parts is overcome in the unity of the animal. They therefore score higher still. Human beings, as yet more diverse and yet more self-governed, rank above animals.[36] The principle of unity in humans is therefore the most dominant.

Balthasar endorses Goethe's idea that a hierarchy of forms can be found in the world: 'Every really existing thing that meets us takes on form in analogous degrees and the "height of the form" is judged according to the greater power of the unity to gather together equal varieties.'[37] In fact, this notion of hierarchy is an important ingredient

---

[33] Goethe, 'Morphologie', in Ferdinand Weinhandl, *Die Metaphysik Goethes* (Darmstadt: Wissenschaftliche Buchgesellschaft, 1965), 100. Waldstein, 'Expression and Form', 82.

[34] Waldstein, 'Expression and Form', 83. Waldstein uses the idea of a heap of sand as another example that falls at the low end of the scale. Such a haphazard collection of individual parts (the grains of sand) does not demonstrate any particular relation among those parts. There is arguably no principle of inner unity at all.

[35] Waldstein, 'Expression and Form', 83.

[36] Waldstein, 'Expression and Form', 84.

[37] *GL* IV, 31. Waldstein also indicates the significance of Christian von Ehrenfels for Balthasar concerning this notion of hierarchy. Ehrenfels is typically acknowledged as one of the intellectual forerunners and founders of 'Gestalt psychology'. For his discussion of form, see his 'Weiterfuehrende Bemerkungen', in *Gestalthaftes Sehen: Ergebnisse und Aufgaben der Morphologie*, ed. Ferdinand Weinhandl (Darmstadt: Wissenschaftliche Buchgesellschaft, 1974), 50–1. Balthasar mentions Ehrenfels briefly in *GL* IV, 28–32.

in Balthasar's own efforts at resisting the 'mechanistic' view of the world used as our foil above. This mechanism, on Balthasar's reckoning, attempts to 'dissolve all phenomena horizontally-quantitatively, in order to make them approximately intelligible and reconstructable'.[38] Whereas Goethe's morphology is able to account for this hierarchy and develop its significance, the mechanistic view of the world, by contrast, flattens any notion of a given, objective structure to the world. It looks to disassemble and reassemble at will.

As significant as Goethe is for Balthasar's notion of form, Balthasar takes Goethe's idea one step further, as noted by Peter Legnowski.[39] Specifically, Balthasar maintains that as one views higher forms in the world, the transcendent centre of the form exposes one to the very depths of being. As Balthasar puts this point, 'The higher and purer a form, the more will light shine forth from its depths and the more will it point to the mystery of the light of being as a whole.'[40] For Balthasar, then (unlike Goethe), form is an ontological concept; it describes the structure of reality at its very deepest level. As Legnowski puts this point, 'From an idea of the understanding (*Erkenntnisbegriff*) in Goethe's morphology, the form becomes an idea for ontology according to Balthasar.' [41] This transition is crucial to Balthasar's project. Indeed, it is for this reason that we can speak of beauty as a transcendental in the first place, as form does not simply reveal *a being*, as discussed above. Instead, through the form one is exposed to the depths of being itself.

In addition to Goethe, Balthasar also draws upon Aristotle's model of the relationship between form (εἶδος) and matter. Form for Aristotle is that which combines with matter in a particular thing. Form, on this understanding, gives structure to 'prime matter'.[42] Form

---

[38] Balthasar, *In the Fullness of Faith: On the Centrality of the Distinctively Catholic* (San Francisco, CA: Ignatius Press, 1988), 14. Originally published in German as *Katholisch: Aspekte des Mysteriums* (Einsiedeln: Johannes Verlag, 1975), 8. Quoted in Waldstein, 'Expression and Form', 85.

[39] Peter Legnowski, 'Die letzte "säkulare Verwirklichung der Herrlichkeit": Zur Goetherezeption Hans Urs von Balthasars', in *Logik der Liebe und Herrlichkeit Gottes: Hans Urs von Balthasar im Gespräch*, ed. Walter Kasper (Ostfildern: Matthias-Grünewald-Verlag, 2006), 134–45.

[40] *GL* IV, 31.

[41] Peter Legnowski, 'Die letzte "säkulare Verwirklichung der Herrlichkeit"', 144 (my translation).

[42] *Metaphysics* VII, 2 (1028b 8–33). Sir David Ross helpfully indicates the range of meanings associated with the term 'form' for Aristotle. ' "Form" for Aristotle embraces a variety of meanings. Sometimes it is used of sensible shape, as when the sculptor is

can therefore be considered a principle of inner organization similar to that described by Balthasar. According to Waldstein, Aristotle also holds a hierarchical understanding of form similar to that developed above. As Waldstein characterizes Aristotle on this point, 'The greater the power of a form, the more the dispersion of matter is overcome. At the same time however, the greater the power of a form, the more such a form is spiritual and removed from matter.'[43] Although Waldstein does not go into greater depth on this topic, scholars of Aristotle will confirm his claims. Sir David Ross, for example, notes that among living things, to Aristotle, the least complex forms are found in tissues, which provide material to create organs, which in turn furnish more complex material for complete living entities. Among these living entities, human beings are the most 'formed', since to them is 'superadded a form [the soul] which is not the principle of structure of the body or of any part of it, uses no bodily organ, and can survive the body'.[44] Above humans are 'the intelligences that move the heavenly spheres', and 'highest of all is the pure substance which is God'.[45]

Many aspects of this Aristotelian view are taken up by medieval figures such as Thomas Aquinas, for whom *forma* performs a similar function as that which brings together diverse components.[46] And, as is true for Aristotle, Aquinas also holds that the power of form increases with its ability to overcome disparate elements. Waldstein draws his reader's attention to a portion of the *Summa Theologiae* in which Aquinas makes this point explicitly: 'To the extent to which a form is nobler, it dominates bodily matter more, is less immersed in it and exceeds it more in its operation and power.... The more one proceeds in the nobility of forms, the more one finds that the power of the form exceeds elementary matter.'[47] According to Waldstein's reading, Goethe, Aristotle, and Aquinas all advance understandings of form as the inner principle that gives structure to things in the world, and they all understand forms as hierarchically arranged.

---

said to impose a new form on his material. But more often, perhaps, it is thought of as something which is an object of thought rather than of sense, as the inner nature of a thing...On the whole, μορφή points to sensible shape and εἶδος to intelligible structure, and the latter is the main element in Aristotle's notion of form.' *Aristotle* (London: Methuen, 1964), 74.

[43] Waldstein, 'Expression and Form', 86. Waldstein refers the reader to Aristotle's *Physics* I.7; *De Anima* III; *Metaphysics* XII.
[44] Ross, *Aristotle*, 169.   [45] Ross, *Aristotle*, 169.
[46] Waldstein, 'Expression and Form', 86. *SCG*, II, 54, 6.
[47] Waldstein, 'Expression and Form', 86. *ST* I, 76, 1, c.

Although D. C. Schindler is broadly appreciative of Waldstein's reading of Balthasar, he offers an important corrective to it. Specifically, Schindler holds that Waldstein emphasizes the 'transcendent centre' of the form at the cost of the 'immanence of that center in its parts'.[48] According to Schindler, Balthasar does not simply hold that form is the inner principle of unity that brings together distinct components. Instead, Balthasar also emphasizes that this transcendence actually works its way into the material constituents of the form. As Schindler expresses this point, 'Gestalt is itself a whole, which is distinct from a principle of unity, even if it includes such a principle as one of its essential elements.'[49] As this whole, the form can never be reduced to its transcendent centre.

According to this reading, Balthasar does not by form mean only εἶδος, as the inner principle that joins with matter in a particular substance. Instead, by form he also means Aristotle's μορφή, as the outwardly visible shape of a thing.[50] Or, to use scholastic terminology on this topic (in which *forma* is used in the opposite sense from that above),[51] Balthasar means by form both *forma* and *splendor*, both the exterior, concrete shape and the inner light that shines forth from within that shape.[52]

---

[48] Schindler, *Hans Urs von Balthasar and the Dramatic Structure of Truth* (New York: Fordham University Press, 2004), 171.
[49] Schindler, *Hans Urs von Balthasar and the Dramatic Structure of Truth*, 172.
[50] At one point in his reading of Goethe's 'The Metamorphosis of Animals', Balthasar claims that the author is interested primarily in the μορφή. According to Balthasar, the text 'is completely dedicated to the immanent natural order; it is concerned not with the εἶδος but also with the μορφή, with how life takes shape under necessary and wonderful limitations'. *GL* V, 367.
[51] Eco helpfully notes the two distinct meanings of the term *forma* for Aquinas. 'Aquinas' idea of form is the same as Aristotle's "entelechy"—that is, a structural principle in things... A somewhat different meaning of the word *form* in Aquinas is that of "shape", or *morphê (figura)*. Form in this sense is a property, namely the quantitative boundary of a body, an external feature which can be empirically experienced'. Eco, *The Aesthetics of Thomas Aquinas*, 69.
[52] Thomas Aquinas is frequently cited as a source for this distinction between *forma* and *splendor* (or, alternatively, *species* and *lumen*), but on this point the thought of Albert the Great should also be considered to be of utmost importance. Albert regards beauty as 'the splendour of substantial or actual form in the proportioned and bounded parts of matter' (*splendor formae substantialis vel actualis supra partes materiae proportionatas et terminatas*). *De Pulchro et de Bono*. The text was first discovered in 1869 and was attributed for many years to Aquinas. It is in fact a *reportatio* of Albert's lectures written in Aquinas' hand. The accompanying confusion caused it to be included in Aquinas' *Opera Omnia*, ed. Roberto Busa, SJ (Stuttgart-Bad Cannstatt: Frommann-Holzboog, 1980), vol. VII, 43–7. Albert's notion of the *splendor*

Balthasar's texts support Schindler's characterization. Throughout his aesthetics, and in many other works, too, Balthasar repeatedly emphasizes the importance of the concrete in mediating being to the human observer. In his *Theo-Logic*, for example, he explains, 'Beauty…is the inexplicable active irradiation of the centre of being into the expressive surface of the image, an irradiation that reflects itself in the image and confers upon it a unity, fullness, and depth surpassing what the image as such contains.'[53] In his aesthetics, too, Balthasar repeatedly makes this idea clear:

> Visible form not only 'points' to an invisible, unfathomable mystery; form is the apparition of this mystery, and reveals it while, naturally, at the same time protecting and veiling it. Both natural and artistic form have an exterior which appears and an interior depth, both of which, however, are not separable in the form itself. The content (*Gehalt*) does not lie behind the form (*Gestalt*), but within it.[54]

The materiality of the form does not in any way compromise or diminish the beauty that shines through it. To Balthasar, the form is understood not as a mere physical signifier for a spiritual content or meaning that lies beyond it. Instead, form carries 'within itself', as it were, the content that it communicates.

In fact, Balthasar holds that, if we think of *forma* (or *species*) and *splendor* (or *lumen*) as at all separable from each other, then '[w]e still remain within a parallelism of ostensive sign and signified interior light. This dualism can be abolished only by introducing as well the thought-forms and categories of the beautiful. The beautiful is above all a form, and the light does not fall on this form from above and from outside, rather it breaks forth from the form's interior. *Species* and *lumen* in beauty are one.'[55] As intimated in Schindler's comments, Balthasar holds a deeply non-dualist understanding of form. As he further expounds on the extent of this unity:

> The appearance of the form, as revelation of the depths, is an indissoluble union of two things. It is the real presence of the depths, of the whole of reality, *and* it is a real pointing beyond itself to these depths…both aspects are inseparable from one another, and together

formae succinctly captures much of what Balthasar attempts to convey in his discussion of form. Balthasar refers to this phrase in *GL* IV, 31, 386.

[53] *TL* I, 142. The first volume of Balthasar's *Theo-Logic* was initially published as *Wahrheit: Ein Versuch* (Einsiedeln: Verlagsanstalt Benziger, 1947).

[54] *GL* I, 151 (translation emended).   [55] *GL* I, 151.

they constitute the fundamental configuration of Being. We 'behold' the form; but, if we really behold it, it is not as a detached form, rather in its unity with the depths that make their appearance in it. We see form as the splendour, as the glory of Being. We are 'enraptured' by our contemplation of these depths and are 'transported' to them. But, so long as we are dealing with the beautiful, this never happens in such a way that we leave the (horizontal) form behind us in order to plunge (vertically) into the naked depths.[56]

Balthasar, then, clearly states that the depths shown by the form cannot be separated from the form through which they are revealed. Rather, the luminosity of being remains inextricably intertwined with the particular, concrete form through which it shines.

An instructive parallel can be drawn between, on the one hand, Balthasar's notion of form as a fundamental unity of *forma* and *splendor*, and, on the other hand, as we saw in Chapter 3, his notion of the human being as one who is indivisibly conjoined in body and soul as a 'unity-in-duality'. In his anthropology Balthasar maintains that one cannot think of 'soul' alone, but rather one must always regard soul as 'soul-of-one's-body'. Similarly, his theory of aesthetics does not allow *splendor* to be detached from its material form. Rather, one must always understand *splendor* as 'splendour-of-a-form'. The light of being, for Balthasar, is always interwoven with its material medium of expression.

This point demonstrates that Balthasar does not simply replicate scholastic thought in his understanding of form. Instead, as Schindler notes, whereas Aquinas thinks of form as a finite limitation, Balthasar regards form as capable of revealing the infinite in the very midst of its finite materiality. 'Balthasar's notion of Gestalt...differs in a profoundly significant sense from the Thomistic and Neoplatonic notion of form precisely by the fact that it is *not* simply finite, but is rather the mysterious "intersection" of finitude and infinity.'[57] In other words, a key consequence of Balthasar's intertwining of material and immaterial components of the form is that the infinite (ordinarily the province of form's immaterial aspect) actually makes its way into the material dimension of the form.

To the helpful explanations offered by Waldstein and Schindler I add one important point. Specifically, I argue that the 'transcendent'

---

[56] GL I, 118–19.
[57] Schindler, *Hans Urs von Balthasar and the Dramatic Structure of Truth*, 173.

portion of the form, according to Balthasar, functions not only as an organizing principle that brings together the form's disparate components. Instead, the transcendent dimension of form is itself also *shown*. Being appears, and when it does so, it appears not only through the concrete aspect of the form. Being also shines forth through the form's transcendent, 'spiritual' component. This crucial feature of Balthasar's thought tends to be underemphasized among commentators on his texts. Waldstein, for instance, attempts to account for it by claiming that Balthasar employs various 'metaphors' to convey his meaning: 'Balthasar uses the metaphor of light…when he says that the depth shines up in a form.'[58] Much depends, of course, on what exactly Waldstein means by 'metaphor' (he does not explain how he is using the term), but there is good reason to resist characterizing Balthasar's use of sensory language as simply metaphorical in character. Instead, on numerous occasions Balthasar indicates that an actual—albeit 'invisible' and 'spiritual'—light shines forth to the human being as he or she witnesses the form.

Balthasar in fact goes to great lengths to make this point. We recall from Chapter 3 our treatment of Romano Guardini, whom Balthasar quotes with approval on this very point: 'This spiritual element [of the form] is not subsequently added to the sensory datum, for instance by the work of the intellect; it is grasped by the eye at once, even if indeterminately and imperfectly at first.'[59] Balthasar summarizes this portion of Guardini's thought with the following assertion: 'The eye *sees* the vitality of the animal. In man, it *sees* (and does not "infer") the soul in its gestures, expressions and actions; indeed it sees the soul even before the body, and the body only in the soul.'[60] In no uncertain terms, then, Balthasar uses Guardini to develop a spiritual dimension to form that is—in spite of its incorporeality—nevertheless perceived.

Balthasar again makes this same idea clear a few pages later in his aesthetics: 'In order to read even a form within the world, we must see something invisible as well, *and we do in fact see it*.'[61] It is difficult to imagine a more straightforward expression of the idea that the invisible aspect of the form makes itself known to the senses. In a similar

---

[58] Waldstein, 'Expression and Form', 91. For other instances in which Waldstein discusses Balthasar's 'metaphor' of light, see 87–92.
[59] Romano Guardini, *Die Sinne und die religiöse Erkenntnis: Zwei Versuche über die christliche Vergewisserung* (Würzburg: Werkbund Verlag, 1950), 19. GL I, 391.
[60] GL I, 391.   [61] GL I, 444 (emphasis added).

manner, elsewhere in his aesthetics Balthasar discusses a 'light' within the form that must be 'seen'. He holds, 'For this particular perception of truth, of course, a "new light" is expressly required which illumines this particular form, a light which at the same time breaks forth from within the form itself. In this way, the "new light" will at the same time make seeing the form possible and *be itself seen along with the form*.'[62] Given what we have discovered about Balthasar's understanding of form, we can see that this 'new light' corresponds to the light of being that shines forth as the invisible splendour of the form. And, most importantly for our purposes, this light must itself be perceived.[63]

In a moment we shall examine more thoroughly the role played by perception in Balthasar's aesthetics. At present, however, we turn to the particular features of the central form on which his aesthetics ultimately focuses: namely, the form of Christ. This aspect of Balthasar's thought is well documented among his commentators, and we can therefore move quickly through a number of important themes. Succinctly put, if the form reveals being, and 'higher' forms have greater revelatory capacities, as we have seen, then Jesus Christ, who is the ultimate or 'super-form' (*Übergestalt*), manifests *absolute* being.[64] Balthasar's much-celebrated Christocentrism shows itself in this claim.[65] Furthermore, given

---

[62] *GL* I, 120 (emphasis added). The passage continues, 'The *splendour* of the mystery which offers itself in such a way cannot, for this reason, be equated with the other kinds of aesthetic radiance which we encounter in the world. This does not mean, however, that the mysterious *splendour* and this aesthetic radiance are beyond any and every comparison. That we are at all able to speak here of "seeing"...shows that, in spite of all concealment, there *is* nonetheless something to be seen and grasped.' *GL* I, 120–1.

[63] Additional examples may be adduced in support of this point. For instance, in a passage from the first volume of his *Theo-Logic* that describes the relation between the form (which is simply described as the 'object' here) and the viewer of the form (the subject), Balthasar holds, 'Just as, on the side of the object, the boundary between the immanent measure of the *morphe* and the transcendent measure of the idea [*Idee*] can never be drawn too sharply, so, too, on the side of the subject, there can be no definite separation between the *two modes of vision*'. *TL* I, 60 (emphasis added). In this early work, then, Balthasar has begun to develop a notion of vision that sees not only the *morphe*, the outward shape, but also the transcendent aspect that lies within the object.

[64] *GL* I, 432. Balthasar reads John's gospel in a manner consistent with this view: '[F]or John the divine glory appears "in the flesh" within one individual, absolutely privileged, finite form...in this form absolute Being itself makes its appearance'. *GL* I, 233.

[65] It is especially on this point that Balthasar can be said to be performing a Catholic version of Karl Barth's *Church Dogmatics*. Barth's Christocentric approach to theology is well known, and Balthasar draws on this aspect of his thought in his own theology.

beauty's transcendental status, according to which beauty is convertible with being, Balthasar can uphold the notion that Christ is absolute beauty.[66] Christ is 'most beautiful splendour' (*splendor pulcherrimus*), as Bonaventure puts it.[67] This absolute beauty, or 'glory' (*kabod*, δόξα), according to Balthasar's usage, bears an analogical relationship with all other beauty, which is relative to the absolute. The beauty of Christ thus exceeds all worldly beauty while also serving as the standard by which such beauty is measured.

Particularly relevant to our theme is Balthasar's notion that the glory of Christ serves as the 'splendour' of his form. For example, as is true for the splendour of the form, the glory of Christ 'shines' to the human being. Balthasar holds that 'the knowledge of the glory of God shines forth from the face of Christ'.[68] In fact, at many points Balthasar directly equates Christ's glory with splendour. For instance, he claims, 'The Bible calls Christ the "splendour, the luminous image of God's glory."'[69] Furthermore, as we saw in Balthasar's treatment of splendour above, this glory is 'invisible', and yet it is nevertheless shown to the human observer. Balthasar develops this idea in a meditation on Romans 1:19 in which he claims, 'This divinity of the Invisible, which radiates in the visibleness of Being of the world, is then immediately called "glory" (*Herrlichkeit*).'[70] Last, just as the splendour of the form is intertwined with the form's material component, so too is Christ's glory inextricably linked to his physical form. '[T]he glory of Christ unites splendour and radiance with solid reality, as we see pre-eminently in the Resurrection.'[71] Christ's glory is not separable from his form.

Balthasar differs from Barth, however, in that he is willing to countenance an analogy of being (and beauty, for that matter) to describe the relationship between God and the world.

[66] 'As the incarnate art of God (*ars divina*), he is the appearing of absolute beauty'. *GL* II, 347.
[67] *Hexaemeron* 21, 1. *Opera Omnia* V, 431a. *GL* II, 347.
[68] *GL* I, 437. Cf. 2 Cor. 3:18–4:6.
[69] *GL* I, 87. Similarly, Balthasar draws from 2 Corinthians in claiming, '[F]or Paul, "Son of God" *a fortiori* always means the Incarnate Word in whose light and glory God's Trinitarian fullness becomes present and fills redeemed creation with its glory. The "image," the "splendour" to which "we look in order to be transformed into the same image, from splendour to splendour," radiates from the Incarnate Lord'. *GL* I, 437.
[70] *GL* I, 431.   [71] *GL* I, 124.

More could be said about Balthasar's theory of form.[72] For our purposes, however, the most significant points to observe are, first, the fact that the form is the medium through which the beauty of being and the glory of Christ are manifested to the human being, and, second, the manner in which the invisible splendour of the form (its 'transcendent centre') is in fact *shown* to the human observer. It is with these two points in mind that we turn to Balthasar's treatment of perception.

BEAUTY IS 'SEEN': ON THE IMPORTANCE OF PERCEPTION (*WAHR-NEHMUNG*)

Balthasar reads—and subtly reinterprets—the history of metaphysics in such a way that perception occupies a central position. Specifically, if the beauty of being is mediated to the human observer through the form, and if both the sensory and supersensory components of the form give themselves to be seen, then perceiving this form in its totality stands out as an absolutely essential task for Balthasar's theological aesthetics. Balthasar himself indicates that perception is central to his project: 'A "theological aesthetics"...has as its object primarily the perception of the divine self-manifestation.'[73] And yet, as we have seen above, this notion of perception is distinct from the status granted the category in medieval thought, and, we might add, much modern philosophy. Balthasar here demonstrates his resistance to, for instance, a Kantian division of reality into a phenomenal realm that can be perceived and a noumenal realm that is wholly inaccessible to the senses.[74] Instead, Balthasar has in mind a more robust idea of what it means to perceive: 'One must possess a spiritual eye capable of perceiving (*wahrnehmen*) the forms of existence with

---

[72] Much attention is paid, for instance, to the 'polarity' and 'tension' between the material and immaterial aspects of the form. See Waldstein, 'Expression and Form', 98–108. Most important, perhaps (although beyond the scope of this inquiry), is the fact that, for Balthasar, forms are situated in time and therefore have an inextricably dramatic component. See Schindler, *Hans Urs von Balthasar and the Dramatic Structure of Truth*, 12–27.

[73] *GL* I, Foreword.

[74] For an extended engagement with the philosophy of Kant in Balthasar, see *GL* V, 481–513.

awe. (What a word: "Perception" [*Wahr-nehmung*]! And philosophy has twisted it to mean precisely the opposite of what it says: "the seeing of what is true"!)'[75] Balthasar echoes this reframing of perception later in his aesthetics: 'The all-encompassing act that contains within itself the hearing and the believing is a *perception* (*Wahrnehmung*), in the strong sense of a "taking to oneself" (*nehmen*) of something true (*Wahres*) which is offering itself.'[76] Balthasar, then, elevates the category of perception from its frequently subordinate position as a limited epistemological faculty, and he places it instead at the very heart of the human being's engagement with reality.

Importantly, too, according to Balthasar's anthropology of unity-in-duality, the human being is indivisibly united in body and soul, and therefore he or she is *unavoidably* a 'percipient being'. That is, Balthasar (in conversation with his modern interlocutors, as shown in Chapter 3) develops an understanding of the human person as a 'corporeal-psychic totality'.[77] On this view, the human being is not 'truly' a soul or a mind who happens to have a body that is ultimately extraneous; nor is he or she in essence a body that happens to have a 'mind' as a mere by-product of physiological processes. Instead, according to Balthasar, the human being is fundamentally united in body and soul. One consequence of this view is that the activities of thinking and perceiving (or, having 'awareness') cannot be sharply divided into separate functions. Quoting Barth with approval, Balthasar insists, 'It is "certainly not only my body, but also my soul which has awareness, and it is certainly not only my soul but also my body which thinks".'[78] In other words, for Balthasar, the unity of the human being requires that neither thought nor perception can occur through only one aspect of the human person. There is thus no realm of 'pure thought' on Balthasar's model. There is no aspect of the human being—not even the soul in its innermost reflections—that is not directed outward toward the body and, more generally, the world.

For Balthasar, then, all thought involves a corporeal dimension, and, importantly for the argument that he makes for valuing perception as an epistemological faculty, the human person in his or her most fundamental nature is percipient. Schindler clarifies the meaning of such claims in relation to the corresponding Thomist position. Although Thomism holds that the 'first act' of the mind is

---

[75] *GL* I, 24.   [76] *GL* I, 120.   [77] *GL* I, 385.
[78] *GL* I, 386. *CD* III/2, 400.

the formation of concepts, for Balthasar 'the first act of the mind occurs only in relation to the first act of the concrete being that stands before the mind.... Thus, Balthasar begins his epistemology with an entry into the revelatory character of everything that exists.'[79] Perception simply *must* be valued highly. There is nothing more basic to who we are and what we do.

PERCEIVING SPLENDOUR: THE ROLE OF THE SPIRITUAL SENSES

Given the terms that Balthasar has set for his theological aesthetics, the significance of the spiritual senses should now be coming into view. The form (*Gestalt*) consists of both sensory and supersensory dimensions (both visible and 'invisible' aspects), and this supersensory component— even though it is invisible—*appears*. Balthasar attempts to rehabilitate perception for his theological aesthetics, but corporeal perception alone clearly will not suffice for the task he has given himself. Instead, as he puts it, 'eyes are needed that are able to perceive the spiritual form.'[80] In order for the supersensory 'splendour' of the form to be perceived, a notion of perception that exceeds the corporeal realm must be developed. It is precisely here that Balthasar makes his appeal to the doctrine of the spiritual senses.[81] He describes the need for a 'spiritualization' of the perceptual faculties of the human being: 'In Christianity God appears to man right in the midst of worldly reality. The centre of this act of encounter must, therefore, lie where the profane human senses, making possible the act of faith, become "spiritual".'[82] Human perception requires

---

[79] Schindler, *Hans Urs von Balthasar and the Dramatic Structure of Truth*, 175–6. Balthasar contrasts Bonaventure with Aquinas on this point, although Balthasar himself goes further than Bonaventure, as discussed above, concerning what is disclosed to the human being through perception: 'Bonaventure (in contrast to Thomas, who above all marvels at the power of abstraction possessed by the *intellectus agens* in the subject, and makes this the object of his research) is occupied entirely with the mystery of the objective self-disclosure of things'. *GL* II, 346.

[80] *GL* I, 24.

[81] Balthasar titles as 'The Spiritual Senses' the concluding, sixty-page portion of 'The Subjective Evidence' (i.e., the first half of volume I of *The Glory of the Lord*), thus gesturing toward its significance as the final word on the theological anthropology he develops in that volume. See *GL* I, 365–425.

[82] *GL* I, 365.

a transformation if the subjective conditions for the receipt of revelation are to be fulfilled. As Balthasar memorably captures this transition, 'Our senses, together with images and thoughts, must...rise unto the Father in an unspeakable manner that is both sensory and suprasensory.'[83] The spiritual senses, then, lie at the very centre of the encounter between the human being and God in Balthasar's thought.

One finds textual evidence for the importance of the spiritual senses throughout Balthasar's aesthetics. In the volumes treating the history of metaphysics (4 and 5), Balthasar speaks of the moment at which, 'for the religious person, Being becomes theophanous... "spiritual (*geistliche*) senses" make him capable of hearing and of seeing the mystery of Being as a whole.'[84] We also see in one notable case that Balthasar's reference to the spiritual senses has been somewhat obscured by the English translation of the aesthetics. In an important passage from 'Transcendentality and Form' in volume 4, Balthasar describes the 'apprehension' of forms as follows: 'All the forms that can be apprehended spiritually [*alle geistig erblickbaren Gestalten*] refer over above themselves to the full and perfect being...the light which shines forth from the form and reveals it to the understanding is accordingly inseparably light of the form itself (Scholasticism speaks therefore of *splendor formae*) and light of being as a whole.'[85] The translators of this volume of the aesthetics have chosen to render the German *erblickbar* (an adjectival form of the verb *erblicken*) with the English term 'apprehended'. This is certainly a reasonable choice, but an equally viable alternative that better preserves the perceptual dimension of Balthasar's meaning could simply be 'seen'.[86] The passage in question can therefore read: 'All the forms that can be *spiritually seen* refer over above themselves to the full and perfect being.' Such a translation more clearly communicates the centrality of the spiritual senses to Balthasar's thought. Moreover, with this translation issue resolved, we can see that it is precisely the *splendor formae* which gives itself to be spiritually seen.

Concerning the glory of God, the importance of the spiritual senses becomes even clearer. In volume 6 of his aesthetics, in which the 'Old Covenant' is examined, Balthasar flatly declares (quoting David Neuhaus) that normal human vision cannot see God's glory: ' "The

---

[83] *GL* I, 425.   [84] *GL* V, 608.   [85] *GL* IV, 31 (translation emended).
[86] The German *erblicken* is typically translated as 'to behold', 'to catch a glimpse', 'to catch sight of', or 'to see'.

natural eye does not see the *kabod* [i.e., glory]. In order to perceive it, in the natural eye there must emerge the supernatural glance."[87] In the introduction to volume 7, in which the 'New Covenant' is treated at length, Balthasar prepares his reader for the task before him or her: 'But here most of all do we need the "vision of the form" with the "eyes of faith" (Augustine), the *oculata fides* ("faith that has eyes", Thomas Aquinas), the "enlightened eyes of the heart" (Eph. 1.18), because only a "simple eye" (Mt 6.22 par.) is able to perceive something of the simplicity achieved by all multiplicity in the final form of revelation.'[88] In another reference to the form of Christ, Balthasar straightforwardly states, 'This form is unique, not graspable by worldly vision, evident only to the eyes of faith.'[89] For all of Christ's resplendence, his glory is easily missed. Indeed, natural vision alone will not suffice. One must perceive *spiritually* if Christ is to be seen for who he is.

Additional phrases associated with the spiritual senses tradition permeate the aesthetics, including of course 'spiritual senses',[90] 'spiritual perception',[91] and 'inner senses'.[92] One also finds repeated references to senses of sight, hearing, touch, taste, and smell that are clearly described in an extra-corporeal, 'spiritual' register.[93] Balthasar's

---

[87] *GL* VI, 35. Neuhaus, 92.

[88] *GL* VII, 14. In similar fashion, Balthasar holds, 'The measure which Christ represents and embodies is qualitatively different from every other measure. This fact need not be deduced; it may be read off the phenomenon itself. To be sure, for this an "eye for quality" is required...In a certain sense such an "eye" may be acquired (Heb. 5.14), but in essence it must be bestowed along with the phenomenon itself'. *GL* I, 481. The reference to Hebrews 5:14 is significant; this biblical passage is one of the two upon which Origen most directly relies for his development of the spiritual senses.

[89] *GL* I, 480. Balthasar also refers to the Christmas preface, which reads, 'Because through the mystery of the incarnate Word the new light of your brightness has shone onto the *eyes of our mind*; that knowing God visibly, we might be snatched up by this into the love of invisible things'. *GL* I, 119–20 (emphasis added).

[90] *GL* I, 249, 365–425, 461; *GL* II, 79, 260, 319–36; *GL* IV, 359; *GL* V, 89, 298.

[91] *GL* I, 153, 238, 267, 362; *GL* II, 164; *GL* IV, 361.

[92] *GL* II, 318, 322; *GL* IV, 353.

[93] The phrase 'eye(s) of the soul' (one of the most prevalent terms in the spiritual senses tradition) can be found at *GL* I, 285, 391; *GL* II, 171; *GL* III, 16; *GL* IV, 394. 'Eye(s) of the heart': *GL* II, 275; *GL* III, 180; *GL* VII, 14, 358. 'Eye(s) of the spirit': *GL* I, 200, 264; *GL* II, 291; *GL* VII, 294. 'Eye of the mind': *GL* II, 99, 107. 'Eyes of faith': *GL* I, 31, 70, 175, 190, 191, 198, 216, 236, 343, 458, 480, 487, 538, 546, 592, 643, 658; *GL* II, 325; *GL* III, 227, 233, 427; *GL* VI, 408; *GL* VII, 14, 18, 28, 89, 260, 328, 368, 493. 'Spiritual eyes': *GL* I, 30; *GL* II, 137; *GL* IV, 328. 'Spiritual sight': *GL* II, 205, 222. 'Spiritual vision': *GL* II, 142, 222. 'Spiritual seeing': *GL* II, 100, 101. 'Spiritual gaze': *GL* II, 291. 'Inner eye': *GL* I, 71, 500; *GL* II, 99; *GL* VI, 348. For references to 'seeing God', see *GL* I, 149, 248, 251, 260, 283, 327, 329, 336, 359, 368, 438, 462, 501, 606; *GL* II, 45, 46, 47, 75, 99, 108, 122, 138, 179, 204, 207; *GL* IV, 37, 66, 68; *GL* V, 82–3, 233; *GL* VI,

reliance on the spiritual senses can thus be demonstrated both systematically and exegetically. The spiritual senses are not simply one feature among many in Balthasar's aesthetics. Instead, they function as the indispensable means through which the human subject perceives the beauty of being and the glory of God.

CONCLUSION

The outset of this chapter insisted that it is through the spiritual senses that one performs the epistemologically central task of seeing the form. We are now sufficiently familiar with the terms used in Balthasar's aesthetics for a more precise formulation of this assertion: it has become clear that, whereas the corporeal senses perceive the material form, it is the spiritual senses that behold the splendour of being and the glory of Christ as revealed in the supersensory aspect of the form. Of course, it should immediately be said that Balthasar's theory of aesthetic form forbids a separation of the material from the invisible splendour that shines forth from it, and it should also be said that Balthasar's anthropology forbids a separation of the corporeal from the spiritual. In truth, then, both aspects of form are perceived in simultaneity by both the corporeal and the spiritual perceptual faculties in the human being. This formulation, however, is of service to us inasmuch as it allows us to put a finer point on the exact role of the spiritual senses in Balthasar's theological aesthetics.

Furthermore, this articulation enables us to see the necessity of a doctrine of the spiritual senses for the fulfilment of Balthasar's goals as he puts them forward in his aesthetics. Balthasar calls for perception of a form that contains both sensory and 'supersensory' aspects (i.e., a material component and a 'spiritual' dimension). Therefore, some account of the way in which this human perception exceeds the material realm is absolutely essential to the success of Balthasar's

---

68, 71, 72, 92, 149, 327; *GL* VII, 14, 25, 55, 287, 319, 483. For hearing, see especially 'ear(s) of the soul': *GL* I, 285; *GL* VII, 542. 'Ear of the heart': *GL* II, 326. 'Ear of the spirit': *GL* III, 135. 'Spiritual hearing': *GL* II, 321. Touch: *GL* I, 285, 307, 323, 362, 368, 369, 371, 376, 380, 397, 402; *GL* II, 319, 322, 324, 341; *GL* III, 112, 143, 457; *GL* IV, 359; *GL* VI, 131. Taste: *GL* I, 100, 289, 307, 425; *GL* II, 321, 347, 349; *GL* III, 257; *GL* V, 229; *GL* VII, 234, 371, 530. Smell: *GL* I, 289, 371, 386, 425; *GL* II, 218, 319, 322; *GL* IV, 359; *GL* VI, 131.

project. In other words, it is precisely because the form itself is possessed of both sensory and supersensory aspects that the *perception* of that form must be both sensory and supersensory. Balthasar's theological aesthetics thus actually requires a doctrine of the spiritual senses; without it, one cannot give a proper account of the reception of revelation in the human person.

It will be clear from the above analysis that Balthasar's countless uses of sensory images throughout his writings should now be read anew. A recurrent question for interpreters of Balthasar's theological aesthetics has been: just exactly *how* should his pervasive use of the language of sensation be understood? One is often tempted to think of Balthasar's dizzying array of sensory terms as purely figurative in character. We saw above that Michael Waldstein interprets Balthasar's various references to the senses—especially his use of the phrase 'the light of being'—as metaphorical. It is here that reference to the spiritual senses proves to be particularly helpful in advancing understandings of Balthasar's thought. Scholarship on the spiritual senses insists that the language of sensation is used in this tradition in a manner that is more than simply metaphorical, as noted in the introduction to this study. Balthasar, then, as one who positions himself in this tradition, should also be understood as frequently using such language in a non-metaphorical sense. Therefore, when Balthasar writes of 'seeing' the Christ-form or 'perceiving' the light of being that shines forth from the depths of the form, reference to the spiritual senses tradition cautions one from dismissing such language as merely figurative or metaphorical speech. Instead, in using sensory terms Balthasar does in fact describe an actual, 'spiritual' perception of the glory of Christ and the splendour of being.

With this understanding of the crucial role of the spiritual senses now established, we explore in the next chapter the far-reaching implications of this claim for Balthasar's fundamental theology and his model of nature and grace.

6

Seeing (Spiritually) Is Believing

The Spiritual Senses and Faith

The previous chapter argued that the spiritual senses are necessary for Balthasar to fulfil the goals he lays out in his theological aesthetics. According to this interpretation, if the human being is to perceive both the sensory and supersensory aspects of the form (both *forma* and *splendor*), then he or she must have not only corporeal perceptual faculties, but also spiritual senses. This chapter develops the far-reaching implications of this claim by spelling out just exactly what it means and why it matters for Balthasar's broader theological project. In order to do this, we shall examine the role the spiritual senses play for Balthasar's contributions to some of the most pressing theological debates of his day. Balthasar's disputes with Neo-Scholastic figures, Catholic 'Modernists', Karl Rahner, and even Karl Barth bring to the fore a number of important theological problems, each of which has to do with Christian faith and, ultimately, the relationship between nature and grace. We shall investigate Balthasar's engagement with these figures, looking in particular at his treatment of natural theology, fundamental theology (or apologetics), and the relationship between the natural and supernatural orders. I argue in what follows that the spiritual senses function as an indispensable component of Balthasar's proposed solutions to key problems that have been laid before modern theologians. Therefore, the treatment of the spiritual senses in this chapter offers ways of advancing theological discussion, not only for Balthasar scholarship, but, more broadly, for a recurrent set of challenges presented to modern theology. To the first of these debates we now turn.

SEEING GOD IN ALL THINGS: THE SPIRITUAL SENSES AND NATURAL THEOLOGY

Balthasar famously chafed against the Neo-Scholastic theology he was taught at the hands of the Jesuits in Pullach and Fourvière, and one of the many aspects of their thought he found lacking was their treatment of proofs for the existence of God.[1] Broadly speaking, Neo-Scholastic theologians hold that examination of the natural world can be used to establish God's existence. In a contested appropriation of Thomas Aquinas' so-called 'five ways', Neo-Scholastic figures claim that unaided reason (i.e., reason untouched by grace) finds in the world sufficient evidence for positing God's existence.[2] On this view, the existence of God can be demonstrated by reason alone.

Balthasar, however, holds such proofs to be utterly unpersuasive. This is, in part, because the very method by which they have been developed depends on a distinction between nature and grace that evacuates the grace from the natural order. This idea of a 'pure nature'

---

[1] The following is a frequently quoted passage from one of Balthasar's retrospectives: 'My entire period of study in the Society was a grim struggle with the dreariness of theology, with what men had made out of the glory of revelation. I could not endure this presentation of the Word of God'. Peter Henrici, SJ, 'A Sketch of von Balthasar's Life', in *Hans Urs von Balthasar: His Life and Work*, ed. David L. Schindler (San Francisco, CA: Ignatius Press, 1991), 7–43, at 13.

[2] See, perhaps most famously, the Neo-Scholastic distillation of Thomas Aquinas' thought known as the '24 Thomistic Theses'. Thesis 22 is particularly apposite to our point: 'That God exists we do not know by immediate intuition, nor do we demonstrate it a priori, but certainly a posteriori, that is, by things which are made, arguing from effect to cause. Namely, from things, which are in movement and cannot be the adequate principle of their motion, to the first mover immovable; from the procession of worldly things from causes, which are subordinated to each other, to the first uncaused cause; from corruptible things, which are indifferent alike to being and non-being, to the absolutely necessary being; from things, which, according to their limited perfection of existence, life, intelligence, are more or less perfect in their being, their life, their intelligence, to Him who is intelligent, living, and being in the highest degree; finally, from the order, which exists in the universe, to the existence of a separate intelligence which ordained, disposed, and directs things to their end.' *DS* 3601–24.

leads to the rather odd question, to Balthasar's mind, that had been asked by modern rationalism: how far can human reason go without divine revelation?[3] In a brief historical treatment of the topic, Balthasar observes, 'Only with Descartes does philosophy become dependent on the scientific ideal of the rising natural sciences... And only from this point onwards do philosophers become eager to experiment with the question of what reason can accomplish without the aid of revelation and what the possibilities are for a pure nature without grace.'[4] Balthasar would be happy to dismiss the question asked by Neo-Scholastic theologians, as it was not asked by the church until it was, to his mind, misdirected to do so by rationalist philosophers of the seventeenth and eighteenth centuries.

Additionally, Balthasar holds that modern philosophy and theology have separated the true from the beautiful, as examined in the last chapter. In so doing, these modern approaches have made truth claims that will, to Balthasar, necessarily ring hollow: 'In a world that no longer has enough confidence in itself to affirm the beautiful, the proofs of the truth have lost their cogency. In other words, syllogisms may still dutifully clatter away like rotary presses or computers which infallibly spew out an exact number of answers by the minute. But the logic of these answers is itself a mechanism which no longer captivates anyone. The very conclusions are no longer conclusive.'[5] Although Balthasar does not develop further his critique—something his reader might have appreciated—he clearly thinks that any talk of proof requires something more than isolated treatments of truth. The Neo-Scholastic method for establishing God's existence focuses too narrowly on an impoverished understanding of reason.

In an important study of Balthasar's religious epistemology, Victoria Harrison similarly observes that Balthasar rejects much Enlightenment thinking, in particular its 'elevation of universal concepts, [through which] it subsumes supernatural revelation under a universal, or naturalistic conception of revelation'.[6] Instead of approaching the question of God's existence from a supposedly universally available, neutral starting point, Balthasar insists that faith is a necessary prerequisite for knowledge of God.

---

[3] *GL* I, 71.   [4] *GL* I, 72.   [5] *GL* I, 19.

[6] Victoria Harrison, 'Putnam's Internal Realism and von Balthasar's Religious Epistemology', *International Journal for Philosophy of Religion* 44 (1998), 67–92, at 67–8.

The crucial question that then arises, as noted by Harrison, is whether Balthasar therefore endorses a form of non-rational fideism.[7] Indeed, in rejecting rationalism, it may appear that Balthasar instead supports the idea that there is no role for reason in belief. Such a position would resist the notion that one can provide any justification of one's religious views.[8]

Balthasar, however, holds that one can and should justify such views, but one first needs to expand one's understanding of key terms such as rationality, evidence, proof, and demonstration.[9] Any 'evidence' that the theologian will provide 'will be different in character from, for example, mathematical proof and evidence'.[10] In the following important passage from his aesthetics, Balthasar develops at length the way in which his view of 'objective evidence' should be understood:

> [W]e must render a precise account of what we mean by 'objective evidence'. It is the kind of evidence that emerges and sheds its light from the phenomenon itself...the form...is convincing in itself because the light by which it illumines us radiates from the form itself and proves itself with compelling force to just such a light that springs from the object itself. Naturally, this does not mean that the form must enlighten just *anyone*, or that this someone must not fulfil and bring along prerequisites which are just as specific as, for instance, those expected (in a wholly different field) from an atomic physicist if he is to understand certain formulas of his science, or from an art historian if he is to recognize the quality of a Teniers and tell it apart from counterfeits. As is clear from these examples, the subjective conditions can be varied and sophisticated; but no one will ever argue that it is a person's formation that actually produces the laws of physics or the beauty and value of the work of art. The fact that Christ 'says nothing to me' in no way prejudices the fact that, in and of himself, Christ says everything to everyone.[11]

---

[7] Harrison, 'Putnam's Internal Realism and von Balthasar's Religious Epistemology', 69.

[8] Harrison, 'Putnam's Internal Realism and von Balthasar's Religious Epistemology', 69.

[9] Harrison, 'Putnam's Internal Realism and von Balthasar's Religious Epistemology', 69.

[10] Harrison, 'Putnam's Internal Realism and von Balthasar's Religious Epistemology', 69.

[11] *GL* I, 464. Harrison, 'Putnam's Internal Realism and von Balthasar's Religious Epistemology', 69–70.

Simply put, for Balthasar a lack of *recognition* does not indicate a lack of *evidence*. An untrained eye would not detect a forged Teniers, but the painting still displays evidence that it is a fake. Similarly, Balthasar insists that there is in fact sufficient evidence in the natural world to support belief in God. That evidence, however, must be properly viewed.

It is precisely at this juncture that supplementing Harrison's analysis with our treatment of the spiritual senses further illuminates Balthasar's religious epistemology. Just as the art historian must be able to see the quality of great artistic works, thereby learning to read the evidence for what it is saying, so too must the Christian be able to detect God's presence in the natural world. And, crucially, the way in which the Christian does this is by viewing the world with the spiritual senses. Balthasar makes this clear at a number of points in *The Glory of the Lord* (many of which draw from Romans 1:18–21), as we saw in the previous chapters of this study. For instance, in Balthasar's treatment of Augustine, as we saw in Chapter 1, he says the following about spiritual sight:

> This training in seeing also leads, when the soul becomes pure and open, to that 'spiritual seeing' of God in his works of which Paul speaks in Romans (1, 20), *invisibilia ipsius per ea quae facta sunt intellecta conspiciuntur*. But this seeing succeeds only when the sight, leaving all finite things behind, has already reached the divine (*sempiterna ejus virtus et divinitas*) and looks back from there on what can become for it an entrance and an epiphany.[12]

Balthasar also quotes Barth with approval when Barth maintains, 'Man perceives and receives into self-consciousness particular things.... But these are important and necessary for man only because God does not usually meet him immediately but mediately in His works.'[13] Additionally, Balthasar summarizes Guardini's position as making much the same point: 'Now we can understand how, by referring to Rom. 1.18f., Guardini can demand of the eye and the senses that they see and perceive God. It is not God's unmediated essence that he means, but God's eternal power and glory, which are expressed in his works.'[14]

According to Balthasar and these other figures, God is in God's works, and creation can indeed show us God. However, for Balthasar,

---

[12] *GL* II, 101.   [13] *CD* III/2, 402.   [14] *GL* I, 392.

it only does so when the human being receives spiritual sight. The natural world gives evidence for God on all sides, but one will remain blind to God's presence unless one has 'antennae', so to speak, through which to pick up on the divine realities to which one is continually exposed. According to Balthasar, as we observed in Chapter 4, when the spiritual senses transform human perception, 'creation as a whole has become a monstrance of God's real presence'.[15]

But, one might wonder, does the committed stance Balthasar presupposes here mean that one's objectivity has been compromised? Although Harrison recognizes the temptation of this reading, she explains that, for Balthasar, 'a theologian cannot distance herself from faith, or "suspend judgment", in order to achieve a neutral standpoint by means of which knowledge can, supposedly, be attained'.[16] This means two things: 'Von Balthasar's epistemology is, thus, contrary to the view that one can reach truth in theology without having faith. But it is also contrary to the view that one can reach truth in theology by means of faith alone'.[17] Balthasar endorses the patristic view that 'all knowledge had to begin with a natural faith and, indeed, that in life's most elementary things a certain trusting "faith" in nature, its laws, and providence, remains the basis for all human conduct'.[18] To Harrison, this means 'all knowledge essentially involves an attitude of "trusting faith"—in other words, belief'.[19]

For Balthasar, then, Neo-Scholastic proofs of God's existence do not succeed because they presume a neutral starting point. In so doing, they attempt to gain knowledge without making any commitments, without taking an attitude of 'trusting faith'. On Balthasar's model, belief does not compromise one's epistemological capacities. It is not that one believes things that one will never know for certain. Instead, it is precisely by believing that one comes to know truth. On this point, we can use the terms developed in Chapter 5 to convey that the splendour of the form is always objectively 'out there', in the

---

[15] *GL* I, 419–20.
[16] Harrison, 'Putnam's Internal Realism and von Balthasar's Religious Epistemology', 70.
[17] Harrison, 'Putnam's Internal Realism and von Balthasar's Religious Epistemology', 70.
[18] *GL* I, 447. Harrison, 'Putnam's Internal Realism and von Balthasar's Religious Epistemology', 70.
[19] Harrison, 'Putnam's Internal Realism and von Balthasar's Religious Epistemology', 70.

world. One who does not see it actually has a *deficient* view of reality. Only the one who perceives splendour through the spiritual senses has accurate knowledge of the true depths of reality and the evidence of God that is always being presented to the human being.[20]

The spiritual senses therefore allow Balthasar to make the claim, crucial to Harrison's treatment, that there is in fact objective evidence of God to behold in the world. And, they make clear that, for Balthasar, faith in God is not about finding any new evidence. Instead, it is about seeing the very same evidence before one with new, spiritual senses.

THE SPIRITUAL SENSES AND FUNDAMENTAL THEOLOGY

Broadly speaking, the field within Catholic theology known as 'fundamental theology' (frequently equated with apologetics) concerns itself with the credibility of Christianity.[21] As such a field, it spends considerable effort examining the 'act of faith'.[22] Among the key questions it

---

[20] Of course, there is a difference between what, exactly, creation shows the human being according to Balthasar and the Neo-Scholastics. Neo-Scholasticism holds that the natural world gives us data that human reason uses to determine that God exists. For example, according to the teleological argument (or, the argument from design), upon investigating the natural world one observes that it is remarkably ordered. This order does not directly show one God, but one can use reason to establish that there must be an intelligent source of that order. Therefore, the fact that God exists, God's 'thatness' can be demonstrated through reason alone. God's 'whatness', however (i.e., what God is like, God's nature) remains unknown to unaided reason, and can only be known through revelation. For Balthasar, by contrast, the human being perceives God in God's works. In so doing, he or she witnesses not just a set of data points that require a subsequent use of inductive reasoning. Rather, one beholds the personal presence of God Himself. One does not, then, get evidence that ultimately points to a God who has orchestrated the workings of the world. Instead, one is exposed to the very reality of God in the midst of the created order.

[21] See, for instance, Heinrich Fries' section on 'Credibility' in his *Fundamental Theology*, trans. Robert Daly, SJ (Washington, DC: Catholic University of America Press, 1996), 18–21; also Erhard Kunz, 'Glaubwürdigkeit und Glaube [Credibility and Faith] (analysis fidei)', in *Handbuch der Fundamentaltheologie*, vol. 4, *Traktat theologische Erkenntnislehre. Schlussteil: Reflexion auf Fundamentaltheologie*, eds. W. Kern, H. J. Pottmeyer, and M. Seckler (Freiburg: Herder, 1988), 414–50.

[22] See especially Roger Aubert's magisterial *Le Problème de l'acte de foi* (Louvain: E. Warny, 1950).

asks are the following: Why would one find the claims made in revelation credible? Why should one believe a Christian worldview? What is the relationship between reason and faith? As we shall see momentarily, Balthasar's distinctive approach to these questions offers an important 'third option' that avoids, on the one hand, the dangers of the Vatican I, Neo-Scholastic treatment of this topic, and, on the other, those figures who oppose it, such as Maurice Blondel and the Catholic 'Modernists'. And, crucially for the central claim of this chapter, we shall see that the spiritual senses lie at the very heart of Balthasar's view of the act of faith. Simply put, to see spiritually is to believe.

One response to the above questions concerning the act of faith, as articulated during the first Vatican Council (1869–70), is to say that faith is assent to the authority of God, who has revealed external, objective signs (in miracles and prophecies) of the truth of Christianity. As the council's *Dei Filius* (1870) proclaims,

> [T]he Catholic Church teaches that this faith, which is the beginning of man's salvation, is a supernatural virtue, whereby, inspired and assisted by the grace of God, we believe that the things which he has revealed are true; not because of the intrinsic truth of the things, viewed by the natural light of reason, but because of the authority of God himself, who reveals them, and who can neither be deceived nor deceive. For faith, as the Apostle testifies, is 'the substance of things hoped for, the conviction of things that appear not' (Heb. 1:11).[23]

According to this understanding, faith is not something that is naturally achieved; the 'natural light of reason' cannot command the act of faith.[24] Instead, faith is supernaturally aided by God. Crucially, however, this divine grace only facilitates assent to authority. Through grace, one comes to believe that the signs revealed by God are trustworthy. That toward which those signs point remains opaque. Faith concerns things that 'appear not'. Grace, then, does not grant one actual knowledge of God in this life, and the truth of Christianity can only be believed because of the reliability of signs that have been revealed by God.

The key danger of this approach, as perceived initially by Victor Dechamps, then Maurice Blondel and others, is that its understanding

---

[23] DS 3008.

[24] Note that 'faith' here is understood to be different from belief in the existence of God, which, as discussed above, can indeed be demonstrated by unaided reason, according to Vatican I and Neo-Scholastic figures.

of revelation is inherently heteronomous, or 'extrinsic' to human beings.[25] That is, according to Vatican I and the Neo-Scholasticism that dominated Catholic theology in its wake, Christianity can only be believed on the basis of authority. One does not, upon searching one's heart, find that the claims of Christianity resonate with the deepest aspects of one's being. Instead, the act of faith is an act of obedience to the authority of God and the church. Therefore, on this model, God's truth will always be extrinsic to the human being, and the content of revelation will never be one's own.

As an alternative, Dechamps insists on the importance of the subjective longing within the human being, in addition to the objective signs external to him or her.[26] There is a correspondence, according to Dechamps, between the claims of the church and the inner spiritual strivings of the human being.[27] In fact, the ability of the church's teachings to fulfil humanity's yearnings suggests, to Dechamps, that the church has been given to human beings by God's providence.[28]

In similar fashion, Blondel famously resists the extrinsicism of Vatican I and Neo-Scholasticism through his 'method of immanence'. Blondel, drawing implicitly from Augustine, claims that the human being has a desire within him or herself that cannot be fulfilled by anything within the natural world. Human beings are thus confronted with a double impossibility: 'It is impossible not to recognize the insufficiency of the whole natural order and not to feel an ulterior need; it is impossible to find within oneself something to satisfy this religious need'.[29] To Blondel, one necessarily feels this insufficiency, and

---

[25] Blondel pseudonymously compared his work with that of Dechamps under the name of his friend, Fr François Mallet. See F. Mallet, 'L'oeuvre du Cardinal Dechamps et la méthode de l'apologétique', *Annales de philosophie chrétienne* 151 (1905–16), 68–91; 'Les controverses sur la méthode apologétique du Cardinal Dechamps', *Annales de philosophie chrétienne* 151 (1905–16), 449–71; 625–45; 'L'oeuvre du Cardinal Dechamps de les progress récents de l'apologétique', *Annales de philosophie chrétienne* 153 (1906–17), 562–91.

[26] Victor Dechamps, *Entretiens sur la démonstration catholique de la révélation chrétienne* (Paris: Tournai, 1861). According to some interpretations of Vatican I, Dechamps' concerns were integrated into the view of faith expounded by the council. See Gerald McCool, *Catholic Theology in the Nineteenth Century* (New York: Seabury, 1977), 223–4.

[27] Aubert, *Le Problème de l'acte de foi*, 142–52.

[28] Avery Cardinal Dulles, *A History of Apologetics* (San Francisco, CA: Ignatius Press, 1999), 255.

[29] Maurice Blondel, *Action: Essay on a Critique of Life and a Science of Practice*, trans. Olivia Blanchette (South Bend, IN: University of Notre Dame Press, 1984), 297.

one necessarily can do nothing about it. This suggests that only the supernatural can satisfy human beings' unlimited desire. Therefore, when the human being encounters divine revelation, he or she finds fulfilment, not a heteronomous imposition. God's revelation is not extrinsic to the human being; Christianity directly speaks to who one most deeply is.

This idea would be intensified among many Catholic 'Modernist' thinkers, for whom the threat of extrinsicism required a radical response: namely, that all of God's revelation be understood as *already within* the human being, never outside of him or her.[30] The following from George Tyrrell characteristically expresses this 'immanentist' extreme:

> [T]he teaching from outside must evoke a revelation in ourselves. The prophet's experience must become experience for us. It is to this evoked revelation that we answered by the act of faith, recognizing it as God's word in us and to us. Were it not already written in the depths of our being, where the spirit is rooted in God, we could not recognize it...without personal revelation, there can be no faith, nothing more than theological or historical assent. Revelation cannot be put into us from outside. It can be occasioned, but it cannot be caused, by instruction.[31]

Whereas the danger of extrinsicism looms ominously for the post-Vatican I approach, the Blondelian-inspired alternative is haunted by the possibility—made reality in the Modernist appropriation of Blondel's insights—that God's revelation will be reduced to that which is already within the human being. Indeed, if 'revelation cannot be put into us from outside', as Tyrrell claims, then one may rightly be concerned that the 'otherness' of God, the way in which God transcends human concepts and capacities, has been severely compromised.

---

[30] Of course, the group of theologians labelled as Catholic Modernists did not draw from Blondel alone (whose thought they actually distort in significant ways), but instead were influenced by a wide array of figures, including many liberal Protestant theologians.

[31] George Tyrrell, 'Revelation as Experience', 305–6, in Alessandro Maggiolini, 'From Modernism to Vatican II', *Communio* 23 (Summer, 1996), 225–43, at 231. Quoted in Rodney Howsare, *Balthasar: A Guide for the Perplexed* (New York: T. & T. Clark, 2009), 13. For complete text, see 'Revelation as Experience', Unpublished lecture of George Tyrrell, ed. Thomas Michael Loome, *The Heythrop Journal* 11 (1970), 117–49.

From Sign to Form

Balthasar enters into this highly contentious debate by locating in both the post-Vatican I method and its Modernist counterpart a common fault that his aesthetic approach is meant to remedy. Specifically, as John Riches has argued, Balthasar finds in both methods a tendency to push *beyond* the signs that have been revealed by God—albeit in different ways—thereby objectionably separating the historical and material from the suprahistorical and spiritual. According to Riches, for both approaches 'there is no place for a more than external or functional relationship between sign and signified. The sign is that which points one to, a means by which one rises to that which is signified'.[32] Such a view of the sign contrasts sharply with Balthasar's understanding of form, as will be shown below.

This tendency can be observed in the post-Vatican I approach, according to which the 'signs' establish only the trustworthiness of God and the credibility of the church's teachings. However, as noted above, those signs do not grant one actual knowledge of God. The inner divine realities remain unknown. One need only believe that the signs are trustworthy. As Balthasar pithily expresses his assessment, 'The signs are understood; what they point and witness to is believed.'[33] In other words, this view opposes faith (πίστις) to knowledge (γνῶσις). One can have knowledge of the signs, but for the reality that lies behind them, one may only have faith. As Riches expresses the shortcoming of this view: 'The understanding of truth is positivist: experience takes us so far but does not lead us into a perception of being. The events of saving history stand in an external relation to the truth which is revealed. They could have been other without affecting the substance of the *revelatum*.'[34] There is a separation between signifier and signified, according to Balthasar's critique, and this separation ends up trivializing the signs, for they are not integral to the object toward which they point.

For the Modernists, according to Balthasar, the inner yearning for God that is so crucial for overcoming extrinsicism ends up surpassing the particular facts of God's revelation in an effort at attaining the object of its desire. As Balthasar puts his criticism, 'This view [i.e.,

---

[32] John Riches, 'Balthasar and the Analysis of Faith', in *The Analogy of Beauty: The Theology of Hans Urs von Balthasar*, ed. John Riches (Edinburgh: T&T Clark, 1985), 35–59, at 54.
[33] *GL* I, 147. [34] Riches, 'Balthasar and the Analysis of Faith', 52.

that of Blondel, Rousselot, Maréchal, and others] is taken to extremes in Modernism, which dissolves the objective facts of revelation into mere functions of the interior subjective dynamism of revelation between God and the soul, and which regards these facts as valid for the believer only in so far and as long as they effectively support and foster this dynamism.'[35] What is important, according to Modernist thinkers, is not whether or not Jesus performed certain miracles or fulfilled certain prophecies, but instead the underlying experience of God that is expressed in those stories.

In each case, then, we have an inadequate view of that which 'shows up', so to speak, in the material world and in history. For the post-Vatican I approach, the signs are separable, external pointers to the divine; for the Modernists, the signs are taken to be ultimately unimportant for faith. As Balthasar issues his judgement on these two errors: 'In the first approach God's historical witnesses do not really stand within the light of divine Being: they merely point to it. In the second approach they become so transparent to this light that in the sign only the signified is of interest, and in the historical only that which is valid for eternity.'[36] For both, according to Balthasar, the signs themselves are not as important as the divine reality that lies behind them. 'For, so the argument goes, if the mystery were visible as such in the signs themselves, then faith would be abolished.'[37]

Balthasar's aesthetic approach, then, should be understood as a corrective to the error shared by both sides of this high-profile debate within modern Catholic theology. For Balthasar, the concrete sign is not something to be left behind as one progresses towards the signified: 'This dualism [between sign and signified] can be abolished only by introducing as well the thought-forms and categories of the beautiful. The beautiful is above all a *form*, and the light does not fall on this form from above and from outside, rather it breaks forth from the form's interior.'[38] The previous chapter described Balthasar's non-dualist understanding of form. We can now see more fully what is at stake in this conjoining. For Balthasar, the concrete (and we should now add, historical) aspect of the form cannot be separated from its interior (and eternal) dimension. Balthasar is concerned that, if faith is actually about what lies behind the form, then that which appears in history and the material world will be dismissed as

[35] *GL* I, 149.   [36] *GL* I, 150.   [37] *GL* I, 150.   [38] *GL* I, 151.

ultimately inconsequential. The problem to this formulation becomes clear when viewed through a Christological lens. As Riches puts this point, 'Balthasar insists that while Jesus may indeed work signs, he himself is more than a sign. He can be known only when his *Gestalt* is seen as the divine-human *Gestalt*; when what appears of him is "seen" or "believed" as the "surfacing" of the personal divine depth.'[39] Or, to put this in the Trinitarian terms Riches also uses, one does not come to know the Son in order to move beyond Him to know the Father. Instead, one knows the Father in knowing the Son Himself.[40] For Balthasar, that which shows up concretely in the world is not a pointer to the divine, but rather God manifested in history.

To Balthasar, then, the act of faith is not about transcending the signs God has provided in the material world and in history; faith instead involves seeing mystery and depth in the very midst of the world. To put the point in this way, of course, positions us well to appreciate the role played by the spiritual senses for faith. Indeed, if faith requires seeing in the concrete form the divine light that shines forth from it, then the spiritual senses clearly must be used in order to behold this depth. Riches comes close to noticing this in his treatment of Balthasar's understanding of faith. To Riches, Balthasarian faith involves 'learning to see in the object of its contemplation the opening up of a deeper dimension [...] learning to see, that is, the *ground* which *appears* in the *Gestalt* which it contemplates. Here "seeing" indeed transcends "normal" sense experience.'[41] Based on Riches' comments about a form of sight that transcends normal perception, we can easily see that the spiritual senses must play a crucial role in this sort of perceiving.

Balthasar himself explicitly, if subtly, yokes together the spiritual senses, faith, and fundamental theology in *The Glory of the Lord*. First, Balthasar insists that faith and the fundamental theology that examines it are about *perceiving*: 'The central question of so-called "apologetics" or "fundamental theology" is, thus, the question of perceiving form—an aesthetic problem.... For fundamental theology, the heart of the matter should be the question: "How does God's revelation confront man in history? How is it perceived?"'[42] For Balthasar, one finds Christianity credible precisely when one has been struck by the

---

[39] Riches, 'Balthasar and the Analysis of Faith', 54–5.
[40] Riches, 'Balthasar and the Analysis of Faith', 55.
[41] Riches, 'Balthasar and the Analysis of Faith', 58.   [42] *GL* I, 173.

beauty of God's revelation. He undertakes his theological aesthetics not simply to rehabilitate beauty as a divine attribute for its own sake, but also because, in his view, aesthetics is the way in which fundamental theology should be done.

In particular reference to the spiritual senses, Balthasar explains that 'fundamental theology…sets out to convey and to make plausible to one who does not yet believe the image of divine revelation. This image really becomes plausible, however, only for the person who sees the true contours of its total form dawn before the eyes of his spirit.'[43] Much of Balthasar's emphasis on form involves seeing the 'whole' of revelation. This is frequently taken to mean that one cannot break the form down into its constituent components. What should also be said, however, is that the 'total form' includes both sensory and supersensory aspects, as we saw in Chapter 5. In reference to the discussion above, we can say that only through the spiritual senses is the 'sign' perceived for what it truly is: namely, a *form*. The eyes of the spirit, then, play a crucial role in recognizing this total form of revelation, and this recognition in turn makes Christianity credible to those who behold the form in its totality.[44] Simply put, seeing spiritually is believing.

More than Meets the (Corporeal) Eye: Supernaturally Elevated Aesthetic Experience

We noted earlier in this chapter that the spiritual senses address a problem common to post-Vatican I and Modernist understandings of faith. They also, as I argue below, play a crucial role in the criticisms Balthasar has for *each* side of this debate. Specifically, the spiritual senses are crucial in overcoming extrinsicism (thus playing a key role in Balthasar's critique of post-Vatican I approaches to theology), and also important in preserving the idea that God's revelation does not wholly conform to human expectations or capacities (thus playing a key role in Balthasar's criticism of Modernism). The spiritual senses, then, allow the human being to behold that which is *other* to him or

---

[43] GL I, 127.
[44] Elsewhere in his aesthetics Balthasar simply claims, '[T]he moment of faith coincides with the vision of the form' (GL I, 524). Given that the form has both sensory and supersensory aspects, the spiritual senses, as that which perceives the spiritual dimension of the form, play a crucial role in the act of faith.

her in a manner that is 'non-extrinsic'. In order to clarify further the meaning of this claim, we turn to Balthasar's criticisms.

To the post-Vatican I approach outlined above, Balthasar insists that the act of faith does not involve heteronomous submission to external authority. In this regard, he is sympathetic with the critique of extrinsicism articulated by figures such as Blondel, Rousselot, Maréchal, and the Modernists (despite his ultimate reservations). As he puts this point in *Love Alone is Credible*: 'The modernist and dynamist approaches no doubt reflect a great Christian tradition: God, who condescends graciously to his creature, does not want to lay hold of him and fulfil him in an external manner, but rather in the most intimate way possible.'[45] To Balthasar, God's revelation must indeed be received subjectively. Balthasar quotes with approval the memorable lines of Angelus Silesius on this point: ' "If Christ were born a thousand times in Bethlehem, but not in you, you would remain lost forever.... The Cross on Golgotha cannot redeem you from evil if it is not raised up also in you".'[46]

At the very same time, however, Balthasar has concerns about the Modernist notion that the inner strivings of the human subject are fulfilled in God's revelation. Specifically, he worries that such an understanding constrains the possibilities for God's revelation. Indeed, those aspects of revelation that do *not* fulfil human yearnings would seem to have no place in such a subject-centred theological method. Balthasar insists that, in revelation, God does not simply give us what we think we need: 'The tradition never set the criterion for the truth of revelation in the center of the pious human subject, it never measured the abyss of grace by the abyss of need or sin, it never judged the content of dogma according to its beneficial effects on human beings.'[47] In an important sense, God's revelation does not depend on anything within us. Instead, it surprises us, reorients us, and causes us to reevaluate all previous understandings we had before it befell us with such life-changing power.

---

[45] *LA*, 42.

[46] Angelus Silesius, *Cherubinischer Wandersmann*, I: 61–2. Quoted in *LA*, 42.

[47] *LA*, 43. Balthasar puts a similar point somewhat cryptically in *The Glory of the Lord*, 'In the Gospel, the strength of the disciples' belief is wholly borne and effected by the person of Jesus, the locus of revelation. Here we no longer detect the slightest trace of a creative, myth-projecting capacity on the part of man.... Jesus' non-inevitability, his overwhelming originality has become infinite and of itself demands assent and effects submission' (*GL* I, 177).

Karen Kilby has observed a similar set of concerns for Balthasar in his engagement with the thought of Karl Barth, on the one hand, and that of Karl Rahner, on the other. Kilby notes that Balthasar wants 'to offer a conception of revelation as containing the genuinely new, the other, even the strange—something that a thinker like Karl Barth is very concerned with.'[48] Kilby then explains the drawback of Barth's view of revelation (which could also be said of the post-Vatican I approach, in a slightly different way): namely, that Barth buys the novelty of revelation at the cost of 'a deep negation of our nature...presenting revelation in terms of a fundamental alienation.'[49] For Barth, according to Kilby, there seems to be nothing in the human being that would find fulfilment in what God reveals. Instead, especially for the early Barth, God's revelation issues only rebuke and judgement of the human being.

If Barth represents something akin to the extrinsicist position, the immanentist alternative is occupied by Rahner in Kilby's analysis. Rahner draws from Blondel, Rousselot, and Maréchal to articulate a theological anthropology in which the human being is 'absolutely opened upwards' to God.[50] In a similar fashion to Blondel's method of immanence, Rahner holds that the human being has an inner dynamism that drives him or her toward the infinite. The risk associated with this approach, as Kilby notes, is that God's revelation will be understood solely as a response to this inner drive, and revelation will be reduced to a mere 'expression of our experience, of that which is already within us'.[51]

Balthasar, then, wants with Barth for revelation to be something genuinely new, not something that can be anticipated by a pre-existing structure within the human being. Or, to put the point in the language preferred by the post-Vatican I approach outlined above, Balthasar insists that revelation be understood as *external* to the human being. And yet, with Rahner and the Modernists, Balthasar also wants revelation to be enrapturing, not alienating. Whereas Barth buys the novelty of revelation at the cost of alienation (and Neo-Scholastics at the cost of extrinsicism), Balthasar looks for a way in which it can fulfil the human being while still surprising him or her.

---

[48] Karen Kilby, *Balthasar: A (Very) Critical Introduction* (Grand Rapids, MI: Eerdmans, 2012), 52.
[49] Kilby, *Balthasar*, 52.
[50] Karl Rahner, 'Current Problems in Christology', in *Theological Investigations*, vol. 1: *God, Christ, Mary and Grace*, trans. Cornelius Ernst, OP (London: Darton, Longman, & Todd, 1961), 149–200, at 183.
[51] Kilby, *Balthasar*, 52.

The fundamental question, then, is: how can the human person be open to the newness of revelation without being deeply disaffected by what he or she experiences? Kilby explains that Balthasar's use of aesthetic categories is meant to address this very issue. As she puts the central point: 'A work of art can be genuinely new and surprising, can present us with a kind of beauty never previously imagined, and yet still hold us transfixed rather than alienated.... A work of art can be genuinely other to us, and yet genuinely make a connection with us.'[52] To Balthasar, God's revelation, on the analogy with a work of art, resonates with the human being, enrapturing and transporting him or her. Aesthetic enjoyment cannot be purely extrinsic, to Balthasar, for beholding beauty speaks to something deep within oneself.

And yet, Balthasar's aesthetic approach insists to the Modernists and Rahner that there is in fact something objectively 'out there', beyond the human being that does not completely overlap with his or her desires, expectations, and capacities. Just as we are taken beyond the predictable and familiar during our most powerful aesthetic experiences, we are confronted by a beauty that surprises and overwhelms us when we perceive God's revelation. One does not simply get what one expects in experiencing great works of art; instead, the very power and genius of such works involves them giving their audiences something that is unanticipated.

Balthasar's aesthetic approach to theology thus lends him tools with which to resist shortcomings particular to each side of the debate highlighted above. The experience of beauty, paradoxically, both overwhelms *and* fulfils human hopes and strivings. Or, to put the point in more technical language, through 'seeing the form' one beholds that which is *other* to the human being in a manner that is nevertheless non-extrinsic.

Kilby's illuminating exposition of Balthasar's thought should be supplemented in one key way. Specifically, we complement it (or, perhaps, make explicit an idea it already implicitly contains) by claiming that the perception of revelation for Balthasar actually involves a particular kind of aesthetic experience: namely, one that is *supernaturally elevated*. To be sure, analogies with art are instructive, but when it comes to *theological* aesthetics and appreciating the beauty of the divine form, natural aesthetic enjoyment will not suffice.

[52] Kilby, *Balthasar*, 52.

Subjectively, the human being does not have, already within his or her nature, an apparatus for encountering the fullness of God's revelation. One cannot be utterly enraptured by the form without supernatural aid. Any ability to do so on the natural plane would be viewed as a pre-existing capacity for God, but Balthasar is worried (with Barth) about reducing God's revelation to human categories, so much so that he does not want to allow for a fully functioning natural capacity. Instead, one must be prepared for God's revelation to challenge radically one's conception of what beauty is. As we have seen throughout this study, at the very moment that the form of Christ is before one's eyes, one is given *by grace* the ability to perceive God's glory.

To be more specific, in this moment of supernaturally elevated aesthetic appreciation, God's grace operates on the human being by giving him or her spiritual senses, or, as Balthasar phrases the same idea in the following passage, a 'new sensorium' with which to behold the divine:

> The love which is infused in man by the Holy Spirit present within him bestows on man the sensorium with which to perceive God […] the new sensorium is infused into the natural sensorium and yet is not one with it: for all that it is bestowed upon man *as his own* (and increasingly so as he is the more unselved), it is equally his only as a gift.[53]

In this passage the interplay between nature and grace is complex, as will be examined in greater detail below, but what is clear is that the natural sensorium *alone* does not perceive God. Instead, a new, grace-given sensorium (which we can see as another name for the spiritual senses) becomes a part of the human perceptual apparatus. The spiritual senses, then, as the centrepiece of Balthasar's understanding of theological-aesthetic experience, emerge as the key to Balthasar's resistance to both the post-Vatican I and Modernist (and Barthian and Rahnerian) approaches to theology.

GIVEN, YET ONE'S OWN: THE SPIRITUAL SENSES, NATURE, AND GRACE

Above we noted that supernaturally elevated aesthetic appreciation is required for the receipt of revelation, according to Balthasar. Putting

---

[53] *GL* I, 249.

the point in this way may cause one to wonder if we have not ultimately tipped toward extrinsicism, despite Balthasar's efforts to avoid this consequence. Indeed, if both God's revelation and the ability to perceive it come to the human being from beyond, then in what way might such a view of revelation involve something consistent with his or her nature? How could it not be a heteronomous imposition? The passage just quoted may actually seem to muddle the issue, not give one a satisfying account of its complexities. For Balthasar, 'the new sensorium [with which one perceives God] is infused into the natural sensorium and yet is not one with it: for all that it is bestowed upon man *as his own* (and increasingly so as he is the more unselved), it is equally his only as a gift'.[54] Balthasar here makes two claims that seem to be mutually exclusive: on the one hand, the sensorium is the human being's own. It is not radically inconsistent with his or her nature. And yet, on the other hand, it also is his or hers 'only as a gift'. It is given as grace. The former claim is important if Balthasar is to overcome extrinsicism, the latter if he is to address shortcomings of the immanentist alternative. However, it would appear that Balthasar revels in the paradoxical nature of his position without actually aiding his reader's understanding of the issues that are in play.

Although Balthasar is not typically credited with a high degree of conceptual clarity on such topics, below I argue that his account of spiritual sensation rests on more rigorously developed theoretical ground than is often thought to be the case. Specifically, the implications of Balthasar's 'personalism', as initially examined in Chapter 3, lend one tools with which to make better sense of his comments concerning the sensorium above. The following analysis also demonstrates that Balthasar deals with the relationship between nature and grace precisely through the spiritual senses. Indeed, when grace descends upon the human being, the point of contact (*Anknüpfungspunkt*) with God is the perceptual apparatus through which he or she perceives the divine. This view of the 'scope' of grace differs greatly from those versions of the doctrine, such as that of Origen, which reserve this particular form of God's grace for the few who are 'perfect'. For Balthasar's democratized version of the doctrine, the spiritual senses are among the very first things given to the ordinary human being when grace befalls him or her.

[54] *GL* I, 249.

By way of a beginning, then, we remind the reader of the findings of the third and fourth chapters of this study. In Chapter 3, we saw Balthasar's appropriation of the 'personalism' of Karl Barth and Gustav Siewerth, according to whom the human being is fundamentally constituted in the encounter with the *Thou*. On this anthropology, the human being cannot be regarded as an individual, discrete entity *prior to* relationship. Instead, the human being is always already in encounter with an other.

We noted in Chapter 4 that Balthasar uses this anthropology to advance a highly creative rearticulation of the spiritual senses for his theological aesthetics. Indeed, Balthasar gives the spiritual senses a profoundly personalist dimension in his understanding that love for the other functions as the definitive arena in which spiritual sensibility is granted.

Another way to put this personalist aspect of Balthasar's anthropology is to say that his understanding of the human being is always at every point a 'meta-anthropology'.[55] The human being only 'finds' him or herself 'outside' of him or herself. Put even more forcefully, as we saw in Chapter 3, the single human being, as such, does not exist. The import of this aspect of Balthasar's thought for our inquiry cannot be overstated. What it means is that any question about epistemological structures of the human being must not be treated in isolation from relation to the other. The most fundamental 'unit', if we can put the point in such a manner, is not a 'monad', but rather a 'dyad'—not one, but always two in relation. As a result, examining the 'knowing apparatus' of the human being inevitably involves asking questions about the nature of relationship with the *Thou*. The key question then becomes: in exactly what way does Balthasar's understanding of interpersonal encounter lend one resources with which to understand better the structures of human knowing?

D. C. Schindler has helpfully analysed this feature of Balthasar's thought by examining his account of the mother's smile in the encounter between mother and child.[56] Balthasar uses this idea (which he adopts from Siewerth, as shown in Chapter 3) at a number of

---

[55] Balthasar uses this term in an interview with Angelo Scola: *Test Everything: Hold Fast to What Is Good* (San Francisco, CA: Ignatius Press, 1989), 24–5. See also Martin Bieler, 'Meta-anthropology and Christology: On the Philosophy of Hans Urs von Balthasar', *Communio* 20 (Spring 1993), 129–46.

[56] D. C. Schindler, *Hans Urs von Balthasar and the Dramatic Structure of Truth: A Philosophical Investigation* (New York: Fordham University Press, 2004).

different points in his work, but his most detailed discussion of the topic occurs in his essay, 'Movement toward God'. In a dense but important passage from that text, he depicts the relationship between mother and child as follows:

> The little child awakens to self-consciousness in his being-called by the love of his mother. The spirit's being raised up (*Emporkunft des Geistes*) to alert self-possession is an act of simple fullness, which can be broken up into diverse aspects and phases only *in abstractio*. It is not in the least possible to account for this event on the basis of the formal 'structure' of the spirit: sensible 'impressions' that bring into play an ordering, categorial constitution, which in its turn would be a function of a dynamic capacity to affirm 'Being in general' and to objectify the determinate and finite existing object present to consciousness.[57]

Schindler notes that Balthasar here opposes his own account of self-consciousness to a transcendental approach, as advanced paradigmatically by Kant.[58] This transcendental method employs a priori structures of consciousness that are, by definition, already complete. The shortcoming of this view, according to Schindler, is that these finished pre-existing structures impose their categories on all they encounter, and in so doing they filter out the depth and complexity of what is actually there. To Schindler, this approach 'never reaches an other *as such* but is always only itself'.[59] The completed structures of consciousness prevent the human being from ever getting beyond him or herself. As Schindler quips, 'It may be "transcendental," but it is never genuinely transcendent'.[60]

In direct opposition to this view, Balthasar holds that the child does not have a pre-existing, transcendental structure of consciousness through which he or she beholds his or her mother. Instead, the smile of the mother completes his or her self-awareness in the very moment of encounter. Schindler focuses on Balthasar's term, 'the spirit's being raised up' (*Emporkunft des Geistes*) to offer the following summary of Balthasar's understanding of the birth of consciousness: 'The self comes *to* itself only by coming *out* of itself or, more concretely,

---

[57] Hans Urs von Balthasar, 'Movement toward God', in *ET* 3: *Creator Spirit* (San Francisco, CA: Ignatius Press, 1993), 15–55, at 15. Translation in Schindler, *Hans Urs von Balthasar and the Dramatic Structure of Truth*, 112.
[58] Schindler, *Hans Urs von Balthasar and the Dramatic Structure of Truth*, 113.
[59] Schindler, *Hans Urs von Balthasar and the Dramatic Structure of Truth*, 113.
[60] Schindler, *Hans Urs von Balthasar and the Dramatic Structure of Truth*, 113.

only by going *to another*; indeed, by being raised up *by* the other, *to* the other.'[61] The smile of the mother, then, functions as the stimulus that brings the child to self-awareness, and, crucially, the structures of consciousness are not formed in isolation from the other. Instead, consciousness is completed in an ecstatic movement *beyond* the self that actually includes the other.

This particular aspect of Balthasar's thought has important implications, according to Schindler's reading: 'The "objectivity" of the object is not in the first place "constituted", "merely" theoretically through merely intellectual rays of intentionality, radiating outward from a static center of subjectivity; instead, the objectivity of the object is *given* to the subject in the subject's going out of itself, or, more accurately, being called outside of itself, to meet the object.'[62] A transcendental approach to knowledge would lead to a model of truth in which *only* the subject is active, imposing its schema onto a passive object.

Balthasar makes no secret of his resistance to this approach to epistemology, but the alternative he gives is not often well understood. Many commentators on Balthasar's texts have erroneously presumed that he simply *inverts* the relationship described above such that the object functions as the active part of the relationship, and the subject remains purely passive.[63] However, in the example of the mother's smile, subjectivity arises through a *combination* of activity and passivity (or 'spontaneity' and 'receptivity', to use Schindler's preferred terms). Schindler summarizes this aspect of Balthasar's thought as follows: 'Consciousness is constituted both from above (receptively) and from below (spontaneously). If it came *merely* from below, it would be a *closed* circle, a finished product, and therefore incapable of receiving.'[64] In relation to our previous discussion, we can see that this understanding of consciousness would fall into the same problems as the immanentist position described above. Specifically, if consciousness were constituted only from below, then nothing surprising, nothing that exceeded the pre-established capacities of the individual, could ever be received.

---

[61] Schindler, *Hans Urs von Balthasar and the Dramatic Structure of Truth*, 112.

[62] Schindler, *Hans Urs von Balthasar and the Dramatic Structure of Truth*, 112.

[63] See Noel O'Donoghue, 'A Theology of Beauty', in *The Analogy of Beauty: The Theology of Hans Urs von Balthasar*, ed. John Riches (Edinburgh: T&T Clark, 1986), 1–10, at 3.

[64] Schindler, *Hans Urs von Balthasar and the Dramatic Structure of Truth*, 118.

And yet the alternative approach faces the difficulties encountered by extrinsicism. As Schindler puts it, 'At the same time, consciousness constituted simply from above would lack the *active* receptivity that characterizes genuine subjectivity and connects it with a free self. It is what distinguishes the receptivity of consciousness from that of putty'.[65] One does indeed receive what comes 'from above' into oneself, according to Schindler's analysis, but one then spontaneously responds to it. If one did not, if one were purely passive, then the gift would always remain extrinsic to oneself, unused and un-integrated.

Consciousness, then, is given to the subject from beyond the subject. As such, it is a 'grace' of sorts that befalls the human being from beyond his or her sphere of control. One cannot come to self-awareness without this gift, but one also cannot produce the gift. And yet, when this gift is received, it is integrated into the self as the subject transcends him or herself in responding to its call. The gift does not *remain* outside, but rather it becomes a part of the human being.

Schindler's analysis of Balthasar's thought gives us important tools with which to understand the interplay of nature and grace in his discussion of the spiritual senses. Specifically, we now have a way of conceiving how this sensorium can be given as a real grace, yet integrated into the self in a non-extrinsic manner. As we saw in Chapter 3, Siewerth himself refers to a 'self-transcending' perception that moves into that which is other: 'Vision (sensory knowledge) has in itself moved out to the open and, thus, into that which is other. Awakened to itself by the light, vision has strayed from its origins and become "lost" in the other and, hence, in the exteriority of spatial extension.'[66] One crucial implication of this idea is that natural, corporeal sensation is actually *incomplete*, much like the inchoate mind of the child before he or she has been raised up to self-consciousness by the smile of the mother. The physical senses need grace in order to be fulfilled. If they did not, if the physical senses were an already complete, pre-existing structure, then, for Balthasar, they would function as a filter that would block God out (much as a priori structures of consciousness preclude actual encounter with an other, in Schindler's analysis). For Balthasar, a pre-existing *capax dei* would not actually be a capacity at all. Instead, precisely because of its pre-existence, it would be incapable of beholding God.

---

[65] Schindler, *Hans Urs von Balthasar and the Dramatic Structure of Truth*, 118.
[66] *WB*, 13. *GL* I, 395–6.

The spiritual sensorium that perceives God, then, must be given as a gift. And yet, when it is given, it does not arrive as a foreign invader. Instead, the spiritual senses are integrated into the natural, corporeal senses, thereby completing the sensorium as it becomes one single, corporeal-spiritual sense apparatus. Recall from Chapter 4 that, for Balthasar, the spiritual and corporeal senses do not function separately from one another, as they do in other dualist accounts of the doctrine. One consequence of this move is that spiritual perception never occurs without its corporeal counterpart. They are always one.

There is, therefore, a consistency and unity between the corporeal and spiritual senses, and this fact, to Balthasar, ensures that the spiritual senses will not be extrinsic to the human being. We are destined to have physical and spiritual perception, even if we cannot attain that destiny by our own natural powers. The spiritual senses are received from 'outside', to be sure, but they are also used 'spontaneously'. The spiritual senses become the human being's *own* in that they are used in an active response to the grace that is granted to him or her. Balthasar expresses this idea as follows: 'The inspiration [i.e., the ability to perceive God], therefore, descends upon believing man from the heights of the absolute…And yet, at the same time, the inspiration rises from man's own most intimate depths: it is the person himself who loves and tastes God, not an alien principle that does this through the person.'[67] The human being is not putty. He or she actively uses that which has been given. The senses, then, find their completion and fulfilment when, in the encounter with God, they—while remaining corporeal—become spiritualized.

CONCLUSION

I have argued in this chapter that Balthasar's use of the spiritual senses contributes importantly to some of the liveliest debates in modern theology, especially discussions of natural theology, fundamental theology, aesthetic experience, and the relationship between nature and grace. Specifically, we have seen that the spiritual senses play a key role in Balthasar's resistance to Neo-Scholastic natural theology by offering an alternative way in which one beholds evidence for God in

---

[67] *GL* I, 250.

the natural world. They are also necessary for overcoming the error common to the post-Vatican I and Modernist approaches to fundamental theology, which to Balthasar is that both mistakenly view the form as merely a 'sign' that can be surpassed on the way to the object of faith. Additionally, we saw that the spiritual senses are a necessary component of Balthasar's aesthetic solution to the tension between extrinsicism and immanentism. Specifically, it is through the supernaturally given spiritual senses that one becomes open to the overwhelming beauty of God's revelation while not being alienated by what one sees. Furthermore, we saw that, although the spiritual senses are given as a grace, this need not mean that they are necessarily extrinsic to the human being. Instead, drawing parallels from Balthasar's personalist rendering of the relationship between mother and child, we argued that the spiritual senses are integrated into the self such that they become a part of the human being.

As a final point, we note that Balthasar's appropriation of the spiritual senses tradition allows us to observe a key feature of his understanding of how grace functions within the human being. Specifically, we see that the effects of grace are not confined to a strictly noetic realm. Grace does not elevate only the mind or the soul. Instead, when grace arrives, the *whole* human being is changed. Sensibility itself is altered, and one receives senses that are 'capable of perceiving the forms of existence with awe'.[68]

---

[68] *GL* I, 24.

Conclusion

This study has advanced two basic claims about Hans Urs von Balthasar's engagement with the doctrine of the spiritual senses. First, I have argued that Balthasar articulates a version of the spiritual senses that is importantly distinct from its patristic and scholastic instantiations. Second, I have claimed that the doctrine of the spiritual senses plays an indispensable epistemological role in Balthasar's theology.

Concerning the first point, we have seen that Balthasar frequently reads the spiritual senses tradition in a manner that anticipates his own distinctive rendering of the doctrine. Chapters 1 and 2 demonstrated that Balthasar consistently pushes his interpretations towards a positive regard for corporeal sensation (to the extent that he can credibly attribute such readings to that exponent). We also observed Balthasar's attempts to locate Christ and the whole of the 'upper world' as the object of the spiritual senses in his reading of Origen, Pseudo-Macarius, Augustine, and Bonaventure. Additionally, we noted Balthasar's lack of interest in those versions of the doctrine that advocate an 'achievement-oriented' asceticism, and we saw a correlative emphasis on Ignatian 'indifference' as the only practice relevant to the spiritual senses. This focus, I argued, indicates Balthasar's resistance to readings of the doctrine that place it in the final stage of the life of faith (the 'enoptic' for Origen, the 'unitive' for Bonaventure). Instead, Balthasar advocates a 'second-stage' reading of the spiritual senses whereby they are granted prior to the so-called 'mystical' experience of God. Whereas Balthasar made a compelling case for this point in his interpretation of Bonaventure, he did not do so in his reading of Origen, thereby displaying (in this particular instance, at least) the version of Balthasar that patristic scholars have come to expect—as one who imports his own theological concerns into the texts he examines.

Ultimately, however, I have suggested that Balthasar's primary interest lies not in repristinating the doctrine of the spiritual senses out of its patristic and scholastic formulations. Instead, I argued in Chapter 3 that Balthasar turns to Barth, Guardini, Siewerth, and

Claudel in an effort at reworking the idea of spiritual perception in a modern idiom. Balthasar most clearly breaks from previous articulations of the spiritual senses when, drawing on the notion of the human being as a being-in-encounter, he integrates this interpersonal dimension into his doctrine of the spiritual senses. Additionally, we saw that all four modern figures articulate an anthropology of 'unity-in-duality' that resists separating 'spiritual' perception from its corporeal counterpart. All these modern figures attempt to ground Christian life in the particularity of the senses. Although each of them reaches his conclusion by a different method, I argued that their collective efforts at unifying body and soul in the human being exerts a profound influence on Balthasar's own rearticulation of the doctrine.

With our understanding of influences on Balthasar in place, we were able to appreciate in Chapter 4 Balthasar's own distinctive rendering of the spiritual senses in his theological aesthetics. Most innovatively, Balthasar integrates the spiritual senses into a 'personalist' anthropology according to which they are bestowed upon the human being in the encounter with the neighbour. Additionally, we noted that Balthasar thoroughly conjoins spiritual and corporeal perception such that the two occur together in a single unified act. Spiritual perception does not occur without its corporeal counterpart. There is no 'inner vision' of God with the 'eye of the mind'. One thing this means is that the object of the spiritual senses cannot be the 'transcendent God', as Balthasar puts it. Instead, the spiritual senses have as their object the form of Christ, who is perceived in four distinct arenas: the world, the Church, liturgy, and the neighbour. We also saw that, whereas the spiritual senses have frequently been interpreted as pertaining to a 'mystical' encounter with God reserved for a few, Balthasar repositions the doctrine such that the spiritual senses are granted among the general gifts of grace. Last, and most importantly for Balthasar's overall goals in his theological aesthetics, we saw that he gives the spiritual senses an explicitly aesthetic dimension such that they are capable of apprehending and appreciating the splendour of the form.

Concerning the second fundamental claim of this study, I argued in Chapter 5 that it is through the spiritual senses that one performs the epistemologically central task of 'seeing the form'. More precisely, I argued that, whereas the corporeal senses perceive the material dimension of the form, it is the spiritual senses that behold the splendour of Christ as revealed in the form's supersensory aspect. Of course, as we have seen, Balthasar's theory of aesthetic form prohibits a separation of the material from the invisible splendour that shines forth from it. Additionally, as we noted in Chapter 4, Balthasar's anthropology disallows a separation of the corporeal from the spiritual in general. Both aspects of form, then, are actually perceived in simultaneity by the corporeal and the spiritual perceptual faculties in the human being. This formulation, however, is of service to us inasmuch as it allows us to describe more precisely the function of the spiritual senses in Balthasar's theological aesthetics.

Equipped with this formulation of the role of the spiritual senses, we were able to observe the necessity of the doctrine for Balthasar's project. Balthasar calls for perception of the form, and that form consists of both sensory and 'supersensory' aspects. It is precisely because the form itself is possessed of both sensory and supersensory aspects that the *perception* of that form must be both sensory and supersensory. Therefore, some account of the way in which this human perception exceeds the material realm is absolutely essential to the success of Balthasar's project. Balthasar's theological aesthetics thus clamours for a doctrine of the spiritual senses. Without it, in fact, one cannot account for the reception of revelation in Balthasar's thought.

This claim for the central role of the spiritual senses led us to a number of important implications that were explored in Chapter 6. There we saw that the spiritual senses are integral to Balthasar's engagement with many of the urgent theological debates of his time. For example, they are key to the Balthasarian alternative to Neo-Scholastic natural theology, especially its proofs for the existence of God. Specifically, the spiritual senses for Balthasar perceive evidence of God in the divine splendour that pervades the created order. Additionally, we saw that the spiritual senses are a crucial component of Balthasar's creative 'third option' in the debate between Neo-Scholastic theologians and their Modernist opponents. On that point, the spiritual senses ensure that the form of Christ not be misperceived as a mere 'sign', or pointer to the divine (a matter on which both sides of this debate err, to Balthasar). Additionally, we showed that the spiritual senses enable a supernaturally elevated aesthetic experience of divine revelation. This aspect of Balthasar's aesthetic theory allows him to develop the manner in which revelation resonates with the human being at the very same time that it surprises and overwhelms him or her. Last, we saw that, despite initial appearances to the contrary, the spiritual senses are a key way in which Balthasar overcomes both extrinsicism and immanentism. Specifically, as the fulfilment of the otherwise incomplete natural senses, the spiritual senses perfect the sensorium for God in the human being.

A number of consequences follow from the preceding analysis. First, this study demonstrates the insufficiency of the scholarly habit of reading Balthasar through Barth as a purely revelation-centred contrast to Rahner, and instead draws attention to Balthasar's pervasive concern with anthropology and epistemology. With that said, however, it is also important to emphasize that Balthasar does not go so far as to interpret the spiritual senses as a subjective, transcendental 'starting point' for theology (as Rahner renders them); rather, they function as an anthropological correlate or receptor to a revelation that is always initiated by God.

Second, a recurrent question for the interpretation of Balthasar's theological aesthetics involves the exact manner in which his use of the language of sensation should be understood. One is often tempted to think of Balthasar's dizzying array of sensory terms as simply figurative in character. It is here that reference to the spiritual senses proves to be particularly helpful in advancing understandings of Balthasar's thought. Specifically, scholarship on the spiritual senses makes a point of claiming that the language of sensation is used in this tradition in a way that is more than merely metaphorical, as was noted in the introduction to this study. Augustin Poulain and Karl Rahner hold that descriptions of seeing, hearing, and touching God in this tradition are not 'mere metaphors', but that these uses of sensory language bear a 'strong resemblance' to corporeal sensation. Balthasar, then, as one who positions himself in this tradition, could also be said to use such language in a non-metaphorical sense. When Balthasar writes of 'seeing' the Christ-form or the light of being that shines forth from the depths of reality, reference to the spiritual senses tradition cautions one from dismissing such language as merely figurative speech. Instead, in using sensory terms Balthasar does in fact describe an actual *perception* of the form of Christ as manifested in the world, Church, liturgy, and neighbour.

Third, in using the spiritual senses in the particular way that he does, Balthasar arguably places them in the most pivotal position they have occupied in their history. Although the spiritual senses are important to the patristic and medieval figures treated in the first portion of this study, only in Balthasar does an entire theological scheme stand or fall with spiritual perception. Indeed, the theologies of figures such as Origen, Gregory of Nyssa, and Bonaventure do not actually *require* spiritual perception for the mediation of divine revelation. (This is a luxury many of them have as a result of keeping the spiritual senses within the province of a few 'mystical' elite.) For Balthasar, by contrast, everything depends on the human being perceiving the splendour of the form of God's revelation. Given the crucial epistemological role that the spiritual senses play in Balthasar's system, this study proposes that the burgeoning contemporary field of theological aesthetics should give more explicit attention to spiritual perception and draw even more deeply than Balthasar himself on the rich and complex spiritual senses tradition.

On a related point, this approach challenges the recent championing of Balthasar as the paragon of a rather restricted type of *ressourcement*. It demonstrates to the contrary that Balthasar—although clearly invested in rehabilitating the patristic corpus in general, and the spiritual senses tradition in particular—nevertheless calls for that tradition to engage in a thoroughgoing manner with modern thought. Balthasar's systematic option involves no naïve or romantic escape back to the pre-modern world of the Fathers. Investigation of this topic therefore shows him at his most characteristically 'Balthasarian': he draws from the spirit (if not the letter) of the tradition in order to advance the audaciously creative version of the doctrine that is required to meet the challenges of his age.

Concerning those challenges, the rendering of the doctrine advanced in this study calls for scholars to revisit the importance of the spiritual senses for some of the most pressing debates in contemporary theology. To Balthasar, the doctrine of the spiritual senses is vital for solving extremely important theological problems, many of which continue into the present day. In particular, with the contemporary resurgence of a refined Neo-Scholasticism (much of which is actually critical of Balthasar for his 'liberal' views), an extrinsic corrective may increasingly be seen as a necessary response to the immanentist accommodations of post-Vatican II theology. Balthasar's use of the spiritual senses in his aesthetics prevents God's revelation from being reduced to human categories, while also ensuring that revelation is not used as a blunt rationale for blind obedience to ecclesiastical authority. Instead, through the spiritual senses one becomes both enraptured and overwhelmed by God's glorious splendour, awakening the desire to follow where God will lead. Theology today should therefore seriously consider Balthasar's resolution of issues that were provoked by the events leading up to the Second Vatican Council, but that remain frustratingly unsettled in the contemporary theological climate.

Bibliography

Aertsen, Jan A. *Medieval Philosophy and the Transcendentals: The Case of Thomas Aquinas.* Leiden, New York, Köln: Brill, 1996.
Albus, Michael. *Die Wahrheit ist Liebe: Zur Unterscheidung des Christlichen nach Hans Urs von Balthasar.* Freiburg im Breisgau: Herder, 1976.
Albert the Great. *De Pulchro et de Bono.* In Thomas Aquinas [sic]. *Opera Omnia*, ed. Roberto Busa, SJ. Stuttgart-Bad Cannstatt: Frommann-Holzboog, 1980. Vol. 7, 43–7.
Alexander of Hales, *Summa Theologica.* Vol. 4: *Prolegomena.* Ed. Collegii S. Bonaventurae, Quaracchi, 1948.
Andres, Friedrich. 'Die Stufen der Contemplatio in Bonaventuras Itinerarium mentis ad Deum und in Benjamin major des Richards von St. Viktor'. *Franziskanische Studien* 8 (1921), 189–200.
Angelus Silesius. *Cherubinischer Wandersmann*, ed. George Ellinger. Halle a. S.: Max Niemeyer, 1895.
Aquinas, Thomas. *Summa Contra Gentiles*, trans. English Dominicans. London: Burns, Oates, and Washbourne, 1934. (*Summa Contra Gentiles*, eds. C. Pera, P. Marc, and P. Carmello. 3 vols. Rome and Turin: Marietti, 1961.)
———. *Summa Theologiae*, trans. L. Shapcote et al. 3 vols. New York: Benziger, 1947 (*Summa Theologiae.* 5 vols. Ottawa: Commissio Plana, 1953.
———. *De Veritate: On Truth*, trans. R. W. Mulligan, James V. McGlynn, and Robert W. Schmidt. 3 vols. Chicago: Regnery, 1952–4. (*De Veritate.* Vol. 1 of *Quaestiones Disputatae*, ed. Raymond M. Spiazzi. Rome and Turin: Marietti, 1949.)
Aristotle. *Metaphysics.* English and Greek text, trans. Hugh Tredennick. Cambridge, MA: Harvard University Press, 1935.
Aubert, Roger. *Le Problème de l'acte de foi.* Louvain: E. Warny, 1950.
Augustine of Hippo. *City of God*, trans. John Healey. London: J. M. Dent and Co., 1967. (*De Civitate Dei.* In Bernardus Dombart and Alphonsus Kalb, eds. *Corpus Christianorum Series Latina.* Turnhout: Brepols, 1955. Vols 47–8.)
———. *Confessions*, trans. Henry Chadwick. Oxford: Oxford University Press, 1991. (*Confessiones.* In Jacques-Paul Migne, ed. *Patrologia Latina.* Paris: J.-P. Migne, 1844–55. Vol. 32, 659–867.)
———. *Expositions of the Psalms*, trans. Maria Boulding, OSB, ed. John E. Rotelle, OSA WSA III/15-20. New York: New City Press, 2000–4. (*Enarrationes in Psalmos.* In D. Eligius Dekkers, OSB, and Johannes Fraipont, eds. *Corpus Christianorum Series Latina.* Turnhout: Brepols, 1956. Vols 38–40.)

———. *Literal Meaning of Genesis*, trans. John Hammond Taylor. *Ancient Christian Writers*. Vols 41–2. New York: Newman Press, 1982. (*De Genesi ad Litteram*. In Jacques-Paul Migne, ed. *Patrologia Latina*. Paris: J.-P. Migne, 1844–55. Vol. 34, 173–484.)

———. *Of True Religion*, trans. Louis Mink. Chicago: H. Regnery Co., 1959. (*De Vera Religione*. In Jacques-Paul Migne, ed. *Patrologia Latina*. Paris: J.-P. Migne, 1844–55. Vol. 34, 121–72.)

———. *On Free Choice of the Will*, trans. Thomas Williams. Indianapolis, IN: Hackett, 1993. (*De Libero Arbitrio*. In Jacques-Paul Migne, ed. *Patrologia Latina*. Paris: J.-P. Migne, 1844–55. Vol. 32, 1221–310.)

———. *Soliloquies*, and *Immortality of the Soul*, trans. Gerard Watson. Warminster: Aris and Philips, 1990. (*Soliloquia*. In Jacques-Paul Migne, ed. *Patrologia Latina*. Paris: J.-P. Migne, 1844–55. Vol. 32, 868–903. *De Immortalitate Animae*. In Jacques-Paul Migne, ed. *Patrologia Latina*. Paris: J.-P. Migne, 1844–55. Vol. 32, 1021–34.)

———. *Tractates on the Gospel of John*. 5 vols. Washington, DC: Catholic University of America Press, 1988–95. (*In Iohannis Euangelium Tractatus*. In D. Rabouts Willems, OSB, ed. *Corpus Christianorum Series Latina*. Turnhout: Brepols, 1954. Vol. 36.)

Balthasar, Hans Urs von. 'Analogie und Dialektik'. *Divus Thomas* 22 (1944), 171–216.

———. *Apokalypse der Deutschen Seele: Studien zu einer Lehre von letzten Haltungen*. Einsiedeln: Johannes Verlag. 1937–39.

———. 'Auch die Sünde: Zum Erosproblem bei Charles Morgan und Paul Claudel'. *Stimmen der Zeit* 69 (1939), 222–37.

———. *Aurelius Augustinus, das Antlitz der Kirche*. Einsiedeln-Köln: Benzinger, 1942.

———. *Aurelius Augustinus, Psychologie und Mystik*. Einsiedeln: Johannes Verlag, 1960.

———. *Aurelius Augustinus, über die Psalmen*. Leipzig: Hegner, 1936.

———. *Bernanos: An Ecclesial Existence*, trans. Erasmo Leiva-Merikakis. San Francisco, CA: Ignatius Press, 1996. (*Gelebte Kirche: Bernanos*. Einsiedeln: Johannes Verlag, 1988.)

———. *Christian Meditation*, trans. Mary Skerry. San Francisco, CA: Ignatius Press, 1989. (*Christlich Meditieren*. Freiburg: Herder, 1984.)

———. *Cosmic Liturgy: The Universe According to Maximus the Confessor*, trans. Brian E. Daley. San Francisco, CA: Ignatius Press, 2003. (*Kosmische Liturgie: Hohe und Krise des griechischen Weltbilds*. Freiburg: Herder, 1941; 2nd edn *Kosmische Liturgie: Das Weltbild Maximus' des Bekenners*. Einsiedeln: Johannes Verlag, 1961.)

———. *Elucidations*, trans. the Society for the Promotion of Christian Knowledge. San Francisco, CA: Ignatius Press, 1998. (*Klarstellungen: Zur Prüfung der Geister*. Freiburg: Herder, 1971.)

———. *Explorations in Theology*. 4 vols, trans. A. V. Littledale, A. Dru, B. McNeil, et al. San Francisco, CA: Ignatius Press, 1989–95. (*Skizzen zur Theologie*. 5 vols. Einsiedeln: Johannes Verlag, 1960–86.)

———. 'The Fathers, Scholastics, and Ourselves'. *Communio* 24 (Summer 1997), 347–96. ('Patristik, Scholastik, und wir'. *Theologie der Zeit* 3 (1939), 65–104.)

———. 'Geist und Feuer'. *Herder Korrespondenz* 30 (1976), 75.

———. *The Glory of the Lord: A Theological Aesthetics*. 7 vols, trans. Erasmo Leiva-Merikakis, Andrew Louth, Brian McNeil, Oliver Davies, Francis McDonagh, John Saward, Martin Simon, and Rowan Williams. San Francisco, CA: Ignatius Press, 1982–91. (*Herrlichkeit: Eine Theologische Ästhetik*. 3 vols. Einsiedeln: Johannes Verlag, 1961–9.)

———. 'Die Hiera des Evagrius'. *Zeitschrift für katholische theologie* 63 (1939), 86–106, 181–206.

———. *In the Fullness of Faith: On the Centrality of the Distinctively Catholic*. San Francisco, CA: Ignatius Press, 1988. (*Katholisch: Aspekte des Mysteriums*. Einsiedeln: Johannes Verlag, 1975.)

———. 'Karl Barth und der Katholizismus'. *Theologie der Zeit* 3 (1939), 126–32.

———. 'Kunst und Religion'. *Volkswohl* 18 (1927), 354–65.

———. *Light of the Word: Brief Reflections on the Sunday Readings*. San Francisco, CA: Ignatius Press, 1993. (*Licht des Wortes: Skizzen zu allen Sonntagslesungen*. Trier: Paulinus-Verlag, 1987.)

———. *Love Alone is Credible*, trans. D. C. Schindler. San Francisco, CA: Ignatius Press, 2004. (*Glaubhaft ist nur Liebe*. Einsiedeln: Johannes Verlag, 1985.)

———. 'The Metaphysics and Mystical Theology of Evagrius', *Monastic Studies* 3 (1965), 183–95. ('Metaphysik und Mystik des Evagrius Pontikus', *Zeitschrift für Askese und Mystik* (1939), 31–47.)

———. *My Work: In Retrospect*, trans. Kelly Hamilton et al. San Francisco, CA: Ignatius Press, 1993. (*Mein Werk: Durchblicke*. Einsiedeln: Johannes Verlag, 1990.)

———. *The Moment of Christian Witness*, trans. The Missionary Society of St Paul the Apostle in the State of New York. San Francisco, CA: Ignatius Press, 1994. (*Cordula oder der Ernstfall*. Einsiedeln: Johannes Verlag, 1966.)

———. 'Le Mysterion d'Origène'. In *Recherches de science religieuse* 26 (1936), 511–62 and 27 (1937), 38–64.

———. *New Elucidations*, trans. Mary Theresilde Skerry. San Francisco, CA: Ignatius Press, 1986. (*Neue Klarstellungen*. Einsiedeln: Johannes Verlag, 1979.)

———. *Mysterium Paschale: The Mystery of Easter*, trans. Aidan Nichols. San Francisco, CA: Ignatius Press, 2000. (*Mysterium Salutis: Grundriss heilsgeschichtlicher Dogmatik*. Band 1. Einsiedeln: Benziger, 1965).

——. 'On the Tasks of Catholic Philosophy in Our Time'. *Communio* 20 (Spring 1993), 147–87. (*Von den Aufgaben der katholischen Philosophie in der Zeit*. Einsiedeln: Johannes Verlag, 1998.)

——. *Origen, Spirit and Fire: A Thematic Anthology of His Writings*, trans. Robert J. Daly. Washington, DC: Catholic University of America Press, 1984. (*Origenes, Geist und Feuer: Ein Aufbau aus seinen Werken*. Salzburg: Otto Müller, 1938.)

——. *Parole et mystère chez Origène*. Paris: Èditions du Cerf, 1957.

——. 'Persönlichkeit und Form'. *Gloria Dei* 7 (1952), 1–15.

——. *Prayer*, trans. Graham Harrison. San Francisco, CA: Ignatius Press, 1986. (*Das betrachtende Gebet*. Einsiedeln: Johannes Verlag, 1959.)

——. *Presence and Thought: An Essay on the religious Philosophy of Gregory of Nyssa*, trans. Mark Sebanc. San Francisco, CA: Ignatius Press, 1995. (*Présence et pensée: Essai sur la philosophie religieuse de Grégoire de Nysse*. Paris: Beauchesne, 1942. 'Présence et pensée. La philosophie religieuse de Grégoire de Nysse'. *Recherches de science religieuse* 29 (1939), 513–49.)

——. 'In Retrospect'. In *The Analogy of Beauty: The Theology of Hans Urs von Balthasar*, ed. John Riches. Edinburgh: T&T Clark, 1986, 194–221. (*Rechenschaft 1965*. Einsiedeln: Johannes Verlag, 1965.)

——. 'A Résumé of My Thought'. In *Hans Urs von Balthasar: His Life and Work*, ed. David L. Schindler. San Francisco, CA: Ignatius Press, 1991, 1–6. 'Essai de résumer ma pensée'. *Revue des deux mondes* (10–12 October 1988), 100–6.

——. *Romano Guardini: Reform from the Source*, trans. Albert Wimmer and D. C. Schindler. San Francisco, CA: Ignatius Press, 2010. (*Romano Guardini: Reform aus dem Ursprung*. München: Kösel-Verlag, 1970.)

——. 'Das Schauvermögen der Christen'. In *Skizzen zur Theologie V: Homo creatus est*, ed. Hans Urs von Balthasar. Einsiedeln: Johannes Verlag, 1986, 52–60.

——. *Science, Religion, and Christianity*, trans. Hilda Graef. London: Burns and Oates, 1958. (*Die Gottesfrage der heutigen Menschen*. Wien: Herold, 1956.)

——. 'Spirit and Fire: An Interview with Hans Urs von Balthasar', trans. Nicholas Healy. *Communio* 32 (Fall 2005), 573–93. ('Geist und Feuer: Ein Gespräch mit Hans Urs von Balthasar'. *Herder Korrespondenz* 30 (1976), 72–82.)

——. *Test Everything: Hold Fast to What Is Good*. San Francisco, CA: Ignatius Press, 1989. (*Prüfet alles: Das Gute behaltet*. Ostfildern: Schwabenverlag, 1986.)

——. *Theo-Drama: Theological Dramatic Theory*. 5 vols, trans. Graham Harrison. San Francisco, CA: Ignatius Press, 1988–98. (*Theodramatik*. 4 vols. Einsiedeln: Johannes Verlag, 1973–83.)

——. *Theo-Logic: Theological Logical Theory*. 3 vols, trans. Adrian J. Walker. San Francisco, CA: Ignatius Press, 2000–5. (*Theologik*. 3 vols. Einsiedeln: Johannes Verlag, 1985–7. Vol. 1 first published as *Wahrheit: Ein Versuch. Erstes Buch. Wahrheit der Welt*. Einsiedeln: Benziger, 1947.)

―. *A Theological Anthropology*, trans. William Glen-Doepel. New York: Sheed and Ward, 1967. (*Das Ganze im Fragment: Aspekte der Geschichtstheologie*. Einsiedeln: Benziger, 1963.)

―. 'Theology and Aesthetic', trans. Andrée Emery. *Communio* 8 (Spring 1981), 62–71.

―. *The Theology of Henri de Lubac: An Overview*, trans. J. Fessio, SJ, M. Waldstein, and S. Clements. San Francisco, CA: Ignatius Press, 1991. (*Henri de Lubac: Sein organisches Lebenswerk*. Einsiedeln: Johannes Verlag, 1976.)

―. *A Theology of History*. San Francisco, CA: Ignatius Press, 1994. (*Theologie der Geschichte*. Einsiedeln: Johannes Verlag, 1959.)

―. *The Theology of Karl Barth: Exposition and Interpretation*, trans. Edward Oakes. San Francisco, CA: Ignatius Press, 1992. (*Karl Barth: Darstellung und Deutung seiner Theologie*. Einsiedeln: Johannes Verlag, 1951.)

―. *Truth is Symphonic: Aspects of Christian Pluralism*. San Francisco, CA: Ignatius Press, 1987. (*Die Wahrheit ist Symphonisch: Aspekte des christlichen Pluralismus*. Einsiedeln: Johannes Verlag, 1972.)

―. *Two Sisters in the Spirit: Thérèse of Lisieux & Elizabeth of the Trinity*, trans. Dennis Martin. San Francisco, CA: Ignatius Press, 1992. (*Schwestern im Geist: Therese von Lisieux und Elisabeth von Dijon*. Einsiedeln: Johannes Verlag, 1970.)

―. 'Der Unbekannte jenseits des Wortes'. In *Interpretation der Welt: Romano Guardini zum 80. Geburtstag*, ed. H. Kuhn. Würzburg: Echter Verlag, 1965, 638–45.

―. *Der versiegelte Quell: Auslegung des Hohen Liedes*. Salzburg: Otto Müller Verlag, 1939.

Barth, Karl. *Church Dogmatics*. 13 vols, eds. G. W. Bromiley and T. F. Torrance, trans. G. W. Bromiley et al. Edinburgh: T&T Clark, 1936–69. (*Kirchliche Dogmatik*. 13 vols. Munich: Kaiser, 1932; Zurich: Evangelischer Verlag, 1938–65.)

―. *Epistle to the Romans*. 6th edn, trans. Edwyn C. Hoskyns. London: Oxford University Press, 1933. (*Der Römerbrief*. Bern: G. A. Bäschlin, 1919.)

Batlogg, Andreas R. 'Hans Urs von Balthasar und Karl Rahner: Zwei Schüler des Ignatius'. In *Die Kunst Gottes verstehen: Hans Urs von Balthasars theologische Provokationen*, eds. Magnus Striet and Jan-Heiner Tück. Freiburg: Herder, 2005, 410–46.

Beauchemin, F. *Le savior au service de l'amour*. Paris: J. Vrin, 1935.

Bieler, Martin. 'Die kleine Drehung: Hans Urs von Balthasar und Karl Barth im Gespräch'. In *Logik der Liebe und Herrlichkeit Gottes: Hans Urs von Balthasar im Gespräch*, ed. Walter Kasper. Ostfildern: Matthias-Grünewald Verlag, 2006, 318–38.

―. 'Meta-anthropology and Christology: On the Philosophy of Hans Urs von Balthasar'. *Communio* 20 (Spring 1993), 129–46.

Bissen, J. M. *Les degrés de la contemplation*. Paris: J. Vrin, 1928–30.

Block, Edward. 'Hans Urs von Balthasar as Reader of *Le Soulier de Satin*'. *Claudel Studies* 24 (1997), 35–44.

Blondel, Maurice. *Action: Essay on a Critique of Life and a Science of Practice*, trans. Olivia Blanchette. South Bend, IN: University of Notre Dame Press, 1984. (*L'Action: Essai d'une critique de la vie et d'une science de la pratique*. Paris: F. Alcan, 1893.)

———. *The Letter on Apologetics* and *History and Dogma*, trans. Alexander Dru and Illtyd Trethowan. New York: Holt, Rinehart, and Winston, 1964.)

Böhm, Thomas. 'Die Deutung der Kirchenväter bei Hans Urs von Balthasar—Der Fall Origenes'. In *Logik der Liebe und Herrlichkeit Gottes: Hans Urs von Balthasar im Gespräch*, ed. Walter Kasper. Ostfildern: Matthias-Grünewald-Verlag, 2006, 64–75.

Bonaventure. *Breviloquium*. In *The Works of Bonaventure*, trans. José de Vinck. Paterson, NJ: St Anthony Guild Press, 1960. Vol. 2. (*Breviloquium*. In *Opera Omnia*. Rome: Quaracchi, 1882–1902. Vol. 5, 199–291.)

———. *Christ, the One Teacher of All*. In *What Manner of Man? Sermons on Christ*, trans. Zachary Hayes. Chicago: Franciscan Herald, 1974, 21–55. (*Christus Unus Omnium Magister*. In *Opera Omnia*. Rome: Quaracchi, 1882–1902. Vol. 5, 567–74.)

———. *Collations on the Six Days*. In *The Works of Bonaventure*, trans. José de Vinck. Paterson, NJ: St Anthony Guild Press, 1970. Vol. 5. (*Collationes in Hexaemeron*. In *Opera Omnia*. Rome: Quaracchi, 1882–1902. Vol. 5, 327–454.)

———. *Commentaria in quatuor libros Sententiarum Magistri Petri Lombardi*. In *Opera Omnia*. Rome: Quarracchi, 1882–1902. Vols. 1–4.

———. *Commentarius in Librum Sapientiae*. In *Opera Omnia*. Rome: Quaracchi, 1882–1902. Vol. 6, 107–235.

———. *On Retracing the Arts to Theology*. In *The Works of Bonaventure*, trans. José de Vinck. Paterson, NJ: St Anthony Guild Press, 1966. Vol. 3, 13–32. (*De Reductione Artium ad Theologiam*. In *Opera Omnia*. Rome: Quaracchi, 1882–1902. Vol. 5, 317–25.)

———. *The Sunday Sermons of Bonaventure*. In *The Works of Bonaventure*, trans. Timothy J. Johnson. Saint Bonaventure, New York: Franciscan Institute Publications, 2008. Vol. 12. (*Opera Omnia*. Rome: Quaracchi, 1882–1902. Vol. 9.)

———. *Soliloquy on the Four Spiritual Exercises*. In *The Works of Bonaventure*, trans. José de Vinck. Paterson, NJ: St Anthony Guild Press, 1966. Vol. 3, 35–129. (*Soliloquium de Quatuor Mentalibus Exercitiis*. In *Opera Omnia*. Rome: Quaracchi, 1882–1902. Vol. 8, 28–67.)

———. *The Soul's Journey into God*. In *Bonaventure*. Classics of Western Spirituality, trans. Ewert Cousins. Mahwah, NJ: Paulist Press, 1978, 51–116. (*Itinerarium Mentis in Deum*. In *Opera Omnia*. Rome: Quaracchi, 1882–1902. Vol. 5, 293–316.)

Bibliography 199

———. *The Tree of Life*. In *Bonaventure*. Classics of Western Spirituality, trans. Ewert Cousins. Mahwah, NJ: Paulist Press, 1978, 117–75. (*Lignum Vitae* In *Opera Omnia*. Rome: Quaracchi, 1882–1902. Vol. 8, 68–87.)

———. *The Triple Way*. In *Mystical Opuscula*, trans. José de Vinck. Paterson, NJ: St Anthony Guild Press, 1960. Vol. 1, 63–94. (*De Triplica Via*. In *Opera Omnia*. Rome: Quaracchi, 1882–1902. Vol. 8, 3–27.)

Bonnefoy, Jean-François. *Le Saint-Esprit et ses dons selon Saint Bonaventure*. Paris: J. Vrin, 1929.

———. *Une somme bonaventurienne de théologie mystique*. Paris: Librairie Saint-François, 1934.

Bonnici, John S. *Person to Person: Friendship and Love in the Life and Theology of Hans Urs von Balthasar*. New York: Alba House, 1999.

Brown, Stephen. Introduction to Bonaventure, *The Journey of the Mind into God*. Indianapolis, IN: Hackett, 1993, ix–xviii.

Buckley, J. J. 'Balthasar's Use of the Theology of Thomas Aquinas'. *The Thomist* 57 (1995), 517–45.

Carton, Raoul. *L'experience mystique de l'illumination interieure chez Roger Bacon*. Paris: J. Vrin, 1924.

Casarella, Peter. 'Experience as a Theological Category: Hans Urs von Balthasar on the Christian Encounter with God's Image'. *Communio* 20 (Spring 1993), 118–28.

Chapp, Larry. *The God Who Speaks: Hans Urs von Balthasar's Theology of Revelation*. San Francisco, CA: Catholic Scholars Press, 1996.

Chia, Roland. *Revelation and Theology: The Knowledge of God in Balthasar and Barth*. Bern; New York: Peter Lang, 1999.

———. 'Theological Aesthetics or Aesthetic Theology? Some Reflections on the Theology of Hans Urs von Balthasar'. *Scottish Journal of Theology* 49 (1996), 75–95.

Cirelli, Anthony Tyrus Gaines. 'Form and Freedom: Patristic Retrieval and the Liberating Encounter Between God and Man in the Thought of Hans Urs von Balthasar'. Doctoral Dissertation, Catholic University of America, 2007.

Claudel, Paul. *Antlitz in Glorie und vermischte Gedichte*, trans. Hans Urs von Balthasar. Einsiedeln: Johannes Verlag, 1965.

———. 'Der Architekt', trans. Hans Urs von Balthasar. *Hochland* 51 (1959), 217–23.

———. *Art poétique: Connaissance du temps, Traité de la co-naissance au monde et de soi-même, Développement de l'église*. Paris: Societé DV Mercve, 1907.

———. *Les aventures de Sophie*. Paris: Gallimard, 1937.

———. *La cantate à trois voix*. Paris: Gallimard, 1943.

———. *Conversations dans le Loir-et-Cher*. Paris: Librairie Plon, 1957.

———. *Corona Benignitatis Anni Dei*, trans. Hans Urs von Balthasar. Einsiedeln: Johannes Verlag, 1965.

———. *Fünf große Oden*, trans. Hans Urs von Balthasar. Freiburg: Herder, 1939.
———. *Gedichte*, trans. Hans Urs von Balthasar. Basel: Sammlung Klosterberg, 1940.
———. *Gesammelte Werke*, trans. Hans Urs von Balthasar. Einsiedeln-Zürich-Köln: Benziger, 1963.
———. *Der Gnadenkranz*, trans. Hans Urs von Balthasar. Einsiedeln: Johannes Verlag, 1957.
———. *Heiligenblätter*, trans. Hans Urs von Balthasar. Einsiedeln: Johannes Verlag, 1965.
———. *Der Kreuzweg*, trans. Hans Urs von Balthasar. Luzern: Josef Stocker, 1940.
———. *Mariä Verkündigung*, trans. Hans Urs von Balthasar. Luzern: Josef Stocker, 1946.
———. *Die Messe des Verbannten*, trans. Hans Urs von Balthasar. Einsiedeln: Johannes Verlag, 1981.
———. 'Paul Verlaine', trans. Hans Urs von Balthasar. *Hochland* 51 (1959), 251–3.
———. *Der seidene Schuh*, trans. Hans Urs von Balthasar. Salzburg: Otto Müller Verlag, 1939.
———. 'La Sensation du Divin'. In Paul Claudel. *Présence et prophétie*. Fribourg en Suisse: Éditions de la librairie de l'Université, 1942, 49–126.
———. *Singspiel für drei Stimmen*, trans. Hans Urs von Balthasar. Einsiedeln: Johannes Verlag, 1965.
———. *Strahlende Gesichter*, trans. Hans Urs von Balthasar. Einsiedeln: Johannes Verlag, 1957.
———. 'Verse der Verbannung', trans. Hans Urs von Balthasar. *Rundschau* 40 (1940), 406–13.
Coakley, Sarah. 'Gregory of Nyssa'. In *The Spiritual Senses: Perceiving God in Western Christianity*, eds. Paul L. Gavrilyuk and Sarah Coakley. Cambridge: Cambridge University Press, 2012, 36–55.
———. 'On the Identity of the Risen Jesus: Finding Jesus Christ in the Poor'. In *Seeking the Identity of Jesus: A Pilgrimage*, eds. Beverly Roberts Gaventa and Richard B. Hays. Grand Rapids, MI: Eerdmans, 2008, 301–19.
———. 'The Resurrection and the "Spiritual Senses": On Wittgenstein, Epistemology, and the Risen Christ'. In Sarah Coakley. *Powers and Submissions: Spirituality, Philosophy, and Gender*. Oxford: Blackwell, 2002, 130–52.
Coolman, Boyd Taylor. *Knowing God by Experience: The Spiritual Senses in the Theology of William of Auxerre*. Washington, DC: Catholic University of America Press, 2004.
Corder, Stephen. The Spiritual Senses in the Exercises of Ignatius of Loyola. Jesuit School of Theology, Berkeley, CA, 2003.
Corset, P. 'Premières rencontres de la théologie catholique avec l'oeuvre de Barth (1922-1932), III Réception de la théologie de Barth', In *Karl Barth: Genèse et réception de sa théologie*, ed. Pierre Gisel. Genève: Labor et Fides, 1987, 151–90.

Daigler, Matthew A. 'Heidegger and von Balthasar: A Lovers' Quarrel over Beauty and Divinity'. *American Catholic Philosophical Quarterly* 69 (1995), 375–94.

Daley, Brian, SJ 'Balthasar's Reading of the Church Fathers'. In *The Cambridge Companion to Hans Urs von Balthasar*, eds. Edward T. Oakes and David Moss. Cambridge: Cambridge University Press, 2004, 187–206.

Daniélou, Jean. *Platonisme et théologie mystique: Essai sur la doctrine spirituelle de Saint Grégoire de Nysse.* Paris: Aubier, 1944.

Dechamps, Victor. *Entretiens sur la démonstration Catholique de la révélation chrétienne.* Paris: Tournai, 1861.

Denziger, Henry and Adolf Schönmetzer, eds. *Enchiridion Symbolorum.* Freiburg: Herder, 1965.

Diadochus of Photice. *One Hundred Practical Texts of Perception and Spiritual Discernment.* English and Greek Text, trans. Janet Elaine Rutherford. Belfast: Institute of Byzantine Studies, 2000.

Dickens, W. T. *Hans Urs von Balthasar's Theological Aesthetics: A Model for Post-Critical Biblical Interpretation.* Notre Dame, IN: University of Notre Dame Press, 2003.

Dillon, John M. 'Aisthêsis Noêtê: A Doctrine of the Spiritual Senses in Origen and in Plotinus'. In *Hellenica et Judaica*, eds. A. Caquot, M. Hadas-Lebel, and J. Riaud. Leuven-Paris: Éditions Peeters, 1986, 443–55.

Directoria Exercitorum Spiritualium: (1540–1599). Rome: Institutum Historicum Societatis Jesu, 1955.

Disse, Jörg-P. 'Liebe und Erkenntnis: Zur Geistesmetaphysik Hans Urs von Balthasars'. *Müncher Theologische Zeitschrift* 54 (1999), 215–27.

——. *Metaphysik der Singularität: Eine Hinführung am Leitfaden der Philosophie Hans Urs von Balthasars. Philosophische Theologie.* Vol. 7. Wien: Passagen Verlag, 1996.

Dobbins, Dunstan John. *Franciscan Mysticism.* New York: J. F. Wagner, 1927.

Drewes, Hans-Anton. 'Karl Barth und Hans Urs von Balthasar: Ein Basler Zwiegespräch'. In *Die Kunst Gottes Verstehen: Hans Urs von Balthasars Theologische Provokationen*, eds. Magnus Striet and Jan-Heiner Tück. Freiburg: Herder, 2005, 367–83.

Dulles, Avery Cardinal. *A History of Apologetics.* San Francisco, CA: Ignatius Press, 1999.

Dupré, Louis. 'The Glory of the Lord: Hans Urs von Balthasar's Theological Aesthetic'. In *Hans Urs von Balthasar: His Life and Work*, ed. David L. Schindler, 183–206. San Francisco, CA: Ignatius Press, 1991. Originally published as 'The Glory of the Lord: Hans Urs von Balthasar's Theological Aesthetic'. *Communio* 16 (Fall 1989), 384–412.

Eco, Umberto. *The Aesthetics of Thomas Aquinas*, trans. Hugh Bredin. Cambridge, MA: Harvard University Press, 1988.

Ehrenfels, Christian von. 'Weiterführende Bemerkungen'. In *Gestalthaftes Sehen: Ergebnisse und Aufgaben der Morphologie*, ed. Ferdinand Weinhandl. Darmstadt: Wissenschaftliche Buchgesellschaft, 1974, 47–60.

Endean, Philip, SJ 'The Ignatian Prayer of the Senses'. *Heythrop Journal* 31 (1990), 391–418.

Engelhard, Markus. *Gotteserfahrung im Werk Hans Urs von Balthasars*. St Ottilien: EOS Verlag, 1998.

Erp, Stephan van. *The Art of Theology: Hans Urs von Balthasar's Theological Aesthetics and the Foundations of Faith*. Leuven, Paris, Dudley, MA: Peeters, 2004.

Evagrius of Pontus. *Chapters on Prayer*. In *Evagrius of Pontus: The Greek Ascetic Corpus*, trans. R. E. Sinkewicz. Oxford: Oxford University Press, 2003, 183–209. (*Ejusdem de Oratione*. In Jacques-Paul Migne, ed. *Patrologia Graeca*. Paris: J.-P. Migne, 1857–66. Vol. 79, 1165–200.)

——. *On Thoughts*. In *Evagrius of Pontus: The Greek Ascetic Corpus*, trans. R. E. Sinkewicz. Oxford: Oxford University Press, 2003, 136–82. (*De Malignis Cogitationibus*. In Jacques-Paul Migne, ed. *Patrologia Graeca*. Paris: J.-P. Migne, 1857–66. Vol. 79, 1200–33.)

Fields, Stephen. 'Balthasar and Rahner on the Spiritual Senses'. *Theological Studies* 57 (1996), 224–41.

Foley, Grover. 'The Catholic Critics of Karl Barth, in Outline and Analysis'. *Scottish Journal of Theology* 14 (1961), 136–55.

Franco, Francesco. *La passione dell'amore: L'ermeneutica cristiana di Balthasar e Origene*. Bologna: EDB Edizioni Dehoniane Bologna, 2005.

Fries, Heinrich. *Fundamental Theology*, trans. Robert Daly. Washington, DC: Catholic University of America Press, 1996.

Gagliardi, Achille. *Commentarii seu Explanationes in Exercitia spiritualia Sancti Patris Ignatii de Loyola*, ed. Constantinus van Aken. Bruges: Desclée de Brouwer, 1882.

Gavrilyuk, Paul L. 'Pseudo-Dionysius the Areopagite'. In *The Spiritual Senses: Perceiving God in Western Christianity*, eds. Paul L. Gavrilyuk and Sarah Coakley. Cambridge: Cambridge University Press, 2012, 86–103.

Gavrilyuk, Paul L., and Sarah Coakley, eds. *The Spiritual Senses: Perceiving God in Western Christianity*. Cambridge: Cambridge University Press, 2012.

Gawronski, Raymond. 'The Beauty of the Cross: The Theological Aesthetics of Hans Urs von Balthasar'. *Logos* 5 (Summer 2002), 185–206.

——. *Word and Silence: Hans Urs von Balthasar and the Spiritual Encounter between East and West*. Edinburgh: T&T Clark, 1995.

Gilson, Etienne. *The Philosophy of St. Bonaventure*. Paterson, NJ: St Anthony Guild Press; Desclée Co., 1965. (*La philosophie de Saint Bonaventure*. Paris: J. Vrin, 1924.)

Goethe, Johann Wolfgang von. 'Die Absicht Eingeleitet'. In Ferdinand Weinhandl. *Das Vermächtnis des Wanderers*. Klosterneuberg: Stifterbibliothek, 1956.

——. *Gespräche mit Eckerman*. Berlin: Knaur, 1924.
——. 'Morphologie'. In Ferdinand Weinhandl. *Die Metaphysik Goethes*. Darmstadt: Wissenschaftliche Buchgesellschaft, 1965.
Gregory of Nyssa. *Commentary on The Song of Songs*, trans. Casimir McCambley. Brookline, MA: Holy Cross, 1987. (*In Canticum Canticorum*. In H. Langerbeck, ed. *Gregorii Nysseni Opera*. Vol. 6. Leiden: Brill, 1986.)
——. *On the Soul and Resurrection*, trans. Catharine P. Roth. Crestwood, NY: St Vladimir's Seminary Press, 2002. (*De Anima et Resurrectione*. In Jacques-Paul Migne, ed. *Patrologia Graeca*. Paris: J.-P. Migne, 1857–66. Vol. 46, 12–160.)
Grünewald, Stanislaus. *Franziskanische Mystik*. Munich: Naturrechts Verlag, 1932.
——. 'Zur Mystik des hl. Bonaventura', *ZAM* 9 (1934), 124–42, 219–32.
Guardini, Romano. *Die Sinne und die religiöse Erkenntnis*. Würzburg: Werkbund Verlag, 1950.
——. *The Spirit of the Liturgy*, trans. Ada Lane. New York: Crossroad, 1998. (*Vom Geist der Liturgie*. Freiburg: Herder, 1921.)
Guerriero, Elio. 'Von Balthasar e Origene'. *Rivista Internazionale di Teologia e Cultura: Communio* 116 (1991), 123–34.
Gutwenger, Engelbert, and Hans Urs von Balthasar. 'Begriff der Natur in der Theologie: Eine Diskussion zwischen Hans Urs von Balthasar, Zürich, und Engelbert Gutwenger, S.J., Innsbruck'. *Zeitschrift für katholische Theologie* 75 (1953), 452–64.
——. 'Natur und Übernatur: Gedanken zu Balthasars Werk über die Bartsche Theologie'. *Zeitschrift für katholische Theologie* 75 (1953), 82–97.
Hallensleben, Barbara, ed. *Letzte Haltungen: Hans Urs von Balthasars 'Apokalypse der deutschen Seele' neu gelesen*. Fribourg: Academic Press, 2006.
Hamer, Jérôme. 'Un programme de 'christologie conséquente': Le projet de Karl Barth'. *Nouvelle revue théologique* 84 (1962), 1009–31.
Harl, Marguerite. 'La "bouche" et le "coeur" de l'apôtre: Deux images bibliques du "sens divin" de l'homme (Proverbes 2, 5) chez Origène'. In *Forma Futuri: Studi in onore del Cardinale Michele Pellegrino*. Turin: Erasmo, 1975, 17–42.
Harrison, Victoria. 'Homo Orans: Von Balthasar's Christocentric Philosophical Anthropology'. *Heythrop Journal* 40 (1999), 280–300.
——. 'Putnam's Internal Realism and von Balthasar's Religious Epistemology'. *International Journal for Philosophy of Religion* 44 (1998), 67–92.
Hartmann, M. *Ästhetik als ein Grundbegriff fundamentaler Theologie: Eine Untersuchung zu Hans Urs von Balthasar*. St Ottilien: Dissertationen Theologische Reihe. Vol. 5, 1985.
Healy, Nicholas J. *The Eschatology of Hans Urs von Balthasar: Being as Communion*. Oxford: Oxford University Press, 2005.

Henrici, Peter. 'A Sketch of von Balthasar's Life'. In *Hans Urs von Balthasar: His Life and Work*, ed. David L. Schindler. San Francisco, CA: Ignatius Press, 1991, 7–43.

Horn, Gabriel. 'Le sens de l'esprit d'après Diadoque de Photice'. *Revue d'ascetique et mystique* 8 (1927), 402–19.

Howsare, Rodney. *Balthasar: A Guide for the Perplexed*. Edinburgh: T&T Clark, 2009.

———. *Hans Urs von Balthasar and Protestantism*. Edinburgh: T&T Clark, 2005.

Ide, Pascal. *Être et Mystère: La Philosophie de Hans Urs von Balthasar*. Brussels: Culture et Vérité, 1995.

Ignatius of Loyola. *The Spiritual Exercises and Selected Works*, trans. George E. Ganss. *The Classics of Western Spirituality*. New York: Paulist Press, 1991. (*Ejercicios espirituales*. Candido de Dalmases, SJ, ed. Santander: Sal Terrae, 1987.)

Imle, Fanny. *Das geistliche Leben nach der Lehre des hl. Bonaventura*. Werl: Franziskus-Druckerei, 1939.

Kant, Immanuel. *Critique of the Power of Judgment*, trans. Paul Guyer. Cambridge: Cambridge University Press, 2000.

———. *Critique of Practical Reason*, trans. Mary Gregor. Cambridge: Cambridge University Press, 1997.

———. *Critique of Pure Reason*, trans. Paul Guyer and Allen W. Wood. Cambridge: Cambridge University Press, 1998.

Kasper, Walter, ed. *Logik der Liebe und Herrlichkeit Gottes: Hans Urs von Balthasar im Gespräch*. Ostfildern: Matthias-Grünewald-Verlag, 2006.

Kay, Jeffrey Ames. 'Aesthetics and a posteriori Evidence in Balthasar's Theological Methodology'. *Communio* 2 (Fall 1975), 289–99.

———. *Theological Aesthetics: The Role of Aesthetics in the Theological Method of Hans Urs von Balthasar*. Bern: Peter Lang 1975.

Keefe, Donald J. 'A Methodological Critique of von Balthasar's Theological Aesthetics'. *Communio* 5 (1978), 23–43.

Kilby, Karen. *Balthasar: A (Very) Critical Introduction*. Grand Rapids, MI: Eerdmans, 2012.

Koenig, H. *De inhabitatione Spiritus Sancti*. Mundelein: Apud Aedes Seminarii Sanctae Mariae ad Lacum, 1934.

Körner, Bernhard. 'Fundamentaltheologie bei Hans Urs von Balthasar'. *Zeitschrift für katholische Theologie* 109 (1987).

Kromer, Hans Martin. 'Hans Urs von Balthasar und Karl Barth im Kontext der "Apokalypse der deutschen Seele": Der Weg zur "Umkehrung"'. In *Letzte Haltungen: Hans Urs von Balthasars 'Apokalypse der deutschen Seele' neu Gelesen*, ed. Barbara Hallensleben. Freiburg: Academic Press, 2006, 265–79.

Kunz, Erhard. 'Glaubwürdigkeit und Glaube (analysis fidei)'. In *Handbuch der Fundamentaltheologie*. Vol. 4, *Traktat theologische Erkenntnislehre*.

Schlussteil: Reflexion auf Fundamentaltheologie, eds. W. Kern, H. J. Pottmeyer, and M. Seckler. Freiburg: Herder, 1988, 414–50.

———. 'Ignatianische Spiritualität in ihrer anthropologischen Durchführung'. In *Gott für die Welt: Henri de Lubac, Gustav Siewerth und Hans Urs von Balthasar in ihren Grundanliegen*, eds. Peter Reifenberg and Anton van Hooff. Mainz: Matthias-Grünewald-Verlag, 2001, 293–303.

Kuschel, Karl-Josef. 'Literature as Challenge to Catholic Theology in the 20th Century: Balthasar, Guardini, and the Tasks of Today'. *Ethical Perspectives* 7 (2000), 257–68.

Van Laak, Werner. *Allversöhnung: Die Lehre von der Apokatastasis, Ihre Grundlegung durch Origenes und ihre Bewertung in der gegenwärtigen Theologie bei Karl Barth und Hans Urs von Balthasar*. Sinzig: Sankt Meinrad Verlag, 1990.

Landsberg, P. L. 'Les sens spirituels chez Saint Augustin'. *Dieu vivant* 11 (1948), 83–105.

Legnowski, Peter. 'Die letzte "säkulare Verwirklichung der Herrlichkeit": Zur Goetherezeption Hans Urs von Balthasars', in *Logik der Liebe und Herrlichkeit Gottes: Hans Urs von Balthasar im Gespräch*, ed. Walter Kasper. Ostfildern: Matthias-Grünewald-Verlag, 2006, 134–45.

Lepers, Etienne. 'L'Application des sens'. *Christus* 21 (1980), 83–94.

Lochbrunner, Manfred. *Analogia Caritatis: Darstellung und Deutung der Theologie Hans Urs von Balthasars*. Freiburg: Herder, 1981.

———. 'Guardini und Balthasar: Auf der Spurensuche einer Geistigen Wahlverwandtschaft'. *Forum katholische Theologie* 12 (1996), 229–46.

———. 'Gustav Siewerth im Spiegel von Hans Urs von Balthasar'. In *Im Ringen um die Wahrheit: Festschrift der Gustav-Siewerth-Akademie zum 70. Geburtstag ihrer Gründerin und Leiterin Prof. Dr. Alma von Stockhausen*, eds. Remigius Bäumer, J. Hans Bernischke, and Tadeusz Guz. Weilheim-Bierbronnen: Gustav-Siewerth-Akademie, 1997, 257–72.

———. *Hans Urs von Balthasar als Autor, Herausgeber, und Verleger: Fünf Studien zu seinen Sammlungen (1942-1967)*. Würzburg: Echter Verlag, 2002.

———. *Hans Urs von Balthasar und seine Literatenfreunde: Neun Korrespondenzen*. Würzburg: Echter Verlag, 2007.

———. *Hans Urs von Balthasar und seine Philosophenfreunde: Fünf Doppelporträts*. Würzburg: Echter Verlag, 2005.

———. 'Romano Guardini und Hans Urs von Balthasar: Integration von Theologie und Literatur'. *Internationale katholische Zeitschrift Communio* 34 (2005), 169–85.

Longpré, Ephrem. 'Bonaventure'. *Dictionnaire de spiritualité*. Paris: G. Beauchesne et ses fils, 1932–95. Vol. 1, 1768–843.

———. 'La théologie mystique de S. Bonaventure'. *Archivum Franciscanum Historicum* 14 (1921), 36–108.

Löser, Werner. *Im Geiste des Origenes: Hans Urs von Balthasar als Interpret der Theologie der Kirchenväter*. Frankfurt am Main: Josef Knecht, 1976.

——. 'Hans Urs von Balthasar und Ignatius von Loyola'. In *Logik der Liebe und Herrlichkeit Gottes: Hans Urs von Balthasar im Gespräch*, ed. Walter Kasper. Ostfildern: Matthias-Grünewald-Verlag, 2006, 94–110.

——. 'Hans Urs von Balthasar und seine ignatianischen und patristischen Quellen'. *Geist und Leben* 79 (2006), 194–203.

——. 'The Ignatian *Exercises* in the Work of Hans Urs von Balthasar'. In *Hans Urs von Balthasar: His Life and Work*, ed. David L. Schindler. San Francisco, CA: Ignatius Press, 1991, 103–20. ('Die Exerzitien des Ignatius von Loyola: Ihre Bedeutung in der Theologie Hans Urs von Balthasars'. *Internationale katholische Zeitschrift Communio* 18 (1989), 333–51.)

Louth, Andrew. *The Origins of the Christian Mystical Tradition: From Plato to Denys*. Oxford: Clarendon Press, 1981.

Lubac, Henri de. 'A Witness of Christ in the Church: Hans Urs von Balthasar'. *Communio* 2 (Fall 1975), 228–49.

Ludolph of Saxony, *Vita Jesu Christi*, ed. L. M. Rigollot. Paris: Palmé, 1870.

Maggiolini, Alessandro. 'From Modernism to Vatican II', *Communio* 23 (Summer 1996), 225–43.

Mali, Franz. 'Origenes—Balthasars Lehrer des Endes?' In *Letzte Haltungen: Hans Urs von Balthasars 'Apokalypse der deutschen Seele' neu gelesen*, ed. Barbara Hallensleben. Fribourg: Academic Press, 2006, 280–90.

Mallet, F. 'L'Oeuvre du Cardinal Dechamps et la méthode de l'apologétique'. *Annales de philosophie chrétienne* 151 (1905–6), 68–91.

——. 'Les controverses sur la méthode apologétique du Cardinal Dechamps'. *Annales de philosophie chrétienne* 151 (1905–6), 449–71; 625–45.

——. 'L'Oeuvre du Cardinal Dechamps de les progress récents de l'apologétique'. *Annales de philosophie chrétienne* 153 (1906–7), 562–91.

Maréchal, Joseph. 'Applications des sens'. In *Dictionnaire de spiritualité ascétique et mystique*, ed. Marcel Viller, Charles Baumgartner, and André Rayez. Paris: G. Beauchesne et ses fils, 1932–95, Vol. 1, 810–28.

——. *Studies in the Psychology of the Mystics*. Albany, NY: Magi, 1964. (*Études sur la psychologie des mystiques*. Brussels: L'Édition Universelle, 1937.)

Maximus the Confessor. *Ambiguorum Liber sive de variis difficilibus locis SS. Dionysii Areopagitae et Gregorii Theologi*. In Jacques-Paul Migne, ed. *Patrologia Graeca*. Paris: J.-P. Migne, 1857–66. Vol. 91, 1031–417.

——. *Capita de Charitate*. In Jacques-Paul Migne, ed. *Patrologia Graeca*. Paris: J.-P. Migne, 1857–66. Vol. 90, 959–1082.

——. *Mystagogia*, In Jacques-Paul Migne, ed. *Patrologia Graeca*. Paris: J.-P. Migne, 1857–66. Vol. 91, 658–721.

——. *Quaestiones ad Thalassium de Scriptura Sacra*. In Jacques-Paul Migne, ed. *Patrologia Graeca*. Paris: J.-P. Migne, 1857–66. Vol. 90, 244–785.

McCool, Gerald. *Catholic Theology in the Nineteenth Century*. New York: Seabury, 1977.

McCormack, Bruce. *Karl Barth's Critically Realistic Dialectical Theology: Its Genesis and Development, 1909–1936*. Oxford: Oxford University Press, 1995.

McCosker, Philip. "'Blessed Tension": Barth and Von Balthasar on the Music of Mozart'. *The Way: A Review of Christian Spirituality Published by the British Jesuits* 44 (2005), 81–95.

McGinn, Bernard. *The Flowering of Mysticism*. New York: Crossroad, 1998.

———. *The Foundations of Mysticism*. New York: Crossroad, 1991.

———. *The Growth of Mysticism*. New York: Crossroad, 1994.

McGregor, Bede, and Thomas Norris, eds. *The Beauty of Christ: A [sic] Introduction to the Theology of Hans Urs von Balthasar*. Edinburgh: T&T Clark, 1994.

McIntosh, Mark A. *Christology from Within: Spirituality and the Incarnation in Hans Urs von Balthasar*. Notre Dame, IN: University of Notre Dame Press, 1996.

———. *Mystical Theology: The Integrity of Spirituality and Theology*. Oxford: Blackwell, 1998.

Mongrain, Kevin. *The Systematic Thought of Hans Urs von Balthasar: An Irenaean Retrieval*. New York: Crossroad, 2002.

Moss, David, and Edward T. Oakes, eds. *The Cambridge Companion to Hans Urs von Balthasar*. Cambridge: Cambridge University Press, 2004.

Müller, Wolfgang W., ed. *Karl Barth—Hans Urs von Balthasar: Eine theologische Zwiesprache*. Zürich: Theologischer Verlag, 2006.

Murillo, Ildefonso. 'Im Dialog mit den Griechen: Balthasars Verständnis antiker Philosophie in "Herrlichkeit".' In *Hans Urs von Balthasar: Gestalt und Werk*, eds. Karl Lehmann and Walter Kasper. Cologne: Verlag für Christliche Kultur Communio, 1989.

Nautin, Pierre. *Origène: Sa vie et son oeuvre*. Paris: Beauchesne, 1977.

Nichols, Aidan. *No Bloodless Myth: A Guide Through Balthasar's Dramatics*. Edinburgh: T&T Clark; Washington, DC: Catholic University of America Press, 2000.

———. *Say It Is Pentecost: A Guide Through Balthasar's Logic*. Edinburgh: T&T Clark; Washington, DC: Catholic University of America Press, 2001.

———. 'Thomism and the Nouvelle Théologie'. *The Thomist* 64 (January 2000), 1–19.

———. *The Word Has Been Abroad: A Guide Through Balthasar's Aesthetics*. Edinburgh: T&T Clark; Washington, DC: Catholic University of America Press, 1998.

Norris, Thomas. 'The Symphonic Unity of His Theology: An Overview'. In *The Beauty of Christ: A [sic] Introduction to the Theology of Hans Urs von Balthasar*, eds. Bede McGregor and Thomas Norris. Edinburgh: T&T Clark, 1994, 213–52.

Oakes, Edward T. *Pattern of Redemption: The Theology of Hans Urs von Balthasar*. New York: Continuum, 1994.

O'Donnell, John. *Hans Urs von Balthasar*. London: Continuum, 2000.

——. 'The Logic of Divine Glory'. In *The Beauty of Christ: A [sic] Introduction to the Theology of Hans Urs von Balthasar*, eds. Bede McGregor and Thomas Norris. Edinburgh: T&T Clark, 1994, 161–70.

O'Donoghue, Noel. 'Do We Get Beyond Plato?: A Critical Appreciation of the Theological Aesthetics'. In *The Beauty of Christ: A [sic] Introduction to the Theology of Hans Urs von Balthasar*, eds. Bede McGregor and Thomas Norris. Edinburgh: T&T Clark, 1994, 253–66.

——. 'A Theology of Beauty'. In *The Analogy of Beauty: The Theology of Hans Urs von Balthasar*, ed. John Riches. Edinburgh: T&T Clark, 1986, 1–10.

O'Donovan, Leo, SJ, 'Two Sons of Ignatius: Drama and Dialectic'. *Philosophy and Theology* 11 (1998), 105–25.

O'Hanlon, Gerard F., SJ, *The Immutability of God in the Theology of Hans Urs von Balthasar*. Cambridge: Cambridge University Press, 1990.

Olphe-Gaillard, M. 'Les sens spirituels dans l'histoire de la spiritualité'. In *Nos sens et Dieu*, eds. Claude Baudoin et al. Paris: Desclée de Brouwer, 1954, 179–93.

O'Meara, Thomas F. 'Of Art and Theology: Hans Urs von Balthasar's Systems'. *Theological Studies* 42 (1981), 272–76.

O'Regan, Cyril. 'Balthasar: Between Tübingen and Postmodernity'. *Modern Theology* 14 (July 1998), 325–53.

——. 'Balthasar and Eckhart: Theological Principles and Catholicity'. *The Thomist* 60/2 (April 1996), 203–39.

——. 'Newman and von Balthasar: The Christological Contexting of the Numinous'. *Eglise et théologie* 26 (1995), 165–202.

——. 'Von Balthasar and Thick Retrieval: Post-Chalcedonian Symphonic Theology'. *Gregorianum* 77/2 (1996), 227–60.

Origen. *Commentary on the Gospel of John*, trans. Philip Schaff. *ANF* 9. Edinburgh: T&T Clark, 1959. (*Commentaria in Evangelium Joannis*. In Jacques-Paul Migne, ed. *Patrologia Graeca*. Paris: J.-P. Migne, 1857–66. Vol. 14, 21–830.)

——. *Contra Celsum*, trans. Henry Chadwick. New York: Cambridge University Press, 1965. (*Contra Celsum*. In Jacques-Paul Migne, ed. *Patrologia Graeca*. Paris: J.-P. Migne, 1857–66. Vol. 11, 641–1630.)

——. *Homiliae in Ezechiel*. In W. A. Baehrens, ed. *Origenes Werke. Die Griechischen Christlichen Schriftsteller*. Leipzig: J. C. Hinrichs, 1925. Vol. 8, 319–454.

——. *Homilies on Jeremiah*. In *Homilies on Jeremiah, Homily on 1 Kings 28*, trans. J. C. Smith. Washington, DC: Catholic University of America Press, 1998, 1–318. (*In Jeremiam Homilia*. In W. A. Baehrens, ed. *Origenes Werke. Die Griechischen Christlichen Schriftsteller*. Leipzig: J. C. Hinrichs, 1925. Vol. 8, 290–317.)

——. *Homilies on Luke, Fragments on Luke*, trans. J. T. Lienhard. Washington, DC: Catholic University of America Press, 1996. (*In Lucam Homilia*. In W. A. Baehrens, ed. *Origenes Werke. Die Griechischen Christlichen Schriftsteller*. Leipzig: Hinrichs, 1930. Vol. 9.)

——. *In Psalmos*. In Jean-Baptiste Pitra, ed. *Analecta sacra spicilegio solesmensi parata*. Parisiis: A. Jouby et Roger, 1883. Vol. 3, 1–364.

——. *On First Principles*, trans. G. W. Butterworth. Gloucester, MA: Peter Smith, 1973. (*De Principiis*. In Jacques-Paul Migne, ed. *Patrologia Graeca*. Paris: J.-P. Migne, 1857–66. Vol. 11, 115–414.)

——. *Prayer, Exhortation to Martyrdom*, trans. John Joseph O'Meara. Westminster: Newman Press, 1954. (*De Oratio*. In W. A. Baehrens, ed. *Origenes Werke. Die Griechischen Christlichen Schriftsteller*. Leipzig: Hinrichs, 1899. Vol. 2, 295–403. *Exhortatio ad Martyrium*. In Jacques-Paul Migne. *Patrologia Graeca*. Paris: J.-P. Migne, 1857–66. Vol. 11, 561–636.)

——. *The Song of Songs: Commentary and Homilies*, trans. W. P. Lawson. Westminster: Newman Press, 1957. (*In Canticum Canticorum*. In W. A. Baehrens, ed. *Origenes Werke. Die Griechischen Christlichen Schriftsteller*. Leipzig: J. C. Hinrichs, 1925. Vol. 8, 26–289.)

Ouellet, Marc. 'The Message of Balthasar's Theology to Modern Theology'. *Communio* 23 (Summer 1996), 270–99.

Peter, Karl. *Die Lehre von der Schönheit nach Bonaventura*. Werl: Dietrich Coelde Verlag, 1964.

Plato. *Symposium*, trans. Richard Hunter. Oxford: Oxford University Press, 2004. (*Platonis Opera*. Vol. 2, ed. John Burnet. Oxford: Clarendon Press, 1901, 172–223. Stephanus Pagination.)

——. *Timaeus*, trans. A. E. Taylor. London: Methuen, 1929. (*Platonis Opera*. Vol. 4, ed. John Burnet. Oxford: Clarendon Press, 1902, 17–105. Stephanus Pagination.)

Plotinus. *Enneads*. 7 vols. Greek and English text, trans. Arthur Hilary Armstrong. Cambridge: Harvard University Press, 1966–88.

Polanco, Juan de. *Monumenta Ignatiana*, Ser. II (1955), 2: 300–3.

Potworowski, Christophe. 'Christian Experience in Hans Urs von Balthasar'. *Communio* 20 (1993), 107–17.

——. 'An Exploration of the Notion of Objectivity in Hans Urs von Balthasar'. *Renascence: Essays on Value in Literature* 48 (Winter 1996), 137–51.

Pouillon, Henri. 'Le premier traité des propriétés transcendentales, La "Summa de bono" du Chancelier Philippe'. *Revue néoscolastique de philosophie* 42 (1939), 40–77.

Poulain, Augustin. *The Graces of Interior Prayer*, trans. Leonora L. Yorke Smith. London: Kegan Paul, Trench, Trübner, & Co., 1950. (*Des grâces d'oraison*. Paris: V. Retaux, 1901.)

Price, Daniel. *Karl Barth's Anthropology in Light of Modern Thought*. Grand Rapids, MI: Eerdmans, 2002.

Pseudo-Dionysius. *The Celestial Hierarchy*. In *The Complete Works*, trans. Colm Luibheid and Paul Rorem. Mahwah, NJ: Paulist Press, 1987, 143–92. (*Corpus Dionysiacum*. *De Coelesti Hierarchia, De Ecclesiastica Hierarchia, De Mystica Theologia, Epistulae*. Vol. 2, ed. B. R. Suchla. Berlin: De Gruyter, 1991.)

——. *The Divine Names*, trans. C. E. Holt. London, Society for the Promotion of Christian Knowledge, 1920. (*Corpus Dionysiacum. De Divinis Nominibus*. Vol. 1, ed. B. R. Suchla. Berlin: De Gruyter, 1990.)

——. *The Ecclesiastical Hierarchy*. In *The Complete Works*, trans. Colm Luibheid and Paul Rorem. Mahwah, NJ: Paulist Press, 1987, 193–260. (*Corpus Dionysiacum. De Coelesti Hierarchia, De Ecclesiastica Hierarchia, De Mystica Theologia, Epistulae*. Vol. 2, ed. B. R. Suchla. Berlin: De Gruyter, 1991.)

Pseudo-Macarius. *The Fifty Spiritual Homilies* and *The Great Letter*, trans. George Maloney, SJ New York: Paulist Press, 1992. (*Homilae Spirituales*. In Jacques-Paul Migne, ed. *Patrologia Graeca*. Paris: J.-P. Migne, 1857–66. Vol. 34, 450–820.)

Rahner, Hugo. 'Die Anwendung der Sinne in der Betrachtungsmethode des hl. Ignatius von Loyola'. *Zeitschrift für katholische Theologie* 79 (1957), 434–56.

Rahner, Karl. 'Current Problems in Christology'. In *Theological Investigations*. Vol. 1. *God, Christ, Mary and Grace*, trans. Cornelius Ernst. London: Darton, Longman, & Todd, 1961. 149–200. ('Probleme der Christologie heute'. In *Schriften zur Theologie*. Vol. 1. Einsiedeln: Benziger, 1954, 169–222.)

——. 'The Doctrine of the "Spiritual Senses" in the Middle Ages'. In Karl Rahner. *Theological Investigations*. Vol. 16. *Experience of the Spirit: Source of Theology*, trans. David Morland. New York: Crossroad, 1979, 104–34. (This article was compiled by Karl Neufeld from two separate essays by Rahner: 'La doctrine des "sens spirituels" au moyen-âge, en particulier chez S. Bonaventure'. *Revue d'ascetique et de mystique* 14 (1933), 263–99. 'Der Begriff der Ecstasis bei Bonaventura'. *Zeitschrift für Aszese und Mystik* 9 (1934), 1–19.)

——. 'The "Spiritual Senses" According to Origen'. In Karl Rahner. *Theological Investigations*. Vol. 16. *Experience of the Spirit: Source of Theology*, trans. David Morland. New York: Crossroad, 1979, 81–103. ('Le début d'une doctrine des cinq sens spirituals chez Origène'. *Revue d'ascétique et mystique* 13 (1932), 113–45.)

Reifenberg, Peter, and Anton van Hooff, eds. *Gott für die Welt: Henri de Lubac, Gustav Siewerth und Hans Urs von Balthasar in ihren Grundanliegen*. Mainz: Matthias-Grünewald-Verlag, 2001.

Rendina, Sergio. 'La dottrina dei "sensi spirituali" negli Esercizi Spirituali'. *Servitium* 29–30 (1983), 55–72.

Riches, John, ed. *The Analogy of Beauty: The Theology of Hans Urs von Balthasar*. Edinburgh: T&T Clark, 1986.

Rickenmann, Agnell. 'La dottrina di Origene sui sensi spirituali e la sua ricezione in Hans Urs von Balthasar'. *Rivista Teologica di Lugano* 6 (2001), 155–68.

Roberts, Louis. *The Theological Aesthetics of Hans Urs von Balthasar*. Washington, DC: Catholic University of America Press, 1987.

Rosenmöller, Bernhard. *Religiöse Erkenntnis nach Bonaventura*. Münster: Aschendorff, 1925.

Ross, David. *Aristotle*. London: Methuen, 1964.

Sachs, John Randall. 'Spirit and Life: The Pneumatology and Christian Spirituality of Hans Urs von Balthasar'. Inaugural-Dissertation zur Erlangung der Doktorwürde. Eberhard-Karls-Universität zu Tübingen, 1984.

Saint-Pierre, Mario. *Beauté, bonté, vérité chez Hans Urs von Balthasar*. Quebec: Laval University Press, 1998.

Sara, Juan Manuel. 'Knowledge, the Transcendentals, and Communion'. *Communio* 28 (Fall 2001), 505–32.

Scaramelli, Giovanni Battista. *A Handbook of Mystical Theology: Being an Abridgment of Il direttorio mistico*, trans. D. H. S. Nicholson. London: John M. Watkins, 1913.(Il direttorio mistico, *indirizzato a' direttori di quelle anime, che iddio conduce per la via della contemplazione*. Venezia: S. Occhi, 1754.)

Schrijver, Georges de. 'Die Analogia Entis in der Theologie Hans Urs von Balthasars: Eine genetisch-historische Studie'. *Bijdragen: Tijdschrift voor Filosofie en Theologie* 38 (1977), 241–81.

Sherwood, Dom Polycarp. 'Survey of Recent Work on St. Maximus the Confessor'. *Traditio* 20 (1964), 428–37.

Schindler, D. C. *Hans Urs von Balthasar and the Dramatic Structure of Truth*. New York: Fordham University Press, 2004.

Schindler, David L., ed. *Hans Urs von Balthasar: His Life and Work*. San Francisco, CA: Ignatius Press, 1991.

——. 'Modernity, Postmodernity, and the Problem of Atheism'. *Communio* 24 (Fall 1997), 563–79.

Scola, Angelo. *Hans Urs von Balthasar: A Theological Style*. Grand Rapids, MI: Eerdmans, 1991.

——. 'Nature and Grace in Hans Urs von Balthasar'. *Communio* 18 (Summer 1991), 207–26.

Seifert, Josef. 'Person und Individuum: Über Hans Urs von Balthasars Philosophie der Person und die philosophische Implikationen seiner Dreifaltigkeitstheologie'. *Forum katholische Theologie* 13 (1997), 81–105.

Servais, Jacques. 'Au fondement d'une théologie de l'obéissance ignatienne: Les Exercices spirituels selon H. U. von Balthasar'. *Nouvelle revue théologique* 116 (1994): 353–73.

——. Une theologie des 'Exercices spirituels': Hans Urs von Balthasar, interprète de saint Ignace de Loyola. Rome: Tipografia Pontificia Universitas Gregoriana, 1992.

Siewerth, Gustav. *Die Apriorität der Erkenntnis als Einheitsgrund der philosophischen Systematik des Thomas von Aquin.* Kallmunz-Regensburg: M. Lassleben, 1938.

———. *Die Metaphysik der Erkenntnis nach Thomas von Aquin.* München-Berlin: R. Oldenbourg, 1933.

———. *Metaphysik der Kindheit.* Einsiedeln: Johannes Verlag, 1957.

———. *Das Schicksal der Metaphysik von Thomas zu Heidegger.* Einsiedeln: Johannes Verlag, 1959.

———. *Die Sinne und das Wort.* Düsseldorf: Schwann-Verlag, 1956.

———. *Wort und Bild: Eine ontologische Interpretation.* Düsseldorf: Schwann-Verlag, 1952.

Spargo, Emma Jane Marie. *The Category of the Aesthetic in the Philosophy of Saint Bonaventure.* New York: Franciscan Institute, 1953.

Splett, Jörg. 'Wahrheit in Herrlichkeit: Auf Balthasar Hören'. *Theologie und Philosophie* 69 (1994), 411–21.

Striet, Magnus, and Jan-Heiner Tück, eds. *Die Kunst Gottes verstehen: Hans Urs von Balthasars theologische Provokationen.* Freiburg: Herder, 2005.

Tedoldi, Fabio Massimo. *La dottrina dei cinque sensi spirituali in San Bonaventura.* Rome: Pontificium Athenaeum Antonianum, 1999.

Thompson, John. 'Barth and Balthasar: An Ecumenical Dialogue'. In *The Beauty of Christ: A [sic] Introduction to the Theology of Hans Urs von Balthasar,* eds. Bede McGregor and Thomas Norris. Edinburgh: T&T Clark, 1994, 171–92.

Tyrrell, George. 'Revelation as Experience'. Unpublished lecture of George Tyrrell, ed. Thomas Michael Loome, *The Heythrop Journal* 11 (1970), 117–49.

Verweyen, Hansjürgen. *Ontologische Voraussetzungen des Glaubensaktes.* Düsseldorf: Patmos Verlag, 1969.

———. *Gottes Letztes Wort: Grundriss der Fundamentaltheologie.* Düsseldorf: Patmos Verlag, 1991.

Waldstein, Michael. Expression and Form: Principles of a Philosophical Aesthetics according to Hans Urs von Balthasar. Doctoral Dissertation, University of Dallas, 1981.

———. 'An Introduction to von Balthasar's *The Glory of the Lord*'. *Communio* 24 (Spring 1987), 12–33.

Walsh, James. 'Application of the Senses'. *The Way Supplement* 27 (1976), 59–68.

Webster, John, ed. *The Cambridge Companion to Karl Barth.* Cambridge: Cambridge University Press, 2000.

Wiercinski, Andrzej. *Between Friends—A Bilingual Edition: The Hans Urs von Balthasar and Gustav Siewerth Correspondence, 1954–1963.* Konstanz: Verlag Gustav Siewerth-Gesellschaft, 2005.

Wigley, Stephen. *Karl Barth and Hans Urs von Balthasar: A Critical Engagement.* London: T&T Clark; Continuum, 2007.

———. 'The von Balthasar Thesis: A Re-examination of von Balthasar's Study of Barth in the Light of Bruce McCormack'. *Scottish Journal of Theology* 53 (2003), 345–59.

Williams, Rowan. 'Afterword: Making a Difference'. In *Balthasar at the End of Modernity.* Lucy Gardner, David Moss, Ben Quash, and Graham Ward. Edinburgh: T&T Clark, 1999, 173–80.

———. 'Balthasar and Rahner'. In *The Analogy of Beauty: The Theology of Hans Urs von Balthasar*, ed. John Riches. Edinburgh: T&T Clark, 1986, 11–34.

Wulf, Friedrich, SJ 'Die Bedeutung der schopferischen Phantasie für die Betrachtung nach Ignatius von Loyola'. *GuL* 22 (1949), 461–7.

Yeago, David Stuart. 'Literature in the Drama of Nature and Grace: Hans Urs von Balthasar's Paradigm for a Theology of Culture'. *Renascence* 48 (Winter 1996), 95–109.

Zeitz, James V. 'Przywara and von Balthasar on Analogy'. *Thomist* 52 (Fall 1998), 473–98.

Index

Aertsen, Jan A. 137 n, 138 n
Albert the Great 148 n
Alexander of Hales 78 n, 79 n, 137 n
Angelus Silesius 175
anthropology
 non-dualist 79, 95, 100–2, 112–15, 125,
 personalist 94, 97–100, 112, 115–16, 120–4, 180–1, 187
 philosophical 83, 98
 theological 1–2, 12, 14, 79–83, 97–102, 104, 112–21, 123–9, 150, 155–6, 159, 176, 180, 187, 189
Aquinas, Thomas 111, 137 n, 138, 139 n, 147, 148 n, 150, 155, 156 n, 158, 162
apologetics, see fundamental theology
Aristotle 31 n, 138 n, 143, 146–8
asceticism 186
Aubert, Roger 167 n, 169 n
Augustine of Hippo 17, 43–7, 52, 53, 76, 108, 127, 132, 139 n, 158, 165, 169, 186

Barth, Karl 2, 5 n, 8, 12–14, 19 n, 52, 66, 83, 94, 95–107, 109–11, 113, 116, 120–3, 127, 152 n, 155, 161, 165, 176, 178, 180, 186, 189
beauty
 of Christ 9 n, 17, 46, 61, 69, 75–8, 132–3, 142, 153–4
 and form 1, 75–7, 79, 133–4, 143–54, 159, 164, 174, 178, 185
 philosophical 135–43, 148 n, 153, 177
 theological 1, 9 n, 28, 43–7, 53, 61, 69, 75–8, 132–3, 142, 153–4, 174, 177–8, 185
 as a transcendental 1, 57, 77–8, 132, 134–43, 146, 149, 153–4, 159, 177
Blondel, Maurice 168–70, 172, 175, 176
body 11–12, 20, 29, 31, 40, 46 n, 51, 58, 76, 78–80, 82–3, 92, 97, 100–2, 105, 107, 111, 116–18, 121–2, 125–6, 147, 148 n, 150–1, 155, 187
Bonaventure 3 n, 5, 8, 11, 12, 30, 46, 52, 55–84, 91–2, 111, 119, 127, 129–30, 132–3, 136, 139–41, 153, 156 n, 186, 190
Bonnefoy, Jean-François 59–61, 74
Brown, Stephen 57 n, 65 n

cherubim 24, 28–9
church 8, 18, 127–9, 133, 168–9, 171, 187, 189
Claudel, Paul 12, 52, 94–5, 116–22, 128, 187
Coakley, Sarah 2 n, 51–2
Coolman, Boyd Taylor 1 n

Daley, Brian 18, 23 n
Daniélou, Jean 50–1
Davila, Gil Gonzalez 87
Dechamps, Victor 168–9
Diadochus of Photice 17, 37–40, 43, 46–7, 50, 53
Dillon, John 29 n
dualism 30–3, 38, 78 n, 79 n, 120, 126, 149, 172
Dulles, Avery Cardinal
Dupré, Louis 5 n

'ear(s) of the heart' 7, 9 n, 10 n, 159 n
Eco, Umberto 139 n, 148 n
ecstasy 64, 67–72, 74 n
Ehrenfels, Christian von 145 n
Erp, Stephan van 137 n
Eucharist 9 n, 49, 117, 119–21
Evagrius of Pontus 17, 36–40, 43, 46–7, 53
extrinsicism 15, 169–71, 174–9, 183, 185, 189
'eye(s) of the heart' 7, 8 n, 158
'eye(s) of the mind' 7, 10 n, 21, 44–5, 52, 158 n, 187
'eye(s) of the soul' 7, 8 n, 32, 52, 108, 122, 126
'eyes of faith' 7, 8 n, 9 n, 10 n, 158
'eyes of the spirit' 7, 9, 174

faith 13–14, 30 n, 31, 57, 62, 64, 66, 88–9, 92, 124–5, 128–31, 156, 158, 161, 163, 166–75, 185–6

Index

Fields, Stephen 5, 52, 56, 64–5, 78 n, 83, 95
form 1–2, 5–6, 12, 30, 38, 75, 77 n, 79 n, 80, 90–1, 106–13, 118, 122, 124, 127–8, 133–5, 139 n, 140–1, 143–54, 156–61, 164, 166, 171–4, 177–9, 185, 187–90
  of Christ 75, 124, 127–8, 133, 152–3, 158, 160, 178, 187–9
  and being 136, 143–54, 159–60
  and beauty, *see* beauty, and form
  non-dualist aspects of 109–10, 148–51, 172
  splendour of 13, 42, 46 n, 56 n, 61–3, 70, 71 n, 75, 122, 134, 139 n, 140 n, 148–50, 152–4, 156–7, 159–61, 166–7, 187–8, 190
Fries, Heinrich 167 n
fundamental theology 66, 160–1, 167–78, 184–5

Gagliardi, Achille 87, 89
Gavrilyuk, Paul L. 2 n, 52 n
Gestalt, *see* form
Gilson, Etienne 58 n, 83 n
Goethe, Johann Wolfgang von 6 n, 143–7, 148 n
grace 7, 13–15, 20, 28 n, 34–5, 40–3, 53, 58, 63 n, 66, 78 n, 80, 89–90, 92, 104–6, 110–1, 122, 128–9, 131, 133, 160–3, 168, 175, 178–9, 183–5, 187
Gregory of Nyssa 17, 31 n, 40 n, 43, 49–52, 190
Guardini, Romano 2, 8, 12, 52, 94–5, 105–11, 113, 119 n, 121–2, 127–8, 151, 165, 186

Harl, Marguerite 25 n
Harrison, Victoria 163–7
Heidegger, Martin 111
Henrici, Peter 50 n, 85 n, 162 n
hearing, spiritual 3–4, 9 n, 10, 22–4, 27 n, 28, 47, 61–3, 68 n, 69, 70 n, 71–4, 82, 86, 118, 157–8, 159 n, 189
Holy Spirit 65, 97 n, 178
Horn, Gabriel 39

Ignatius of Loyola 11, 55–6, 84–92, 111, 131
immanentism 185, 189
Incarnation 40, 86–7, 90, 119–20
'inner ear' 9 n

'inner eye(s)' 8 n, 9 n, 10 n, 45, 91, 158
'inner senses' 7, 10, 25, 76 n, 79, 82, 158
intellect 28, 48, 52, 67–8, 78 n, 79 n, 106–7, 145 n, 151

Kant, Immanuel 5, 6 n, 136–8, 143, 144 n, 154, 181
Kilby, Karen 176–7

Laak, Werner van 19 n
Legnowski, Peter 146
liturgy 49, 108, 110, 127–9, 133, 187, 189
Lochbrunner, Manfred 4 n, 8 n, 105 n, 111 n, 117 n
Löser, Werner 19 n, 84 n, 85 n, 88–9
Lubac, Henri de 49, 50 n, 84 n, 111
Ludolph of Saxony 90 n

Maréchal, Joseph 85 n, 172, 175–6
Maximus the Confessor 8, 17, 40 n, 43, 47–50, 53, 128
McCool, Gerald 169 n
'Modernism', Catholic 13, 161, 168, 170–8, 185, 188
Moses 68
mother's smile 115–16, 180–4
mysticism 4, 14 n, 20, 23 n, 26, 34–5, 37, 49–50, 55, 57, 65–8, 88, 90, 92, 103 n, 110–11, 119, 122, 127, 130–1, 186–7, 190

nature, pure 162–3
Nautin, Pierre 23 n
neighbour 12, 51, 94, 100, 102
Neo-Scholasticism 13, 15, 26, 45, 161–3, 166–9, 176, 184, 188, 190
Nyssen, *see* Gregory of Nyssa

O'Donoghue, Noel 31 n, 182 n
Origen of Alexandria 5, 7–8, 11, 16–40, 43, 45, 50–3, 56, 65, 74 n, 75, 91–2, 111, 119 n, 125, 127, 129–30, 158 n, 179, 186, 190

Paul 24, 27, 45, 68 n, 108–9, 153, 165
personalism 12, 94, 97–100, 112, 115–16, 120, 122–4, 179–80
Peter, Karl 77, 139–41
Plato 29 n, 30, 31 n, 33, 101, 139 n
Plotinus 29 n, 139 n
Polanco, Juan de 86–7

Index

Pouillon, Henri 137 n, 138 n
Poulain, Augustin 3, 4 n, 20–1, 23, 25, 86–7, 189
presence 4 n, 45, 86, 87 n, 110, 126–8, 139, 149, 165–6, 167 n
Pseudo-Dionysius 17, 40, 43, 49, 51–2, 68, 139 n
Pseudo-Macarius 17, 39–41, 43, 50, 53, 127, 198

Rahner, Karl 2–6, 11, 13–14, 16–18, 21, 25, 35–7, 39–41, 43–4, 47, 50, 56–60, 63–74, 78 n, 79 n, 83–4, 91, 95 n, 143 n, 144 n, 161, 176–7, 189
ratio pulchri 138–42
rationalism 163–4
reason 26, 28, 31, 48, 87, 108–9, 114–15, 162–4, 167 n, 168
revelation 1–2, 9 n, 14, 30, 57, 61–2, 64, 75, 96, 97 n, 110 n, 132, 134–6, 142, 149, 157–8, 160, 162 n, 163, 167 n, 168–79, 185, 188–90
Riches, John 171, 173
Rickenmann, Agnell 5, 19–20
Ross, David 146 n, 147

sensation, language of
 'analogical' 3–4, 20–3, 25, 73, 87 n, 151, 153, 160, 189
 'metaphorical' 4, 14, 20–3, 25, 36, 72–3, 109, 151, 160, 189
senses, corporeal 30, 90, 102, 104, 108, 122, 125, 126, 129, 133, 156, 187
sensus spiritualis 59, 61, 73
seraphim 24, 28–9
Schindler, D. C. 148–50, 154 n, 155, 156 n, 180–3

Siewerth, Gustav 2, 12, 52, 84 n, 94, 95, 111–16, 120, 122, 180, 183, 186
sight, spiritual 2–3, 9 n, 10 n, 23–4, 28, 32, 37, 45–7, 60, 62, 63 n, 68 n, 70 n, 71 n, 73–6, 86, 112, 118, 157–8, 165–6, 173
Simeon 31
smell, spiritual 3, 9 n, 10, 22–4, 27, 48, 52 n, 61–2, 63 n, 69 n, 71, 75 n, 76 n, 81, 86, 91, 118 n, 158, 159 n
Spargo, Emma Jane Marie 77, 140 n
Spiritual Exercises 55 n, 76, 84 n, 85–8, 131
splendour, *see* form, splendour of

taste, spiritual 3, 8 n, 9 n, 10, 22–4, 27, 44, 47–8, 52, 60–2, 63 n, 69–71, 75 n, 76, 81, 86, 118, 120, 158, 159 n, 184
touch, spiritual 3, 4 n, 7, 8 n, 9 n, 10, 22–4, 27–8, 48, 52 n, 60–2, 63 n, 68–74, 76, 81, 86, 118, 158, 159 n, 189
transcendentals 1, 57, 77–8, 132, 134–43, 146, 149, 153–4, 159, 177
Trinity 99, 100 n, 124
Tyrrell, George 170

Vatican I 168–78, 185
Vatican II 190–1
Verweyen, Hansjürgen 4 n
vision, spiritual, *see* sight, spiritual

Waldstein, Michael 143–8, 150–1, 154 n, 160
will 52 n, 68, 78 n, 79 n